From Ecstasy to Agony and Back

From Ecstasy to Agony and Back

Journeying with Adolescents on the Street

Barnabe D'Souza

 **SAGE** www.sagepublications.com
Los Angeles • London • New Delhi • Singapore • Washington DC

First published in 2012 by

SAGE Publications India Pvt Ltd
B1/ I-1 Mohan Cooperative Industrial Area
Mathura Road, New Delhi 110 044, India
www.sagepub.in

SAGE Publications Inc
2455 Teller Road
Thousand Oaks, California 91320, USA

SAGE Publications Ltd
1 Oliver's Yard
55 City Road
London EC1Y 1SP, United Kingdom

SAGE Publications Asia-Pacific Pte Ltd
33 Pekin Street
#02-01 Far East Square
Singapore 048763

Published by Vivek Mehra for SAGE Publications India Pvt Ltd, Phototypeset in 10/13pt Minion by Tantla Composition Private Limited, Chandigarh and printed at Chaman Enterprises, New Delhi.

Library of Congress Cataloging-in-Publication Data Available

ISBN: 978-81-321-0703-3 (PB)

The SAGE Team: Gayatri Mishra, Pranab Jyoti Sarma and Anju Saxena

To all the children who have touched my life.

Thank you for choosing a SAGE product! If you have any comment,
observation or feedback, I would like to personally hear from you.
Please write to me at <u>contactceo@sagepub.in</u>

—Vivek Mehra, Managing Director and CEO,
SAGE Publications India Pvt Ltd, New Delhi

Bulk Sales

SAGE India offers special discounts for purchase of books in bulk.
We also make available special imprints and excerpts from our
books on demand.

For orders and enquiries, write to us at

Marketing Department
SAGE Publications India Pvt Ltd
B1/I-1, Mohan Cooperative Industrial Area
Mathura Road, Post Bag 7
New Delhi 110044, India
E-mail us at <u>marketing@sagepub.in</u>

Get to know more about SAGE, be invited to SAGE events, get on
our mailing list. Write today to <u>marketing@sagepub.in</u>

This book is also available as an e-book.

——————୫)C୫——————

Contents

List of Figures

Preface

I tried to improve my practice ...

There is no magic for the street boys, just a long painstaking process of support which has enabled some to turn their lives around. I have worked in Mumbai supporting street boys since 1982. In order to establish a program (which would eventually be replicable all over the country), I sought a focused response to the plight of street children. The need to respond to their addiction was an obvious starting point: drug abuse was visible, harmful, and leading to medical deterioration and helplessness.

As a practitioner researcher, my experience has prompted me to question the thinking and the mindsets of these male street adolescents and evaluate my practice. My account connects my personal experience to the cultural, placing myself within the social context of the street adolescent. I wish to identify effective practice, and to share and develop this with colleagues on whom the future of the work depends.

In my quest, I stayed at treatment centers around the country, studied their models of intervention, and questioned and reflected with the management and staff on their practice. My organization, Don Bosco, is committed to the youth sector and its main educational pedagogical thrust lies in prevention. I have been trained during my formation period in this pedagogical ideology and hence saw the significance in having a program of rehabilitation that had a strong preventive element in it.

Given the increasing emphasis on the voice of the child, I felt the need of a participative approach in my practice, to develop and evaluate the child centeredness of the program.

As a practitioner researcher, assisted by the staff and the boys, I investigate my own practice. In the process, I developed theories, which I have shared with my colleagues and through their critical feedback tested their validity. Having devised, developed, and evaluated this innovative process, I decided to base this study's design on the principles of Participatory Action Research to analyze, evaluate, and improve upon the Treatment Model of Rehabilitation I began in September 1999 at Lonavala (Maharashtra, India). The Therapeutic Centre addresses not merely the phenomenon of drug use, but facilitates a holistic rehabilitation process "off" the streets, a movement toward positive options for a qualitative improvement in lifestyle, by countering addiction and finding alternatives.

This book studies its development and effectiveness. It was designed after extensive investigation into working practices with street children.

Organizational resources, networks, and support systems are in place to help the street adolescent into a normal rehabilitation or reintegration into mainstream society. Yet, why is this movement "off the streets" such a difficult process, often getting entrapped in a cycle of attempts and failures? Is inhalant substance abuse the hindering factor? Do other factors pull them back? Are they addicted to this lifestyle? Do street boys have a fixed mindset?

There was a need to examine and reflect upon these questions and seek answers with my colleagues and with the boys. Participatory Action Research is followed here not only as a research methodology but also as a philosophy of life that would convert my practice into living and thinking.

The spiral of action research cycles follows a process of action, observation, and reflection to achieve greater understanding, followed by further action and reflection. Ascribing to the "living theory" approach of Jack Whitehead (2006), I tried to "improve my practice" by engaging in cycles of action and reflection, wherein I have created an action plan that enabled me to reflect and construct the values I live more fully.

Across my 26 years of interaction with male street adolescents, I observed that three-quarters were addicted to inhalant volatile solvents. In a sample size of 30 adolescents, I observed that there was a relapse rate of 50–60 percent, which led me to question the very efficacy of our program. I felt that the process of focusing on the whole was at the expense of individualized, specialized care that these adolescents required. It is this issue that motivated me to look beyond mere service provision intervention and instead focus upon working on the mindsets of street adolescents, as a vehicle of life-altering change.

Situations and cases came up that were repetitive and rooted in the past, and I realized that I needed to draw on insights and learning from my experience of working with these children. To reflect on current practice, it is necessary to understand past practice.

I used autoethnography, which is the qualitative study of one's own experiences through systematic observation and reflective note-keeping using the voices of other participants, as an analytical/objective personal account (Bennett, 2004). The various types of reports (annual report, camp report, value education camp, focus group discussion [FGD] reports, case files, and other records) became part of the accumulating data and the source of insights and experience. These resulted in eight research studies, several paper presentations, and 10 publications. These research and publications helped my investigation and updated my practice, "to live my 'I' in my living theory" (Whitehead, 1993) with regard to street adolescents.

Whenever I reflected on a situation relating to the adolescents, I felt the need to do something about it, following Freire's dictum, "reflection without action is sheer verbalism or armchair revolution and action without reflection is pure activism, or action for action's sake" (Freire, 1970: 41).

In the first year of my stay in the Residential Home, Siva, a street boy set me thinking about my assumptions when he said,

I did not want the job, the Father in-charge sent me for it; I am feeling tired today, I do not want to go to work. When I was picking scrap, I worked when I wanted. This job does not give me that freedom. I did not want this job.

I began reflecting on why the boys did not take up what was so lucidly planned and offered for their betterment. "*Should I work on his identity shift from a street boy to an identity of stability?*"

If the adolescents were not involved in planning and deciding their future, they did not take responsibility for the choices given to them (they did not get involved in the action). Their option was to run away (or cause a problem at the workplace that prompted the owner to ask them to leave). The situation was not of their making; hence the dropout rate was high. With them, reflection and action had to be simultaneous, or it would become "sheer verbalism." The dropout rates made the staff frustrated. I rationalized that it was part of these children's lifestyle, and that they "lived for the day" and could not think of their future. My staff rationalized that they were not educated enough or old enough to plan their future so they had to be told; but the "pull of the streets" was too strong. They only looked for "instant gratification."

Was there another method of working with the boys? We were reflecting on their situation but not with them. The children did not participate in that reflection or in the plans for their own future. In an action research approach, there was a felt need to involve the views of the adolescents in the rehabilitation program.

The power of transformation is "central to Participatory Action Research." The case of Siva required a transformation not only in my attitude, understanding, perspective, and vision, but also in those of my staff and the street adolescents I dealt with. Participatory action research provided the flexibility required for quick adaptability to changing situations. It led to looking at children as their own psychologists, creating meanings for themselves out of their own experiences and understanding.

The term "mindset" encourages generalizations that will stimulate thinking in other street adolescent programs across the world and establish principles of mindset change. By owning their actions, they begin to structure their moving off the streets (with support from significant others), to facilitate their rehabilitation and reintegration into society, and thereby improve their status. This forms the basis of my critical enquiry and the core of this study.

It seeks to bring together action and reflection, theory and practice, in participation with others, in the pursuit of practical solutions to issues of pressing concern, and more generally, the flourishing of individual persons and their communities.

Acknowledgments

At the completion of this book, I have sentiments of being overwhelmed by the support I have received from the people around me. My gratitude to God for giving me these good people and the opportunity to become one of His tools to make a difference.

I have always had a multitude of things happening alongside this work. It needed a well-seasoned captain to steer my research "ship" in those tidal waves, to take me out of those cloudy moments. I could not have had a more insightful, precise, understanding, and patient Captain in Dr Stephen Bigger—you will always have a special place in my heart. Dr Nanette Smith's constant encouragement, concern, special help, and insights make me want to continue my research journey.

To put it in a typical Indian philosophical vein, "My past karma must have helped me in this life." I do not know what good I did to deserve your dedication, zeal, diligence, and commitment to this study. Thanks Dakshayani, you are one to be shared but not parted with! Your teaming with Sudha, my gentle yet firm driving force, Asha my constant motivator, and the entire team past and present, though I do not mention each of you by name, I am in deep appreciation of your contribution, dedication, and commitment. You all have never let me down. Our entire team of the Shelter and most especially each one of you, from Dutta to all who have been part of this research; your silent yet backbreaking 24 × 7 days is an exemplar in dedication and love for the children. I will always be in awe and deep gratitude for your untiring support.

I thank the community of Shelter for their encouragement, and Rev. Fr. Giles, Fr. Paul, and all those good people at Our Lady Queen of Peace (OLQP), Worcester, UK. I could not have asked for a better home away from home to do this study.

Don Bosco once said, "For you my dear boys, I work, breathe, eat and live." I wish to imitate him, in all humility. If it were not for the *raison d'être* of my work, you my dear boys, there would not be so much meaning in my life. Right from that memorable rainy day when I was sent to my first apostolate in Lonavala and was saved from a lightning strike with those children, you have intrigued me, challenged, motivated, and enraptured me with your ability to teach me through your lives. This research is my wish for your future off the streets. I would like to say a special thanks to Ms Rekha Natarajan and all at SAGE Publications, New Delhi, for bringing this work to a wider audience. To all those who have been responsible for directly or indirectly making this research such a wonderful experience, though you are not mentioned in person, my gratitude and appreciation will always be with you.

1

Through the Mist

INTRODUCTION

The phenomenon of street children has been in existence for many years. Historically, orphans, homeless, and street children were cared for by religious organizations such as churches, temples, and mosques as part of their charity mandate. These children were regarded with pity and sympathy, and the somewhat paternalistic approach to their sustenance through handouts was well supported by the public. The 20th century saw a politicization of the street children "problem," shifting responsibility away from religious groups, more towards the government. In the light of increasingly negative images of street children as delinquents, a number of institutions have emerged world over, which have tried to treat these "difficult" children in isolation. [1]

The most significant change in attitude came with the advent of the United Nations Convention on the Rights of the Child in 1990 that viewed children as active social subjects with rights to participate in decisions affecting their lives. This prompted the development community to usher in new guiding principles for their care.

Much of the uproar concerning the issue of street children stems, in part, from their visibility on the streets (Dimenstein, 1991; Hecht, 1998; Scheper-Hughes and Hoffman, 1995) and has been exacerbated by an alarming increase in the number of street youth around the world in

---

[1] Consortium for Street Children (2004), "Annual Report." Retrieved from www.streetchildren.org.uk

recent years. With increasing awareness among non-governmental, governmental, national, and international agencies, "street children" are differentiated into categories and seen as an especially vulnerable group worthy of specialized interest, attention, and intervention.

The phenomenon of street youth is a visible manifestation of a disrupted political and socioeconomic society. The forces that lead growing numbers of youth to the street are numerous and complex. In developing countries, few social services exist for the youth who have lived or worked on the streets. It is important to understand not only who these youth are, but also how they function. These insights provide a better understanding of their needs which, in turn, will provide them with the opportunity to be included in decision-making processes pertinent to their future as contributing members of society.

The street has its own security, unwritten norms, and survival modes. The stigma attached to the streets, spatial mobility, and the multiple deprivations of the streets are all an intrinsic part of an environment over which the adolescent seeks to gain mastery to survive. His entry on to the streets occurs at the most vulnerable moment of his life; he learns to survive and as he gets "inducted" into its culture, his coping strategies help him sustain his life on the streets. These strategies include the appropriation of urban niches in the city in which he is able to earn money, feel safe, and find enjoyment.

PROFILE OF STREET CHILDREN— DEFINING TRAITS

Contrary to popular belief, street children are not necessarily society's dropouts, but victims of unfortunate circumstances. Most street children come from the lower socioeconomic strata and have clouded family histories. In India, nearly one out of every three persons in urban areas lives below the poverty line. Their children are rootless, without education, care, affection, or guidance. These children experience abuse from nearly everyone: they are treated with contempt by the community, exploited by parents and employers alike, harassed and arrested by the police, even brutalized by older street children, and are victims of family violence including physical and sexual abuse (Panicker, 1993). They fall easy victims to drug dealers, who turn them into addicts and force them to peddle drugs. These circumstances cause them to lose their self-confidence and self-worth.

SELF-WORTH

Self-worth is frequently based on an individual's feelings of worth in terms of his skills, achievements, status, financial resources, or physical attributes. When an individual finds himself not measuring up to society's yardstick, his self-worth depreciates dramatically. The illusion of being successful and admired gives way to disillusionment as he pass through the rites of eking out a living.

The reality in many areas of the world is that large numbers of street children still express and demonstrate psychosocial difficulties such as low self-esteem, lack of will power, and depression, with a persistent tendency to resort to drugs when facing problems such as hunger and abuse. However, research in a number of different contexts suggest that rather than being passive victims of abandonment, many street children demonstrate strong feelings of self-efficacy in performing tasks required to control their life and environment in positive ways (Veale et al., 1997).

In their search for a safe haven and their strong need to establish a secure base, street children tend to form attachments to people, animals, objects, and institutions. Attachment is an emotional bond to another person. Psychologist John Bowlby was the first attachment theorist, describing attachment as a "…lasting psychological connectedness between human beings" (Bowlby, 1969: 194). Bowlby believed that the earliest bonds formed by children with their caregivers have a tremendous impact that continues through life. The central theme of the attachment theory is that mothers who are available and responsive to their infant's needs establish a sense of security. The infant knows that the caregiver is dependable, and this creates a secure base for the child to explore the world. Failure to form secure attachments early in life can have a negative impact on behavior in later childhood and throughout life. Those who have secure attachments in childhood tend to have good self-esteem and strong romantic relationships.

Street children's attachments are personal connections to people, animals, objects, and institutions. Having a close bond with at least one person and a feeling of acceptance has been found to be vital to developing a sense of positive self-esteem. A street child is more likely to develop strong attachments to other people if he spends a lot of time with them; he performs well in that group in any activity and is consistently rewarded by the group. In such a situation, street children are less likely to begin using substances and more likely to stop using them; the same holds true if their strongest attachments are with people and things not connected with substance use. Unfortunately, the situation of many street children makes it difficult for them to keep in touch with their families, to succeed at school or at work, or to surround themselves with friends who do not use substances. A desire for acceptance makes a street child vulnerable to close relationships with people who can have a negative influence.

Many situations and events that pushed these children onto the street in the first place (like natural disasters, man-made disasters, exploitation, and conflicts) have a lasting impact on their well-being. For example, the family conflict that pushed the child onto the streets continues to deprive the child of emotional and material support for years. When the child has his or her own child, neither the new parent nor the baby has the benefit of the previous generation's support. The trauma they face impacts directly on their thought processes and behavior patterns.

LIFESTYLE

Street children lead an unhealthy and often dangerous life that leaves them deprived of their basic needs for protection, guidance, and supervision and exposes them to different forms of exploitation and abuse. For many, survival on the street means begging and physical or sexual exploitation by adults.

1. *Socially unacceptable behavior:* Though the majority of street children manage to earn or scavenge their daily food, they are denied the basics of survival, and are often forced into thieving, drug peddling, and prostitution. Often children on the street are regarded as juvenile delinquents and anti-social elements: they

are often falsely accused of crimes and sent to Correction Homes, or worse, put into prisons for adults. Besides being cut off from parental influence and guidance, they are deprived of education leading them to behave in socially unacceptable ways.

2. *Health concerns:* The World Health Organization (WHO) studies show that street children suffer from health problems ranging from cholera to tuberculosis and anemia, and that they are exposed to a variety of toxic substances, both in their food and in the environment around them. Most street children suffer from diseases like scabies, infestation of lice, chronic dysentery, worms, tuberculosis, epilepsy, lung/ear/dental/nose/throat infections, chronic cuts, unhealed abrasions, and sexually transmitted diseases, all caused by extreme poverty, exploitation, malnutrition, and unhygienic surroundings in which the children are forced to live. I have made several independent studies on issues of health, food, and drug abuse to learn more about this phenomenon (D'Souza 2008a, 2008b, 2008c).

3. *Lack of trust:* These children are often shunned by society as they are ragged, filthy, smelly, and infested with lice. They are suspicious of everyone and do not believe that anyone can give them unconditional support. They are afraid of the police and give false names if arrested. When they are arrested, they are put in "lockups" where many are physically and sexually assaulted and abused. This makes them scared and ashamed to return to their homes.

4. *Support system on the street:* As there is no guardian figure for a street child, the police represent one of the children's main points of contact for services such as medical attention, food, and legal support, and a possible gateway to "training." Though many of them speak of their experiences of violence, death squads, sexual abuse, harassment, bribery, extortion and corruption, arrest, "round-ups" by the police, some have positive experiences and look to the higher cadre of police for support.

In most instances, his peer groups support him, those individuals who share common interests and needs. Peer groups tend to be homogeneous in age and gender. The peer group has a strong influence on street children because of the child's need for acceptance, belonging, and protection. The group often determines the process of change, socialization, and development among street children by providing emotional and material support. Street children often join to form emotional and material support networks, which can range from a simple circle of friends to an organized business network. Experienced street children teach newcomers how to survive. Members of the group share food, clothing, shelter, information, and psychoactive substances. This research is based on peer group enabling and behavior modification.

EMPOWERING TOWARD DEVELOPMENT

Children are encouraged to reflect on their current realities (for example, why they run away from home to live on the streets and work for their survival). Children's participation involves complexities which require us to "deepen our perceptions" of what the construct of childhood means to the many different people in children's lives. Moreover, children's own perception of themselves and their peer group plays an interacting role in determining how children think and behave.

While reviewing relevant studies for the identification of questions for an inquiry of childhood in the Indian context, Kumar (1993) highlighted the nature of adult–child relations in the Indian sociocultural context. One theme that emerged from several sources (Anandalakshmy and Bajaj, 1981; Bernstein, 1975; Murphy, 1953) was that adult–child continuity has been a dominant feature of the child's cultural ethos. Adults and children are generally not separated in space, moreover, the handling or responsibility is often not age-related. Street children live much of their lives in peer groups, largely without adult supervision, and have been described as children who are "out of place." However, despite the freedom that such life offers, their lives continue to be influenced by a wide range of adults.

Children's interpretations of their roles and relationships as well as of how members of society view them and treat them, of how they are often "scapegoated" with a negative image, and the range and complexity of their relationships with different groups of adults reflect on the nature of their childhood and their behavior patterns. How the adults in specific social settings conceptualize children and childhood determines the extent of children's powerlessness.

Thus, there is a need to address the dynamics of power to enable access and space for them to be citizens for social change, to value diversity and to work constructively with conflict. As opposed to a welfare (or charity) perspective which views street children primarily as victims or delinquents in need of basic services and rehabilitation, an empowerment approach views children as citizens of our society with rights to survival, protection, development, and participation. Through the rehabilitation program, street/working adolescents are empowered to reflect upon their experiences, articulate their views, plan effective programs, and advocate for their own rights; these youngsters are challenging the *status quo* regarding their place and power in society.

MOBILITY

An important element in the lives of many street children is movement: from home to street, rural area to city, rural area to border and across borders. Such movements can result from kidnapping or trafficking, parents' migration, self-migration, abandonment, flight from conflict (communal or familial), or being sent away to work. The actions of parents, family, and school or problems in the local community also are major causes of movement and separation from family. Once on the move, and especially in unfamiliar circumstances without the care or protection of parents or other adults, children are particularly vulnerable to different kinds of exploitation such as prostitution, child labor, and other equally hazardous circumstances.

The mobility of street children is affected by a number of external factors and internal group dynamics, which affect the nature, structure, and composition of these groupings. The external factors often include police attacks, weather conditions, and change in the nature of commercial or economic activities from one district or an area to another. Internal factors, on the other hand, help in changing or modifying the nature, composition, and structure of street children. These factors often include escape of group members for some reason, death, capture by police, or induction of new members. The need to reside in areas with a special supportive environment and characteristics that neither conflict with their lifestyle nor pose threats against their existence is essential for the survival of street children. Contrary to the assumption that street children are always moving or "on the run," research and data collected from NGOs (indirectly and on the basis of discussing rates and frequency of attendance of street children from particular districts to the drop-in centers) indicated that street children tend to "settle down" in areas where they feel secure, protected from violence, and with the possibility of earning a living and having fun. There are those children who alternate between the street and home in a "relay" (Lucchini, 1997). They leave home to check out the possibility of long term staying away. It is what I call the "dry run." It is after such dry runs that the child finally takes the step to run away permanently from home.

Sudesh dreaded the dark hours when his father would come home drunk and beat him up if he did not have his books in hand. One night, he was beaten severely and he ran away to the village temple. It was a dark frightening experience; the call of the jackals was spine-chilling and the temple shut and lonely. He spent the night alone, hurt and scared, only to return home at dawn. A few days later, his father beat him up again. He stole some money and ran away, and took a bus to the nearest town. Hungry and unable to withstand the abuse of the vendors, he returned home in a few days. The next time, he robbed his father's entire pay packet and took the connecting bus from the town to the city. He was initially frightened, but stayed on. Now this has become his home. He has learnt "the ways of the street"—to fend for himself and to survive.

IMPULSIVE BEHAVIOR

Children need the imposition of limits which help to control behavior and to cope with impulses, internal stresses, and external frustrations. Impulsive behavior is common to adolescents and occurs as a way of exploring and testing the limits of adult authority, but in the case of street children, the lack of consistent and externally imposed limits serves only to intensify these normal confusions. In the absence of consistent adult supervision, street children impulsively indulge in drinking, drug abuse, and sexual behavior more typical of adults in their attempt to overcome feelings of anxiety, frustration, and inadequacy. The varying role of impulsivity, a trait related to "dis-inhibition," approach motivation, novelty seeking, and sensation seeking, is seen as a temperamental vulnerability factor for substance use. Eysenck and Eysenck (1985) considered impulsivity as an important risk factor in substance abuse and tried to specify relatively stable characteristics of temperament that predispose individuals to initiate and continue substance abuse. In recent years, studies have linked impulsiveness to higher risks such as smoking, suicide, drinking, and drug abuse. Aggression, compulsive gambling, severe personality disorders, and attention deficit problems are all associated with high impulsiveness.

Gaining control over impulsive behavior involves grappling with powerful internal forces. While talking about addictive or impulsive behavior, individuals do exercise some sort of choice over whether or not to engage in these types of behavior. Most types of behavior are not persistently or addictively pursued. Rather, the healthy individual tries to achieve a balanced variety of reinforcing behavior.

INSTANT GRATIFICATION

"To live for the day" is a typical characteristic of the "present-oriented thinking" of street children. They lack future perspective, but as they grow into adolescence, they demonstrate greater concern towards their future. The nurturing of a future perspective takes place with the help of external supports such as parents or other responsible adults. However, in the case of street children and runaways, these supports are virtually nonexistent, and in their daily struggle to keep body and soul together, these children exhibit a perspective that is more focused on the present, on immediate wants and needs rather than on long-term consequences. Drawn by a longing for adult status and a sense of omnipotence and invulnerability, street children find it difficult to postpone immediate gratification for future reward. They give little thought to the consequences of their actions. Although this "instant gratification" may be understood in the light of the situation faced by the children on the street, the lack of sustained adult supervision hinders their ability to make decisions autonomously.

The concept of instant gratification, "to live for the day" is one of the factors that hinders their reflection and understanding of consequences. The choices and opportunities the street child gets are decisions made to satiate his immediate need but not a meditated reflection for his future progressive movement.

DECISION-MAKING

Decision-making is the process by which an individual makes a choice between two or more rational alternatives in order to select the one that will produce the most desirable consequence relative to unwanted consequences. Children have a body of experience and knowledge that is unique to their situation and harbor certain views and ideas which are a result of that experience. Many countries fail to recognize the legitimacy of the contribution of children to decision-making and develop policies, little knowing how it will affect the day-to-day lives of children and their present and future well-being. In consequence, children's opportunities for play, friendship, growing independence, and exploration are denied in the name of their protection.

Street and working children are not objects of concern but people. They are vulnerable but not incapable. "They need respect, not pity" (Ennew, 1994b: 35).

The development of interactive and participatory research methods has hinged upon the realization that children have social agency and competency and are capable of making informed decisions about their lives and of expressing views and aspirations that may differ from the views held by adults (Johnson et al., 1995, 1998; Hutchby and Moran-Ellis, 1998).

O'Kane (2003) remarks that in response to the challenge of reaching out to street children, who clearly did not fit western notions of childhood nor experience "golden age childhoods," some local NGOs developed new ways of working with children on the streets in ways which built upon their capacities. As street children became active partners in programming, new movements developed, such as Children's Parliament (*Bal Panchayat*), Children's Voice, child participation, and so on, through which they were able to raise questions regarding their participation in the institutions' programs; in society; in economic, social and political life; and consequently make important decisions affecting them.

The social context, the nature of the decision, the particular life experience of the child and the level of adult support affect the capacity of a child to understand the issues before him. Children are often less cynical, more optimistic, and flexible in their approach to the future and in their capacity for change. Street kids are constantly balancing short-term coping strategies against potential risks and future consequences of their actions and decisions. I have interacted with the children in a way that would accord priority to their perspectives and allow for their participation in the design and implementation of research objectives.

ROLE MODELS

Someone whose character, life and behavior is taken as a good example to follow, someone worthy of imitation; every child needs a role model. Children need models rather than critics. (Joubert, 1899)

Street children are significantly influenced by their peers and street drug abusers and tend to establish relatively long-term relationships with them, which include a range of shared activities, often illegal. Research has demonstrated that whenever individual drug users attempt or achieve risk-reduction behavior change, it often depends on whether this change is endorsed or encouraged by their peer group. The rehabilitation of drug abusers, therefore, has to look beyond merely filling a void in their lives. It is important to help the rehabilitated person to establish new networks comprising people he admires and respects and whom he views as positive role models. These role models are often his peers or ex-drug addicts who effect changes in knowledge, attitudes, and practices at the individual level. However, they may also create change at the group or societal level by modifying norms and stimulating collective action that contributes to changes in policies and programs.

Role models offer a measure of social bonding and social support which promote the establishment of more pro-social networks. These networks consist of persons whom the recovering street addicts respect, whom they enjoy seeing and with whom they can feel close, share their time and thoughts, and exchange help on a reciprocal basis.

"Overcome and help" has been the idea behind my recruiting ex-drug addict boys (who have gone through the program) to help those in the period of detoxification in the capacity of attendants, understanding, sympathetic, and yet, firm. It was a way of telling them, "You can contribute to society right here, right now. You can help pull him through his 'meditative pause,' his period of reflection in hospital with your example. You are his role model."

Role models are an intrinsic element to the street adolescents' motivational movement off the streets. They take the example of these role models, deeming it possible to achieve the desired status. "If he can do it, why cannot I."

COPING STRATEGY

"Taking to the streets is a way of searching for identity, earning a living out of it, and contributing to the family's income" (WHO, 1993). A variety of strategies may be adopted for coping with street life. Some of these strategies and skills are pro-social, while others demonstrate skills and strategies used within anti-social activities. However, the skills themselves and the planning capacities used in the anti-social activities may be transferable to pro-social ends, if such ends are perceived as valid and rewarding alternatives.

Some street children express concern about their long-term future, but most see this as being largely beyond their control. Street children who are "successful" in moving off the streets have learned and practiced a wide range of coping skills, which in most other social contexts would be recognized as highly desirable. For example, abilities to negotiate difficult situations, to bargain, and to assert themselves are attributes that might suit many small enterprises. Many street children are perceived as small entrepreneurs. The problem for these children is connected with the deprived and transitory nature of much of their life on the street and their inability to gain an education or other work skills or qualifications to take them off the streets. Street children who do not readily become "street smart" have a particularly difficult time and are unlikely to survive the streets.

Most of the street boys, in my experience, have developed coping strategies which include finding a niche in the economic market that gives them sufficient income to eat and clothe themselves. They engage in high-risk behavior and in commercial/survival sex, learn how to cheat potential exploiters, develop the ability to manipulate the authorities effectively, and use their imagination, intelligence, and creativity to solicit alms. They are also able to find and take advantage of programs that serve them, are sufficiently informed about their physical health to stay reasonably healthy, form close friendships with peers supporting each other emotionally and materially, and maintain some form of connection to their family of origin. Other strategies include the use of drugs to self-medicate fear and depression, to kill hunger, to provide strength to live in difficult circumstances, or as indications of a pathological need for immediate gratification. There have been instances where street children inhaling glue have maintained their ability to cope with the demands of working on the streets in poor, crowded conditions. The ability to survive, however harmful the consequences of his action, and to find responses in coping with difficult situations, is testimony to the street child's resilience. My research has tried to make use of the factors of resilience, coping strategies, practical intelligence, and turn them around to their advantage for a positive growth off the streets.

INHALANT ABUSE

Solvent abuse, more accurately called Volatile Substance Abuse (VSA) has been defined as the "deliberate inhalation of gases, chemical fumes or vapors for mind-altering and recreational purposes in order to get a 'high' similar to the intoxication produced by alcohol." Solvents are chemicals that change from liquid form into gases or vapors at ordinary room temperatures (UNODC, 2004).

For many children in developing countries, the street is home. For most vulnerable children and youth, substance abuse, sexual abuse, and violence are all part of a complex series of factors affecting their lives. There is evidence that the number of vulnerable children and youth is increasing and the age at which they begin abusing substances is decreasing. Their abuse of substances begins with those that are most readily available and inexpensive namely, inhalants. The number of vulnerable children and youth increases with cultural shifts from rural to urban societies, economic and social instability, and decreased importance of nuclear families (NIDA and WHO, 2000).

Substance abuse among street children might be viewed as part of their coping mechanism to deal with street life, to endure stress and to deal with problems of food, hunger, pain, and restless nights and peer influence. A study conducted by the United Nations System in Pakistan—"Solvent Abuse among Street Children in Pakistan" (UNODC, 2004)—showed that the major factor leading to the use of solvents, as reported by more than half of the children (53.4 percent) was friends and peers. Another finding of the study was the way society perceived street children. Children felt that society had a negative attitude towards them, which in turn inculcated feelings of neglect and hatred. Children felt that to repay society, they needed strength not only from outside but from within, which came from the abuse of solvents or other drugs. Consumption of drugs among street children is observed to be affected by market principles and the availability and commonality of certain types of drugs. This activity among street children often entails congregating in gardens, isolated places, empty wastelands, or under bridges, away from the public eye.

Inhalants can be divided into four general categories: volatile solvents, aerosol, gases, and nitrites (NIDA, 2001). The most common and legally available inhalants are products such as glues, nail polish remover, lighter fluid, spray paints, deodorant and hair sprays, whipped cream canisters, and cleaning fluids. Glue sniffing is habitually carried out by most street children. Children using inhalants are also likely to use alcohol and/or marijuana.

Inhalants are appealing to street children for a variety of reasons: they are relatively inexpensive, can be purchased legally, and are readily accessible. Moreover, the "high" from inhalants sets in and disappears quickly, in comparison to other drugs of abuse. The practices of "sniffing," "huffing," "bagging," or inhaling to get high are various forms of inhalation abuse popular among users (*Environmental Health Perspectives*, 2005). The adolescents of my study breathed volatile substances through the mouth, "huffing" from a cloth or their shirt soaked in "solution."

Unfortunately, inhalant abuse poses definite dangers to the health of young children, including cognitive, neurological, and physiological disorders. The immediate effects of inhaling volatile solvents, fuels, anesthetics, or nitrous oxide are similar to the early stages of anesthesia. The user feels an initial stimulating "rush," then is light-headed, uninhibited, excitable, and prone to impulsive behavior. During the intoxification period, it is not possible to stimulate thinking. However, when the street inhalants are not under the drug's influence, it is more conducive to stimulate reflection and change by placing negative role models before them.

TREATMENT PROGRAMS

Treating inhalant abuse among street children involves first gaining an understanding of the "pathways" to the street and certain protective factors. Prevention programs include community readiness models; street outreach programs; drop-in and residential treatment centers; and individual, group, and family counseling in a variety of settings. It is important to develop programs that deliver targeted, comprehensive, coordinated, integrated, age-appropriate, low-cost, and effective services modeled on best practices. While there might be a tendency to see these children as "victims" and they are often presented with situations clearly beyond their control, they could as well be seen as resourceful human beings, many of whom have decided to seek a better life. Their behavior and choices can be viewed as a complex interplay of multiple survival strategies in which these children are "informed" actors. Children who constitute this highly stigmatized population are independent, curious, rebellious, and often make conscious decisions "here and now" about their actions, without reflecting upon their consequences. It is this quality in them that I sought to work with in my approach to inhalant abusing street children which constitutes one of the main queries of my book.

The life of street children may be described as cyclical from which some try to break away. The initial honeymoon period is characterized by freedom and excitement, with drugs becoming a part of this as experimentation. This is followed by a coping period, where basic day-to-day survival becomes the total preoccupation, with drugs being used to assist coping. Next is the routine period, when they come to view their lives as monotonous and in need of change, and drug use also becomes routine and non-fulfilling. Working on their mindsets at this stage through sustained cognitive inputs and exercises in thinking and reflection can bring about long-term change.

Through my study of various treatment models, I have developed the Five Phase Rehabilitation Model. The issues of reflection, mindset change, participation, empowerment, personal agency, self-worth, and movement off the streets through an educative pedagogy were a consequence of studying and tailoring the program to these street adolescent inhalant abusers.

DEPENDENCY ON THE INSTITUTION

The dependency syndrome is an attitude and belief that a group cannot solve its problems without outside help. It is a weakness that is made worse by charity and perpetuated on the streets or in the institution. If exit policies and personal plans and progress charts are not in place, the movement of the adolescent off the streets or out of an institution is made all the more difficult. Their participation in this process is a necessary element for a mindset movement from dependence to independence.

CHANGING BEHAVIOR

Motivation lies at the core of biological, cognitive, and social regulation. People's motivation to act may stem from internal or external sources. The self-determination theory of Ryan and Deci used empirical methods to investigate innate growth tendencies and psychological needs underlying self-motivation and personality integration as well as the conditions that promote these processes. The continuum of self-determination ranged from amotivation or lack of action, resulting from not valuing an activity (Ryan, 1995), not feeling competent to do it (Bandura, 1986), or not expecting it to yield a desired outcome (Seligman, 1975) to the highly autonomous state of intrinsic motivation.

The social cognitive theory explains how people acquire and maintain certain behavioral patterns, while also providing the basis for intervention strategies (Bandura, 1997). Behavioral change depends on factors of environment, people, and behavior. These three factors constantly influence each other. Behavior is not simply the result of the environment and the person, just as the environment is not simply the result of the person and behavior (Glanz et al., 2002). The environment provides models for behavior. *Observational learning* occurs when a person watches the actions of another person and the reinforcements that the person receives (Bandura, 1997). The concept of behavior can be viewed in many ways. *Behavioral capability* means that if a person is to exhibit a certain behavior, he must know what the behavior is and have the skills to demonstrate it.

There are two major factors influencing the likelihood that one will take preventive action:

1. A person must believe that the benefits of performing the behavior outweigh the costs (that is, a person should have more positive than negative outcome expectancies). More importantly, the person must have a sense of personal agency, or self-efficacy with respect to performing the preventive behavior and must believe that he or she has the skills and abilities necessary for performing the behavior under a variety of circumstances. This fits in with my enquiry into the mindsets and thought processes of the adolescent.
2. Social Cognitive Theory defines human behavior as a triadic, dynamic, and reciprocal interaction of personal factors, behavior, and the environment. The mind is regarded as an active force that constructs one's reality, selectively encodes information, performs behavior on the basis of values and expectations, and imposes structure on its own actions. According to this theory, an individual's behavior is uniquely determined by each of these three factors.

Many cognitive theories assume that learning results from interaction with the environment. Thus, the situation the street inhalant is in, the street culture and his experiences are an important part of his learning and a determinant of his positive movement off the streets.

Mindsets

A mindset refers to a set of assumptions, methods, or notations held by one or more persons or groups of people. This established mindset creates a powerful incentive within these people or groups to continue to adopt or accept prior behaviors, choices, or tools. This phenomenon of cognitive bias is also sometimes referred to as mental inertia or "groupthink" and it is often difficult to counteract its effects upon analysis and decision-making. A single mindset is unlikely to possess the flexibility and adaptability needed to address all future events.

The process by which the child adapts to street life may be illustrated by the diagram in Figure 1.1.

Figure 1.1 Adaptation to Street Life

VULNERABILITY ⟶ SURVIVAL ⟶ COPING STRATEGIES

The street drug consumption phenomenon in Mumbai reveals a cycle of entrapment and release. In Mumbai, two major employment activities of the street children are drug enhancing.

1. The recycling industry wherein a majority of the traders pay the street ragpickers partly in cash or partly in drugs and hold back some of the money due, so that he is forced to return.

2. The *wadi* or seasonal marriage party celebrations, which involves an overnight engagement for catering and decor, brings together large numbers of this homologous group. Sexual abuse, gambling, and drug abuse are by-products.

Nearly 70 to 80 percent are addicted to inhalant volatile solvents. Inhalant abuse is the intentional inhalation of a volatile substance for the purpose of achieving a euphoric state. It is also known as solvent abuse, volatile substance abuse, glue sniffing, sniffing, and huffing. It is an under-recognized form of substance abuse with significant morbidity and mortality. Dependence is severe and has both behavioral and biological aspects. Behaviorally, dependence is often characterized by loss of control over one's use of substance. Dependent people may organize their lives around getting and using a substance. Biological or physiological dependence is typified by tolerance, withdrawal symptoms, or both (American Psychiatric Association, 1994).

The street adolescent's drug consumption may be regarded as an outcome of his limited awareness of options to spend the money he earns. He lives in a group that protects him from police beatings and from bigger bullies who rob or abuse him. His drug consumption, therefore, is not a physiological necessity but a survival strategy to conform to and belong to the clique, who in essence becomes his nucleus, a mechanism to street life-survival patterns, assigning him a collective identity and credibility.

Drug consumption is not a marginalizing element among his peers; rather it is one that brings him acceptability and initiates him into mainstream street culture. Thus it is the consequence of a number of street-cultural factors all acting together—the need to conform to societal norms, the need for security from oppressive forces and guardian control. Ironically, it is an encouragement to social deviance by street elders and peers. On the street, the core values of sobriety, ambition, conformity, and economic independence are replaced by hedonism, defiance of authority, and the quest for "kicks." This then may be regarded as elements of a "street culture" that exists as a sub-culture within the domains of a larger culture, the compromise between the contradictory needs of expressing autonomy and maintaining parental identification. Matza and Sykes (1961) found embedded in youth culture those subterranean values (the search for risk, excitement, and adventure) which served to underpin certain aspects of street culture (postponement of gratification, routine).

It is a fact that more and more street children are becoming addicted to drugs, especially solvents. Drug use is inextricably intertwined with the adolescent's survival on the street. The addict moves from a honeymoon usage of the drug, through habituation to a stage of deterioration. Movement through these stages is aided by a number of factors. The constellation of the street adolescent's relationships juxtaposes a sub-culture unique to the streets; gambling, sexual abuse and promiscuity, the consumption of chemical substances are interwoven into this very fabric. Within this ambience, the street child's addiction may be perceived on a continuum, ranging from a period of honeymoon with the drug to persistent usage, a habit that is compulsive and moves inexorably into progressive deterioration (see Figure 1.2).

Figure 1.2 Continuum of Drug Addiction

HONEYMOON USAGE⟶ HABITUAL USAGE ⟶ PROGRESSIVE
DETERIORATION

Certain issues and concerns about inhalant substance abusing male street adolescents and their lifestyle need to be addressed:

1. Their instant decision-making: What are the thought processes that underlie this? What factors trigger this process? What impact does guidance have on such decision-making? Do factors such as length of stay on the street or traumatic past family experience have an effect? Is instant decision-making only an impulse or can it become a pattern?
2. Is there a constraint to thinking beyond the immediate consequences of their actions?
3. What are the thought processes of those who are reintegrated? What precipitates their movement off the streets? What motivates them to seek to improve their lives?
4. Is going back to the streets the only option available, according to the adolescents?
5. Where exactly can I, as a guardian, make decisions for them?

LIFESTYLE OF A STREET ADDICT

Street children experience different lifestyles in different environments and therefore undergo a very different kind of socialization unique to the streets; gambling, sexual abuse and promiscuity, and the consumption of chemical substances are interwoven into this very fabric. These sociocultural complexities of the street characterize their survival modes (Beazley, 2003).

In Mumbai, the street drug addict looks to his peers as a supportive mechanism for his existence on the street. Ennew for example, notes how street children, in the absence of parents, bring each other up and "develop supportive networks, coping strategies and meaningful relationships outside adult supervision and control" (Ennew, 1994a: 409–10).

It is the pressure exerted by this group on the street adolescent to conform to their lifestyle, combined with the adolescent's own need to "belong," that most often precipitates their drug-taking behavior.

Substances used by street children are inexpensive. Glue, solvents, and petrol are affordable by street adolescents. "Solution" costing ₹20 per bottle (in 1999) crashed to ₹2 per bottle (in 2003) and ₹10 per bottle in 2007. Thus, market forces fluctuate to accommodate price changes and still generate demand, and together with easy availability, sustain addiction.

External agencies and authorities in Mumbai are not very effective in controlling the growth of this phenomenon. There is reluctance on the part of the law-enforcing authorities to arrest drug users and offenders, due to the problems caused by withdrawal-related consequences in lock-ups. There is an inadequacy of treatment centers for this category of youngsters whose ability to pay is uncertain.

The inability of the street adolescent to ensure the safety of the money he earns means that he spends whatever he gets that day, most often on an increased intake of drugs. This further intensifies his craving, not merely for the drug but also for the environment that offers him the freedom to sustain his habit. Therefore, he becomes addicted to the streets.

FIVE PHASE THERAPEUTIC PROGRAM

The addiction to the streets and its environment is a strong "pull factor" in the life of the street child. His introduction to "solution" marks his honeymoon period with the drug. It is during his middle and later adolescence, when he consumes the drug on a sustained basis, experiences health problems, and witnesses the trauma of older street addicts, that he begins to perceive his drug use as a problem (D'Souza, 2003). Based on this study, my experience in the field, and the pilot experiment with street addicts that I had conducted in 1993, I developed a Five Phase Therapeutic Model to help street adolescents overcome their drug and street addiction problem (see Figure 1.3). Valuable insights and suggestions from the staff and the children helped develop a syllabus for each phase of the program.

Figure 1.3 Five Phase Therapeutic Approach

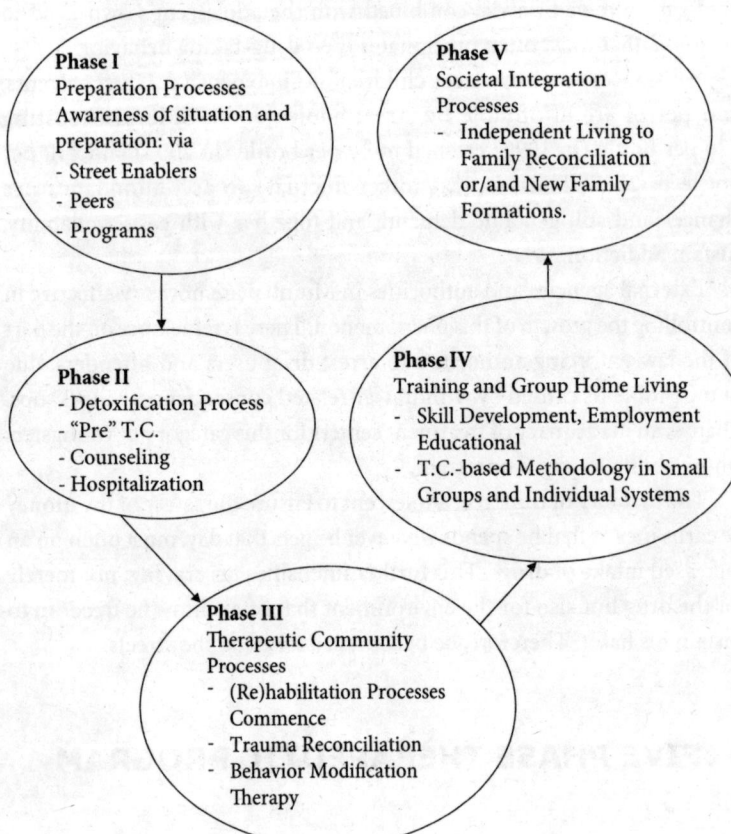

The Five Phase Therapeutic Approach aims to impart family values, controls, security, and guidance. It seeks to address the vicissitudes of street culture and build upon past existential experiences through reflective and therapeutic approaches, thereby building a societal integrative congruence for the child within the program. It marks a paradigm shift from not just viewing drug consumption as the problem but taking a more holistic view, that of addressing street subculture itself. It has individual as well as collective dimensions. The individual seeks to move to socially acceptable patterns of living through his own resolve and capacities within a supportive peer environment.

This rehabilitation model lays stress on facilitating a paradigm shift: "From the Streets" to "Off the Streets," "From Relapses and Having No Alternatives" to "Positive Possibilities." This approach addresses not merely the phenomenon of drug use but helps the child "off" the streets; a movement to positive options to counter addiction and qualitative improvement in lifestyle.

The program helps the street adolescent to build his self-esteem and confidence, show him that he has self-worth towards a positive future. Children possess an inner potential, wealth, and strength of personality which needs developing. Each child needs to be made aware that he is a normal human being, who possesses multiple talents, emotions, and above all, a future. This program seeks to inculcate self-worth, pride, and motivation in these street adolescents.

The Therapeutic Program recognizes the following:

1. Drug consumption is not the problem but rather a consequence of a combination of factors intrinsic to street life.
2. Majority of street adolescents' occupations sustain their street lifestyle.
3. Relapse and sustenance of street culture is due to a lack of shift in the mindset.

The key factor is working with the adolescent's mindsets and thinking to prompt a rehabilitative life. The program builds on past existential experiences through reflective and therapeutic approaches and seeks to encourage a move towards integration into mainstream society. The program follows five connected steps or phases, all participatory in nature.

Phase I: *The Preparatory Phase*

The outreach contact phase, when the street enablers first build rapport with the adolescent street inhalant abusers on the streets. They bond with the outreach team at their "locales" of congregation, get symptomatic services such as medical aid, recreation, counseling, have reflective games, "thinking exercises." The monthly fairs (*melas*) too are a tool for building rapport and establishing a relationship of trust with the street children.

For many of them, this contact is the first time they begin thinking about changing their lifestyle. They are then offered an orientation to the Five Phase Program for two–three days at camps away from the streets. Once an addict expresses the desire to improve the quality of his life, he is encouraged to adhere to that decision. He is then guided through to the next stage, that of medical detoxification in a public hospital.

Phase II: The Medical Detoxification Phase

In this phase, the street adolescent male inhalant abuser is examined by a physician to determine the general state of his health. He is oriented as to what to expect during the abstinence and detoxification stage. I call this stage the "meditative pause," when he begins thinking about his future. Being confined to a hospital bed, the adolescent has the time to reflect on an alternative lifestyle. These adolescents can be helped to overcome the "withdrawals of street life" through counseling, recreation, and most importantly, by being with them. Their decision to enter the program is based more on experimentation (for most first timers), "let's see" rather than a firm decision.

Phase III: The Therapeutic Community Living Phase

The adolescent goes through a residential, rehabilitative orientation of counseling, goal-setting, talent identification, career guidance, discipline, and a psycho-spiritual program for a period of approximately 6 to 8/10 months depending upon individual progress. There is a systematic plan for each child. Towards the end of this phase, there is aptitude testing, wherein his expressed field of interest is matched with his practical skill. Thus his moveout from his context in Phase III to workshops in the neighborhood is further motivation to change his mindset and modify his behavior.

From dependence during the third phase, he moves to becoming independent enough to take his own decisions and responsibility for his actions. His movement into the next phase is depicted in the diagram shown in Figure 1.4, wherein his past "psychological brokenness" is mended for his future; his mindset has shifted towards his movement off the streets.

Figure 1.4 Transformational Change

WORKING ON THE PAST ——————→	WORKING FOR THE FUTURE
DEPENDENCE ON A ——————————→ STRUCTURED PROGRAM	LIFE OF RESPONSIBILITY AND DECISION-MAKING

PHASE IV: *THE TRAINING PHASE*

The street inhalant abuser begins to live in an institutionalized boarding for specialized courses or in a room under the supervision of the resident staff, during which he takes minor decisions. This phase helps bring about active change in lifestyle. He is more purposive and his change of lifestyle is a process of resilience building. Factors that promote resilience in children that are best equipped to overcome adversities, especially those which occur during periods of transition which I refer to as the "limbo state," include the ability or the opportunity to "make a difference" by helping others, enrollment in skill-training courses for employment, undertaking part-time work, and exposure to challenging situations which provide opportunities to develop both problem-solving abilities and emotion-coping skills. He is trying to establish his identity as a respectable citizen and reintegrate himself in society by performing duties and chores that are socially acceptable.

PHASE V: *THE REHABILITATION/REINTEGRATION PHASE*

There are three "pillars" of social reintegration: housing, education/ vocational training, and employment. Once each individual completes his training/education according to his interest, he moves into the next stage where he begins to live independently and manages his savings and career moves. This phase marks a mindset change from his life on the streets, where he thinks and acts as a reintegrated member of society.

The street adolescent addict who comes into the Five Phase Program rootless, roofless, insecure, vulnerable, and unsure, leaves the program with a sense of belonging, stronger, more confident, and ambitious, having finally found a dream and purpose in life. With the skills and talents he develops, he can now support himself.

BEHAVIOR MODIFICATION

There have been several models, responses, services, and other interventions addressing the use of inhalants by street adolescents. Freire's seminal work, *Pedagogy of the Oppressed* (1970), provides inspiration for those who have traditionally worked with people who do not have a voice, which includes street children. A powerful notion in Freire's work is "conscientization," a process for developing critical consciousness that can transform reality and make the street adolescent critically conscious of his reality, vulnerability, and self-worth. This consciousness leads to a desire to change his behavior and subsequently a mindset change from his street pattern of thinking.

Behavior modification refers to using strategies to get a child to change by providing tools to reinforce positive behavior and change the negative ones. Such techniques tend to be highly effective in young children as they are not set in their ways. I found it effective in creating and sustaining long-term change in male street inhalants. Behavior modification needs emotional intelligence, which these children have developed due to their exposure and by handling survival pressures on the streets.

> Emotional intelligence is the ability to perceive emotions, to access and generate emotions so as to assist thought, to understand emotions and emotional knowledge, and to reflectively regulate emotions so as to promote emotional and intellectual growth. (Mayer and Salovey, 1997: 9)

The street adolescents' enhanced emotional intelligence enables them to understand themselves, their goals, intentions, responses and behavior, understand others and their feelings. This helps the adolescent to begin unlearning his street patterns, handle his own feelings, and respond to his peers in an acceptable manner.

REFLECTIONS ON MY JOURNEY

The feet that walked tirelessly through life's many streets...

I call them street children, street adolescents, street inhalants, and street youth. These terms have been used interchangeably. "*Children in street situations*" refers to those who are on the streets, alternating between the street and institutions, and still possess and are governed by the mindset of street life. "*Children in institutions*" include those whose mindsets have altered as a result of sustained stay at an institution, who are focused on their goals, and are on the road to repatriation or rehabilitation. When referring to "*Children at home*," I mean those who have a network of relationships to sustain their bonding to their families.

In my study, the young male street inhalant abusing adolescents whom I contacted on the streets from Phase I and those who joined the program and belonged to the age group of 14 to 17 years are referred to as street adolescents.[2]

They came in numbers, in twos and threes ... how many were they in all?

Participants in qualitative research studies are collaborators not "subjects." I initially worked with 30 adolescents (male inhalant abusing street adolescents) who were part of the rehabilitation program. This number eventually worked out to 15, whose changing mindsets I recorded, studied, and analyzed. Of the 15, six completed the Five Therapeutic Phases and were rehabilitated, two dropped out after Phase II, two during Phase III and two more during Phase IV. One each returned and stayed on in Phases II, III, and IV of the program.

Data collection was lively and interactive, and the exercise of originality and reflective critical judgment of the participants contributed to the richness and diversity of the data. It included naturally occurring ethnographic data, focus group discussions (FGDs), formal and informal meetings with the team members, unstructured interviewing, and group interviews. Gaining their trust and informed consent was my main refrain.

I have reflected and drawn from my vast experience of the past 26 years of living and working with these children. This experience has aided my insights and reflections, and guided my inquiry.

As they walked the streets of life, as they sang the song of life, I recorded, reflected, and rewrote the script for a better tomorrow...

---

[2] I took a sample of 30 adolescents for my study, since from my experience; I expected 50 percent to drop out, not be accessible thereafter or be reluctant to participate in the study.

Chapter 1 introduces the mood, sets the tone and reflects the rhythms of the street adolescents.

The competing and often conflicting influences on the street form the crux of Chapter 2, which focuses on the street adolescents' *Self-worth* and its multifarious components. This chapter essays the fluid nature of their identities, and the process of development and transformation of their self-worth.

In Chapter 3, I have focused upon *Personal Ownership*, which to me, is an iterative process for the street adolescents and includes elements such as freedom, personal autonomy, personal possessions, preferences, decisions, attitudes as well as street culture.

Chapter 4 explores the processes determining the adolescent's decision to *Move off the Street*; the factors that precipitate such movement, the impact that such a movement has on the street adolescent and the factors that may attract him back to the streets.

Chapter 5 highlights the role of *Organizations* as primary caregivers, the spectrum of service provision, the ethical dilemmas that confront organizations, criteria for inclusion and exclusion, and problems relating to staff and management. It concludes with recommendations for monitoring, evaluation, program appraisal, advocacy, and policy measures.

Chapter 6 relates to the final cycle of the research focusing on a sample of 15 adolescents. The focus is on *Mindsets*, on cognitive inputs designed to stimulate reflective thought, enhance emotional intelligence, and search for alternatives leading to sustained behavioral change among street inhalant abusers. It is the crux of the research that traces the mindset change and thought processes of the street adolescent.

Finally, in Chapter 7, I have tried to answer the research questions that have dogged my mind from the commencement of my work. It also includes recommendations for further work.

> The landmarks were Reflect, Reorganize, Reinstate, but they took on different hues, different trends—downward, upward, and inward—through my meanderings.

2

Shadows and Silhouettes

SELF-WORTH

> Socialization refers to an interactive process of transmitting and learning "acceptable" ways of acting, interpreting and feeling. This process is viewed as occupying a central place in the lives of children. Sociologists analyze socialization as an important clue to determining how children construct their identities, interpretations and social relations ... (Visano, 1990: 139)

Individual and group identities are constructed in relation to others. Therefore, our sense of self is established through the boundaries we create to exclude that which is different. The formation of the self-image begins very early in a child and is developed and modified by others in the family and, as the child ventures outside the family, by other groups and individuals. The early development years are critically important for the development of self-regulation; the set of abilities that enable children to control their emotions and behavior, interact positively with others, and engage in independent learning. The ability to cope with stress can be nurtured by helping children develop self-esteem, which is a fairly accurate assessment of oneself, leading to the realization that the self has worth. It is in achieving this self-esteem or sense of self that we achieve psychosocial growth and maturity. This self-image is the basis of self-worth, affecting the child's self-concept, parent's perception of the child and parent's behavior toward the child.

The constant affirmation by significant people in the child's life further reiterates his self-concept and mindset. However, street boys are products of "nature" and seldom beneficiaries of "nurture," growing up with the sole belief in the "survival of the fittest." The street boys are aware of their abilities and potential, but never had a chance to achieve what they had planned when leaving home. All the boys experience physical and mental growth, harsh personal encounters on the street, and changing social situations that affect their identity. Identity is a person's sense of placement in the world; that which tethers one to one's self-worth. The street boys' identities are created by the way they are treated in the city. The police abuse them, the common people think they are a nuisance and look down upon them, and this denial, disdain, and derision crushes their self-esteem. Objective testing of self-esteem is difficult as street children are self-derogatory and this is two-sided—on the one hand, it lowers their self-esteem, and on the other, it serves to enhance their earning potential from begging or related activities.

Individual and collective identities of street children are often fluid, arising out of their daily interactions and are understood in terms of a mental and physical escape from numerous negative experiences and as a solution to their personal troubles. Through the various stages of assimilation to street life, street boys have been able to construct alternative identities and collective strategies among themselves as a form of resistance to the outside world. These strategies provide a matrix within which street children can contest the marginalization imposed on them by mainstream society and regain feelings of belonging and self-worth. Thus, even though their lives are regularly portrayed in a negative way, and as a "problem" which needs a solution, their decision to leave an impoverished or abusive home should, in fact, be understood as the child's own solution to a personal predicament. Street children do not lack agency, but take responsibility for their own actions and have some control over their lives. The creation of street children's self-worth and the maintenance of their own subcultures should be viewed not as a problem but as a response to their stigmatization and a solution to the variety of problems that they face in a world which is hostile to their very existence.

> Often if you ask street children with whom they roam, they will reply, "alone with God," although they are normally in the company of their peers. Street life is marked by both wrenching solitude and intense solidarity. (Hecht, 1998: 46)

IMAGES AND MASKS—IDENTITIES
OF THE STREET CHILD

Street children have developed a whole repertoire of survival strategies and an alternative social reality that symbolize solidarity. These strategies include the appropriation of urban niches in the city in which they are able to earn money, feel safe, and find enjoyment, in addition to the "winning of space." It is within these marginal niches that street boys have constructed their own subculture, as a strategy for both collective and individual survival. For street children, the spaces they have carved out for themselves have become territories in which collective identities are constructed, and where alternative communities have formed. These typify street subcultures. Street subcultures have their own patterns of behavior and a discernable system of values and beliefs.

Socialization to a subculture helps a young person redefine negative self-concepts by offering a collective identity and a reference group from which to develop a new individual identity. A community of children who have similar background problems and experiences can provide new children on the street with comfort, support, and vital knowledge necessary to survive without adult supervision. Similarly, seasoned street children help to socialize newcomers to the street. The socialization provides new children with peer support and survival skills as well as a collective identity that assists them in their construction of a new positive self-image.

An analysis of a child's socialization to the street is important, as it provides significant evidence for determining how children construct their collective identities as "street children." Once on the street, children engage in specific social processes that socialize them to street life and adapt to a lifestyle which differs from the normal "accepted" lifestyle. Owing to the environment in which they live, street children experience a lifestyle different from that of an average child: they sleep, eat, play, and work on the street. They therefore require and undergo a very different kind of socialization.

As a child begins to identify himself as a street kid, he usually changes his name or he is given a new one by his friends. As one boy said, "*you never give your real name on the street, because if there is trouble you don't want to be implicated.*" Giving oneself a new name is also a form of resistance to being abused, and a way of creating a positive self-identity. Most street boys are given nicknames by other children, which they accept as part of their inclusion in the social group, even if they do not like the nickname.

Sashi Rodricks wanted to enroll himself in the NIOS system of education. His admission form needed details, but he was wary of revealing his background. He did not want us to trace his roots because he did not want to return home. Very reluctantly, he said that he came from a Muslim community, and that he had changed his name.

Changing one's name may be recognized as part of the psychological process of a child's repersonalization, as his self-identity undergoes changes and he begins to categorize himself in terms of a new social identity.

The street subculture offers a child who has fled home, a new identity as a child of the street or a street child. As they construct their new collective identities, the children are also expected to adopt appropriate attitudes, values, and perspectives in order to conform to established street etiquette and be accepted as members of the group.

COLLECTIVE VERSUS INDIVIDUAL IDENTITIES

Compliance with peer norms and expectations is an essential aspect of street subculture. Collective identity, security, and personal survival are subject to acceptance by the group. A street child must learn to balance his collective identity with other fluid identities, often resulting in the fragmenting of the presentation of the self. This is due to the multiple identities street children present for various activities and needs across different spatial areas, and the contradictions between these presented identities.

I observed Ramesh who looks much younger than his age (12), and assumes different identities. He acts tough and masculine when he is with older boys, and they like him as he is street smart, despite being small. When he is shining shoes, however, he assumes a more polite and deferential identity. At times he "acts cute" to obtain credit from stall owners or money from adults on the street. Sometimes he just enjoys being a child, which he so often has to keep in check.

There are, therefore, disparities between street children's collective and multiple self-identities; commitment to the subculture is often in the form of the adoption of an identity that is in contrast to the image of a child. This tough, masculine, adult-type behavior, or "assumed adulthood" has been used as evidence of street children having "lost childhood." Such constructions are based on adult concepts of childhood and belief in the need for the "innocence" of childhood. Although street children may, in some ways, have lost their "innocence," they have not lost their childhood, but are merely experiencing them differently.

The formation of a boy's street identity is a fluid process. The importance of spatial processes in the creation and development of their identities cannot be overlooked. The relationships that the street boy engages in also play an important role. Interaction with diverse environments influences identity formation; identities are influenced by social interactions that occur in particular spaces and by the way individuals see themselves as part of that interaction.

Late evening on the traffic island at the busy junction, Rafique, Pyarelal, and Hitesh were holding the piece of cloth that had their dose of "solution" in one hand, while with the other, they were sorting out the recycling material they had collected that afternoon. The traffic, the pedestrians crossing the junction were oblivious of their presence. I had known Pyarelal earlier and approached them for a chat. Within a few minutes, a sizeable crowd of twelve to fifteen people gathered. Pyarelal said, "Let's go uncle, you have attracted a lot of attention— now the traffic police will come and beat us."

By themselves these boys were not considered as objects of curiosity; my involvement gave passersby an interest in them. That traffic island was their "space and safe spot" to sort out their daily scrap materials at that time, they were familiar with the area and, for the past few months, were a familiar sight at that junction. What did Pyarelal and his friends think about the reaction of the people and the sudden attention they garnered due to my presence with them, I asked.

Pyarelal said,

These people do not care about us uncle, they must have thought you were a policeman in plain clothes who had come to arrest us.

Street children are comfortable being left alone. Their mixing with "other class people"[1] attracts suspicion. They are perceived as ones who come in contact with these "other class of people" only to cause harm. Hence their identity is constructed by the public. The street child tries to be as inconspicuous as possible. The "best time for outreach"[2] is at night when the streets are deserted and the adolescent is vulnerable to notice. His insecurity of being noticed at night is alleviated by his staying with a group. He only begins to change this mindset when he moves into a home or an institution. He now feels he is not doing anything wrong. He is not living on the streets and hence moves about more confidently.

This is typified in Ramana's attitude as an outreach peer educator. Ramana, a former street boy, lived in a residential home for six years. He was now working as a peer educator on outreach work and was assigned night duty. He was questioned several times by the police for working so late at night. He said, "*When I was sleeping on the streets, the image of seeing a policeman 20–30 meters away was enough for me to wake up and run for my life. Now I am proud to show him my identity card and wait for him to approach me.*" His self-image changed along with a shift in his identity. Earlier he feared the police; now he felt he was helping the police in keeping children off the streets. It gave him a sense of positive self-worth. Society's perception of street children when they try to relate to this "other class people" is well illustrated in this case.

Street children are rarely treated with respect, and their views and opinions are seldom taken into consideration by anyone. They go unnoticed in public places, their presence is not acknowledged; to warrant attention they would have to be doing something unusual or be given special attention by someone other than their kind. They are chased away from shops and restaurants by both owners and customers. Some street children are highly visible, and the subject of public concern because they are "out of place." Some see such children as victims; others see them more as small criminals. Often, society chooses not to see them at all.

The socialization process of the group can shape and direct a wide variety of behavior and, as the influence of parents wanes, that of the

---

[1] "Other Class People" are considered to be those people who do not generally mix with the street children. It could be the middle and upper class people.

[2] "Best time for outreach": The night time is considered as the most suitable time to meet the street child. While the city sleeps, he is a conspicuous by his presence on streets with very few or no people. He does not have work and is often in a group by night.

peer group increases. Acquiescence to/acceptance/exhibition of another's power appears to be the inevitable price of becoming a member of the group. Inclusion or acceptance into the group demands proving oneself and converting to the overriding peer point of view. For instance, peer support can take the form of peer pressure, which converts individuals to the view that certain drug-taking is safe, accepted by the group, and even prestigious. Thus, drug consumption becomes a requirement for group entry. Through his drug habit, the street boys develop identities that are directly opposed to the acceptable societal structure. This marginalizes them further and gives them a feeling of low self-worth in comparison with the larger society, while at the same time it establishes them firmly in mainstream street culture.

COMPONENTS OF SELF-WORTH ON THE STREETS

Self-worth gives a new dimension to the street adolescent whose image consciousness inspires him to groom himself, begin having dreams of a future and look for a relationship with the opposite sex with a desire to be successful. Attire constitutes an important aspect of self-worth among street boys. Typically, street boys are seen as slovenly, dirty, and unkempt, and this greatly determines the way others behave towards them. Being regarded in the same light as the rags they pick is a further blow to their self-esteem and sense of self-worth. They become conscious of the "dirty" nature of their ragpicking and scrap-collecting work and make efforts to look for other "less dirty" occupations.

In an effort to overcome this, the street boys attempt an image makeover—they dress up and attract the attention of the opposite sex, particularly the female street enablers. Appreciation by these female street enablers enhances their pride in themselves and bolsters their self-esteem. Gautam said, "*I like it when Saku didi says you are looking good.*"

The desire to be clean and well-groomed may also be attributed to the adolescent street boys' sexual activity. Those who have active sex lives are observed to bathe every day, maintain their hair and are well-dressed. Engaging in sexual activity with a prostitute or with a smaller boy and the sense of being wanted by someone, for whatever purpose, forms an important dimension of enhanced self-worth. On the other hand, there are some who, out of fear of being targeted for sexual abuse, try to appear as dirty and filthy as possible, in the hope that they will be left alone. Appearing dirty and filthy also would mean that they could get easy money by begging.

Role preservation is at the root of the image that the street boy adopts and conveys. He establishes a mindset of being appealing to others to attract attention to the image he wants to show.

PERCEPTION OF FREEDOM ON THE STREETS

Street children usually have a love–hate relationship with street life. On the one hand, it is a perilous existence; they are permanently exposed to violence and aggression and have to struggle to survive. On the other hand, many children are very attached to the streets: they live an adventurous and carefree existence with their peers. The street is their life, their home, their family. They have built their own world, which is often far removed from the society that cast them aside.

The strongest factor that ties the children to the streets is the freedom it offers. That freedom is often their only possession and, therefore, it is the last thing they would like to relinquish. Street children are not used to living within the boundaries of four walls with strict rules and regulations, and regard this as a threat to their freedom. It is one of the factors that time and again attract these children back to the streets, and the reason why so many children cannot sustain a prolonged stay in a home or an institution. I have tried reflecting with them and asking them what are the positive aspects of living on the streets compared to the positive aspects of living in a home/institution. They said that "at Home we get ₹100, while on the streets we get 10 Rupees worth of life!" Yet after one such session, five of the bigger boys, the very ones who had enumerated the positive aspects of living in the Home, decided to leave. Later, I realized that among the negative aspects of street life, they had mentioned "money" which enticed them into drugs and visiting prostitutes. For them, it was a "here and now" situation, where they wanted "instant gratification" with little thought for its negative consequences. I understood that self-discipline is not acquired immediately or with a change of scene, but is learnt over a period of time.

During the stay at the detoxification camp, the boys see a way of life that is disciplined, with limited mobility and not being able to do as they desire. It is in contrast to what they have been experiencing on the streets. Although they see no positive future by continuing on the streets, they are still not yet ready to change their mindset. They view it as "a giving up" rather than "a gaining something" for themselves. In fact, two-thirds of the boys decide to go back to the streets after the detoxification orientation camp.

STREET BROTHERHOOD

The socialization process, very often, initiates the street children into culturally deviant behavior such as drug abuse, frequent and unsafe sex practices and illegal procurement of money. Relationships that evolve among the street children are marked by trust and distrust, love and hate, loyalty and betrayal.

Conforming to street life involves drawing and coercing street boys into performing particular behavior. They often develop a special relationship with those who are respected and feared in the group and tend to imitate the older boys.

Chotu was made to dance to a Bollywood tune regularly which he used to do in an amusing manner. Being in the constant company of the bigger boys, he picked up abusive language from them and would use it on those slightly older to him. A volunteer from Europe saw this and remarked, "He is being used like a puppet." He was often acting this way, to obtain the favors of sweets, toys, or special food from some of the bigger boys who doted over him.

Chotu's case brought to mind what psychology regards as positive reinforcers of behavior that is food and approval, those stimuli which increase the possibility of responses being repeated.

A bigger group of 10 to 15 boys may sleep together, yet the street child will form a close bond with one or two peers, whom he considers his close friends and whom he will stand by even if they are wrong. This I witnessed during one of my outreach rounds in Mumbai.

Ali and Hussein, both 13–14 years old were sleeping with a group of 13 other boys, when a fight broke out between them. Ali accused Hussein of robbing him when he was sleeping. Imran (Hussein's friend) supported Hussein and said that it was Hussein's money. Hussein argued that he had won the money gambling that evening. Three to four other boys from the group woke up with the commotion, and, using abusive words, urged them to go to sleep, while the others just opened their eyes and then went back to sleep ignoring the fight.

— Night Outreach, September 2004

There is a loose togetherness within a larger group, often to be protected from a bigger bully, a thief, or the police at night. In reality, the street boy may bond with just one or two close friends who are his intimate colleagues. His behavioral patterns revolve around this small group.

Rajeevbhai, 24 years, was the "dada" (don) of 14 odd boys at the city suburban station. The boys had to hand over a part of their daily earnings to him. In return, he "protected" them—if they were taken away by the police, he tried to release them by paying off the police. He laid down a few rules; any new boy on that station had to be brought to him first, there was to be no stealing, no taking drugs, any "uncle or didi" (male and female street enablers) was to be introduced to him first. He had to be informed immediately of any new developments affecting the boys.

—Street Contact Program, Monthly Report, November 2005

Rajeevbhai believed that drug-taking and participating in any criminal activity would get the police to disturb the group's existence in the station and hence he decided not to "allow" any unwanted activity by the boys. My team suggested placing Rajeevbhai as a role model for other group leaders. We invited him for the "mela" and asked him to speak to a gathering of 500-plus boys. The use of positive role models has been an effective tool for street children's learning.

Fear of the bigger bullies is a constant for the street boy. The older street boys terrorize the younger boys into sharing their earnings, and out of fear, they give in without any argument or resistance. The older boys feel that they are entitled and thus help themselves to it. The bullies or protectors often abuse the younger boys sexually. Some regard themselves as "positive role models" for the younger boys, giving them useful suggestions in matters of survival—where to find free food distribution outlets, where to keep their change of clothes, what event to go for, and which institution is good for them—and at the same time, coerce the younger boys into gambling, taking drugs, prostituting themselves, spying on other peers, and forcing money out of them. The street boy is not always in a position to resist the seductions offered by the "protector," as they offer him a sense of security, camaraderie, and peer support. It is a strange interpolation of fear–anger–hatred–security as well as awe and suppression.

This type of a relationship carries on in their other interactions, too. The scrap merchants in the city's central area employ large numbers of street boys to bring in recycling materials, and try to keep them bonded by paying them partly in cash and partly in drugs for their services. In the institution too, the resident younger boys are bullied by the older boys, if not for sexual favors then for other favors such as food, attention, and money.

There is a sense of solidarity and brotherhood that the group appears to substitute for family. The boys use inhalants to initiate and enhance friendships. However, there may be an element of distrust within the street group. Evidence points to the fact that most violence and abuse of children is perpetrated by the very people in whom children are entitled to trust thus destroying their security and leaving them defenseless and vulnerable. There is the strong prevalence of the "protector–utility boy relationship" with its concomitant use–abuse cycle. The removal of trust takes away the ability to believe in others; isolation, uncertainty, and suspicion replace happiness and security. The coexistence of these sentiments highlights the precariousness of surviving on the street; of having to remain in groups for safety, fun, and recreation; and also having to bear the constant struggle and possibility of rupture and betrayal within the group.

These situations sometimes force the street boy to seek self-protection from the prevalent street culture of gambling, promiscuity, and addiction and may precipitate a mindset change to his first tentative motions and thoughts towards moving off the street.

DEALING WITH THE MEN IN UNIFORM

Street children are frequently detained arbitrarily simply because they are homeless or criminally charged with vague offenses such as loitering, vagrancy, or petty theft. They are tortured, beaten, not allowed to earn a wage by police due to not possessing a license, or held as a preventive measure, as they are seen as a high-risk criminal group. They make up a sizeable proportion of those children who enter the criminal justice systems and are committed finally to correctional institutions (remand homes) that are euphemistically called correctional schools, often without due process.

In my first four years at the Residential Home (1995–99), I was frequently called towards the end of the month, in the early hours of the morning, or late night to come and sign for the release of a boy from the Residential Home who was returning from his night duty. There was *naka bandi*.[3] The police had to have "x" number of cases in their registers and it was common knowledge that they would pick up street youngsters under false charges and release them after procedures were complete. If they could not pay for their release, they had to spend a few days in the police lock-up. Often I had to intervene with the police to release them.

Raghu (19 years) was our peer educator. His assignment was to go twice a week on night outreach from 8.00 pm to 12.00 midnight. One day, I received a call from the CST police station at 3.00 am to come and sign as guardian for Raghu to be released from police custody, as he was arrested on one of his outreach rounds. I was told that he was loitering suspiciously and was disturbing the peace of the area. These were false charges. Raghu, later, told me that he was caught while applying a bandage to one of the boys in the station. The constable beat him up, tore his Social Worker ID card, and he was slapped and falsely charged.
—Case File, Residential Home, 1997

This has been a common occurrence for the children and sometimes for the peer educator or street enabler, too. I questioned a few beat constables on how they viewed the street child. Their response was, "*Do not waste your time, these children are only cheats and criminals, it is useless trying to change them.*" They translated this view in their treatment and relationship with the children.

Arif, a shoe shine boy, refused to shine a policeman's shoes for free. He was beaten up and his money was taken away. He became a target for several other policemen

---

[3] *Naka bandi*: Police check point at a traffic junction.

*even when he did other odd jobs like selling pens in the train. They would take
away five to ten pens from his bag without paying for them. Arif said, "They are
not letting us earn honestly; if anyone is making us thieves, it is these policemen."*

Often the street child develops a scorn or contempt for authority,
though he may not get the opportunity to express it. Contempt comes
from being pushed around and finding himself helpless. The street child
feels he is incapable of helping his situation and feels a low sense of self-
worth. If you ask the street boy, who is your number one enemy, he will
invariably mention the police.

The helplessness and submissiveness towards the one wielding
unquestioned power and authority reflects the vulnerability of the street
child. He has no one to turn to. Instances of policemen sexually abusing
street boys are also rampant. The authority supposed to protect him
turns to be his exploiter. This leaves him dejected and further makes him
mistrust power structures and authority. When I questioned one such boy
as to why he did not complain, he replied, *"How can I, he is a policeman,
whom else could I go to?"*

THE LETTER OF THE LAW

The Juvenile Justice Act of 1986 (Amendment in 2000) seeks to consolidate
and amend the law relating to juveniles in conflict with law and children
in need of care and protection, by providing for proper care, protection,
and treatment by catering to their development needs. It adopts a child-
friendly approach in the adjudication and disposition of matters in the
best interests of children and for their ultimate rehabilitation through
various institutions established under this enactment. It has promulgated
that the police protect the rights of the child. The reality for street children
however, is that no such rights exist.

Senior police officers understand the plight of the children and refer
them to social workers, to the state-run correctional institutions, or to
a residential home. Unfortunately, though there has been some change,
much is left to be desired. The attitudinal change has yet to percolate down
to the beat constable.

TAINTED IMAGES

Street children do not suffer merely from physical homelessness, but also from a psychological homelessness since they have "nowhere to belong." The misconception is that street children are addicts, uncontrollable and violent, and have no emotions or moral values. As a result of these misconceptions, people tend to be unsympathetic and indifferent to the actual plight of street children. This lack of social acceptance pushes them away from mainstream society and forces them to survive on the fringes of the social system. Street boys internalize and take cognizance of the stigma of their street life and form negative opinions about themselves.

After the FGD session at the Detoxification Orientation Camp, I asked Samad, a peer educator, why the boys began with such a negative picture of themselves. He said, "*They just repeat whatever opinion the public harbors about them.*" This was a case of their inability to reflect on themselves. They live by their feelings and tend to go along with what the group/friends choose. Would opportunities and situations make them think and reflect upon their situation and bring change in their mindsets, despite a difficult transition?

SHADOWS OF THE PAST

Most street children have traumatized backgrounds. Their peers on the streets neither understand nor care about why they are acting strangely; often their method of cure is beating, teasing, or ostracism from the group. Owing to lack of education and awareness on mental health issues, the street peers do not consider these important, in fact, they even find them amusing.

About eight years earlier, Rahul's (13 years) mother immolated herself to escape the beatings of her husband. She tried to clutch Rahul while aflame but he managed to wriggle free and ran out to call the neighbors. This incident left a lasting impression on him. His father remarried and Rahul ran away at the age of 10 as he could not get along with his step-mother. Subsequently, whenever Rahul saw a fire lit, he would begin to scream and cry. To have "fun," his peers would then purposely keep a small pile of papers, cover his eyes, light the pile of papers and make him watch it and scream.

— Street Contact Program Report, March 2003

Homes too have not paid adequate attention to the mental health issues of the street child. There is an emphasis on education and future goal-setting and their achievement. This pushes aside the treatment of the trauma, the subtle psychological challenges that the child, who apparently appears "normal," faces. It is important that the institution too shifts its priority from education to treating mental health issues.

SHRINKING SELVES

A considerable number of street boys have low self-esteem or low self-concept, with a tendency to be negative.

At the first session of the orientation camp, I asked the boys to highlight two positive and two negative qualities. Not one was able to highlight a positive point, but faced no such problem with regard to their negatives; "We are bad people, we use bad words, we gamble, we take drugs, we have done something wrong by leaving home, we fight a lot, we are good for nothing." I asked them, "What about your good points, do you not have any positive aspects to say about yourselves?" They again mentioned, "We have many bad habits, we get on to the wrong side of the police."

I said, "Already here I can see some good—first of all, you are very honest in what you have said. Second, the fact that you all have come for this camp voluntarily shows that you desire to be good, you want to change for the better. Third, you are obedient, you have all come and sat through this session without disobeying, causing fights or using bad words." They began taking off from there, "Yes, I am a good friend of Krishna," said Somnath, "I looked after him and gave him food when he was sick." "I sent two new boys from the street to the Residential Home, otherwise they would become like us on the streets," said Anik.

— FGD Session, Detoxification Orientation Camp, June 2004

The first session of this camp made them feel proud of themselves and there were visible changes on their faces and in their behavior. They started believing that they did have good qualities and were not so bad after all.

Their inability to reflect has much to do with the stigmatization label that they appropriate. One of the reasons for depression and low self-worth is when these children lose out on opportunities.

Faizal (21 years) wanted to go to school. Since he did not have elementary education, it was not possible to admit him to any school at that age. He became very frustrated. Faizal decided to join an NGO in which he would be able to pick up reading and writing quickly and then do the NIOS[4] exams. However, no NGO was willing to admit a boy above the age of 15–16 years. He tried to get into technical trade schools but there too age was against him. This created a sense of low self-worth.

— Street Contact Program Report, 2001

The boys' low self-esteem leads them to care less about their own selves and to adopt what society considers deviant behavior. Accepting that they are not good is indicative of their reluctance to change. It is a defense mechanism that they use to escape humiliation. Much of this is influenced by their being labeled by society as aggressive and hostile. They feel that "this is our *karma*" and that change is not possible.

STREET MINES

The environment on the streets is exploitative and street children are subject to street fights, abuse, and bullying from older youth and the protector, harassment from the beat constable. They are not allowed to work and earn and are forced into deviant behavior (drugs, sex, theft, and fights) against their will. The degree of prevalence of these factors in their external environment further marginalizes and shapes their identity. It also determines whether their spatial mobility is derived voluntarily or is coerced. The vulnerability of one situation in reality puts them into another exploitative situation. It is a case of the proverbial "from the frying pan into the fire."

---

[4] National Indian Open School (NIOS) is an adaptive curriculum and formal education system set up by the Delhi Board of Education to help children who cannot go to formal school due to various reasons.

According to the staff team, most of the boys found ways to escape being sexually abused. One was to present a disheveled, dirty, and bedraggled appearance; the other was to forego the comforts of sleep to survive.

Birju, 12 years, was given a meal daily in return for staying up at night and looking after a street vendor's cart which was tied to a lamppost. Birju used to sit awake on the footpath the whole night and wake up the vendor's helper who used to sleep nearby, if anyone attempted to steal the cart. If the vendor's helper happened to wake up and catch Birju sleeping, he would hit him. Occasionally, Birju had to stand under the shop roof guarding the cart through the night, in the rain. But he was happy to do this in return for being safe and for lunch the following day from the cart-owner.

— Street Contact Program Report June 2005

The external environment goes a long way in making up the street child's psyche and perception of society. It is a constant struggle of survival and of choosing the lesser evil.

PHANTOMS OF THE MIND

In some instances, respect may be accorded by street boys to their peers and other adults, primarily due to fear. Often, street boys indulge in substance abuse and sexual promiscuity, out of the compulsion to please an older, stronger bully, or their "protector" whose respect they seek. For the same reason, the younger boys permit the older boys and other adults to abuse them sexually.

Riaz (10 years) would not talk about what he and Munaf (24yrs) were up to. When Munaf called him, he would go without protest, when he got back he would sit silent for a few hours.

Riaz was being sexually abused by Munaf. Occasionally he would give him a few sweets. Riaz hated yet feared him. When he got into any fights with his peers, he would call Munaf to settle it. His sitting in silence indicated his feeling of helplessness, fear, and resignation to his situation. The "protector" rules the mind of the "utility boy" by wielding power and fear.

The street boys' physical development is undermined by irregular diet and sniffing glue for which they do not mind missing a meal or two. Skin and respiratory diseases and dental decay weaken the growing child. However, what they suffer from most are the psychological effects of life on the streets.

In my first year in the Residential Home (September 1995), we had boys dying of various ailments, almost one each, on a monthly basis. Sunder, 19 years old, an inmate of the Residential Home, was pushed out of a running train. He went into a coma and after three weeks, succumbed to his injuries. Since we were not his legal guardians and did not have the address of his next of kin, we requested the coroner permission for us to be present for his cremation. Sunder's body was brought for burial after two months in the morgue with twelve other unclaimed bodies, a result of railway or road accidents. Some had their torsos cut in two, some were limbless and some disfigured beyond recognition. All were piled together in a heap on a pyre and cremated. It was one of the most psychologically disturbing experiences for the ten boys who accompanied us. It left a lasting impression on them. They kept asking questions: "Do we matter at all to anyone? We are worthless; we will die uncared for."
We counseled them for the next few months individually and in small groups.

IDENTITIES OF A STREET CHILD

The experience was used as a motivator to change their situation, to propel the boys of that group to begin making themselves useful to society, to begin learning skills so that they could go into mainstream work or return home. It left deep emotional scars on them and their low self-worth was further intensified if they failed at learning skills or faced adjustment problems in their work situations or with their families.

Beneath the show of bravado, life on the margins is bleak and street boys suffer from intense feelings of despair and extremely low self-esteem. There are no role models to look up to, no parents to show them a different lifestyle. Everyone they know shares the same experiences and they gradually accept the emotional void and loneliness as normal. "*There is no one who cares about us*" was a common statement we heard after the cremation experience. These experiences often strengthen the mindset of the boys that they are "not meant to be useful."

What makes the world of street children so tragic yet so fascinating, is that they inflict on themselves what has been done to them by others.

SELF-DESTRUCTIVE BEHAVIOR

Substance abuse, particularly inhalant abuse, is just one expression of their self-destructive behavior. Street boys invariably organize their survival around the purchase and consumption of harmful substances. Some boys say that these substances help repress feelings of hunger, cold, and abandonment. It is also seen as a way of coping with the many adversities of street life, some resulting from their own actions such as deteriorating health, the deaths of their friends, quarrels with loved ones, stigmatization, and other negative societal reactions. The boys are conscious of the fact that substance abuse is destructive. They are well informed of the consequences and inform each other of the risks involved. Even if they do not, there are always some outreach staff or street educators who routinely inform the boys about the risks. I have observed that they take delight in doing things they know they ought not to do. For instance, "I am upset about the fight, so I am eating tobacco in front of you." Another reason they express is the sense of "community" they get when they share drugs. It also provides a route towards an elevated social status, which their low self-worth craves for.

ALIASES AND HIDDEN IDENTITIES

Street boys seek anonymity within the streets. One of the main reasons for boys leaving home is conflict with the family or the law. They safeguard themselves by assuming aliases. It is quite common to find several Rajus, Babus, Santoshs, Mohammeds, and Salims. I have come across hundreds of boys using these names on the streets. The choice of names tends to be common, run-of-the-mill, designed not to draw attention in any way.

Street boys tend to tell lies for several reasons: out of fear of being traced back to their abusive homes or their disturbed past catching up with them or to maintain group cohesiveness. They tend to betray each other only if they have a past grouse with the person. Hence, lying about themselves or their circumstances frequently becomes a way of covering up their identity, to take on a new beginning, and to quell feelings of inadequacy and low self-worth. Siddharth (7 years) kept telling us that his native residence was the central city station and that he did not have parents as he "fell down from the sky."

One day while I was having an important discussion with a colleague, Siddharth started playing with a paper weight and disturbing the discussion. While giving him a drawing sheet and color pencils, my hand hit a statue of Mother Mary on my table. Siddharth immediately said, "Don't hit her, she is 'Big Mother'. Don't be like my father, he catches my mother's hair and bangs her on the wall, he takes me by the leg, swings me around and throws me in the field. As for my sisters, Saku and Meera, he shoves their heads near the fire stove when he is drunk…"

Siddharth did not want to go back to the abusive situation of his home and so made up a story that his seven-year-old mind could come up with. He hid behind it for as long as he could. I thought if we kept confronting him about the untruth of his story, he would leave the Home and be exposed to the dangers of the street. Hence, we gave him an opportunity to erase the lie in his own time and played along with it till he trusted us and was assured that we would not send him back to his abusive situation.

Another defense mechanism is to point a finger at a peer with whom there is an ongoing rivalry to detract attention from one's own misdoings. For instance, Shivnarayan, a resident, who resented the popularity of Jagdish, a responsible peer, chose to tell the European volunteers who were inquiring into cases of abuse, that Jagdish was abusing the younger boys in his care. This was an attempt by Shivnarayan to cover his tracks. Another ploy is to pretend innocence and be ingratiating.

From my window, I watched Mushtaq who was 15 years old, smoking. I called him, and he quickly tried to hide his cigarette. When I asked him about his smoking, he began swearing, taking the name of God and his mother. He touched my feet saying, "Why are you doing this to me? I do not touch cigarettes, how could you see me? I was just talking to someone downstairs." Then he asked me to sniff his hands and breath. They smelt of cigarette smoke, and when I asked two other boys to smell them, the bigger boy agreed that they did smell of cigarette, but the smaller boy denied it.

— Residential Home, February 1999

Often such incidents, despite having concrete evidence, make me harbor doubts. The lying behavior of the street boy is akin to drug-taking, and is an integral part of the survival repertoire on the streets. This learnt behavior forms a mindset, that being dishonest is important for survival. It is valued more as an art and a skill to learn and use when needed.

TO DO OR NOT TO DO?

Decision-making can often be a confusing experience. At the training phase of the drug rehabilitation program, when asked in a group, what they would like to do, eight of them said that they would like to be mechanics, seven drivers, and 15 wanted to study and work. It is very rare to get anything other than a "chorus answer," a choice they make because their friends have chosen the same. They are confused when asked to decide and hence take whatever decision they have heard the others taking. This confusion perpetuates feelings of low self-worth, especially when they are confronted with a need to make an informed decision. They are often the victims of impulse which underlies most of their actions, take security in the others' decision and make it their choice, too. It once again shows that lack of reflection and thinking about themselves is a drawback for their positive growth.

"IT IS MY *KARMA*..."

Younger boys seldom complain to authorities about being abused physically or sexually. They prefer to remain silent. It is a tacit form of acceptance of power over them. Physical force appears to exert greater influence over them than skill, talent, or intelligence. This is because power, which is valued and respected by street boys, is commonly associated with physical force. Good looks among the smaller boys are not always regarded as positive for it only makes them vulnerable to sexual abuse. Those who are handicapped are taken advantage of more often than "normal" boys, and given "a benefit" in exchange for their services.

Street children accept the fact that their lives on the street go hand in hand with exploitation and there is neither the belief that they can do anything nor the spirit to fight back. They suffer from the "can't do" syndrome, an outcome of their sense of insecurity which is again derived from being deprived of parental protection and guidance, food, home, and other basic amenities of life. It is the acceptance of unfairness, the helplessness in situations of overpowering force that keeps their self-opinion low. Their views about themselves are ambivalent; although they view themselves as helpful, they also think of themselves as bad boys doing "bad things." Hitesh typifies the opinion that a street boy has about himself, "*I am like this only, I am a bad boy, not good.*" He developed a mindset that he was bad and that change was not possible.

Mohan (16 years) had been sexually abused by his employer. When asked why he did not complain, he told me, "They are educated people, we are illiterate; we do not know anything. How can we say anything against them?"

Mohan's illiteracy was his vulnerability and this prompted a silent acceptance of his abusive situation. Education, therefore, was perceived by him as being only for "decent people." He thought nobody would accept his complaint because he was illiterate.

The concept of *karma* is deeply embedded in India's cultural ethos. In a simplistic sense, it implies a fatalistic belief that "certain things are ordained by fate" and that there is no way one can hope to change them. Some street boys harbor the notion that since their parents were enslaved by their circumstances, so are they. Thus, by embracing street life which seems inevitable to them, street boys feel they are choosing what has already been in their destiny and often give up efforts to change the situation. Such a mindset depreciates the street child's self-worth even further.

Sunny (10 years) had entered my room through the window while I was out of station. He managed to find a spare set of keys to my drawer and safe and robbed the petty cash savings of 40 boys. Sunny fed his companions lavishly and purchased small electronic goods with that money. When I returned, I called some of the big boys of the Residential Home, whose money was stolen. Sunny admitted to stealing. I asked them, "What do you want me to do now?" They replied, "Forget it, let it be, we have been always robbed on the streets, and here too this is nothing new; this is our life story."

— Case File, Residential Home, 1997

This seemed to indicate not merely the forgiving attitude and resilience of the boys who were wronged, but their fatalistic attitude towards this incident. A majority of those who think this way end up living all their lives on the streets. The others who are encouraged by social workers and institutional care, try to translate obstacles into opportunities and are successful.

IMAGE BOOSTERS

Street boys attempt to overcome their low self-worth by overt displays of machismo, trying to create an impression that they are strong and powerful. Some of this behavior may be traced to the rebellion redolent of the adolescent stage, while a good part of it owes its origin to the impact of Bollywood films that dominate much of their recreational outlets.

Lehfer (19 years) had premature grey hair when he was hardly 15; lazy by nature, he never tried to pick up a trade, got a little money from "wadikaam" at the end of the wedding season and if he wanted some money in between, he took a loan. A transformation took place when he was 18; he colored his hair black, shaved and bathed regularly, and got a new set of clothes. He wanted to look like Salman Khan (a Bollywood actor), enrolled for a driving course, and was on the look out for a stable job. He began "hanging around" the common water tap of the pavement dwellers. He was interested in a girl from one of the pavement families. He was taking steps to ensure that no one called him "lazy, good-for-nothing" anymore; if anyone did, he would get into a fist fight with them. Being well-built, he soon started earning their respect and was happy to show off his strength. He began doing weight training at the Residential Home.
— Case File, Residential Home, 2002

Thus, imitating reel-life heroes and getting into a relationship with the opposite sex helps enhance the boys' self-esteem by motivating them to set goals and improve their lives. Their mindset changes when there is an external stimulus such as the development of a relationship with the opposite sex. This change is at the feeling level and not after reflection and thinking. If his relationship is not reciprocated, it gives him a low self-worth and plunges him into deviant behavior such as drug abuse, gambling, or being destructive or depressive.

Younger boys accord respect to older and bigger boys. A positive aspect of such respect is the security that older boys frequently provide to the younger ones from harassment by law enforcers or other bullies and also help them in securing food and shelter. At the Residential Home, as is also the case on the streets, the experience varies according to age—the younger a new boy is, the more he is cared for.

When 5-year-old Chotu did not come back after an evening game in the nearby park, Tony, the self-styled leader of the boys, dispatched six boys to various railway stations and market areas. He called a meeting of the small boys' group to find out where Chotu was last seen and by whom.

There seems to be an unwritten code of protecting small boys from the vulnerability and harshness of the streets. There have been several incidents such as the above (both at the Residential Home and on the streets), where the big boys have been extremely concerned in ensuring that the little boys between 4/5 and 8/9 years are protected and cared for.

While forming relationships, street boys constantly seek different ways to earn the respect of their peers, visitors, outsiders, and street enablers, as this makes them feel good about themselves. What is uppermost for the street child is the money he can earn to survive. On the streets, the more he earns means the greater his chances of getting into gambling, drug abuse, and being robbed. Living in a Home or on his own in a rented room means greater respect and a stable future that involves an identity change from a street child to a contributory citizen.

Respect may be derived from the kind of job the street boys are engaged in. For instance, a street boy who works in a canteen and gets to wear a uniform to work, elicits greater respect compared to those engaged in ragpicking, washing vessels, or cleaning drains. As one boy remarked about another who cleaned toilets, "*He is like a worm from a dirty drain.*" Similarly, a boy who works as a salesman in a shop is regarded with respect, due to the relatively "clean" and less menial nature of his occupation.

Rahim, a sales representative for an Aqua guard company, wears a uniform consisting of a tie, with a blue shirt, black trousers and black shoes. He comes into the Residential Home after work, walks around in his uniform, and is the object of admiration and commands great respect. Although he gets ₹500 less than what he was earning in his earlier job as a carpenter's helper, he is proud to have this sales job.

A peer who has moved on to a skilled job after acquiring the requisite skills and training, also commands respect and serves as a role model for those on the streets and in the institution.

For the street boy, therefore, a stable job and working with "normal" citizens are a benchmark of success, of getting respect, and of making it into mainstream society. Mir (23 years) had worked as a paraprofessional with a street children's organization. Owing to some difficulties, he applied to some other NGOs but failed to get an appointment. He worked as a courier agent and later as a salesman, and wants a higher income. He says, "*I am not a street boy, I have enough of respect, I have enough of experience to get any job. I will never get back to the streets.*" He has broken out of his street image; achieving self-respect has given him a sense of self-worth, he identifies with "normal society" and this mindset change propels him to look into various options of staying within this newfound identity.

Respect on the street is usually linked to displays of aggression and power. It serves as an outlet for releasing frustrations. Aggression becomes an accepted form of behavior for street boys in their quest for respect.

I was introduced to Guru at a railway station, "That is Guru, he was involved in a murder in the big metropolis; he has come here now, see the knife scar on his face," Ronak told me with awe and fear, "He has already shown his knife threateningly to 3–4 boys."

I have spent long hours with street children who slept on roof tops or in trucks, observed them, chatted with them, and studied their behavior. Once they had taken me into their confidence, they spoke about their habits and experiences on the streets. Sex, which was a taboo topic, was openly shared. Nearly three-quarters of the street children are abused sexually or physically by the persons with whom they interact. They would say, "*You have to learn to bear with it.*" While for the abused child, it was a feeling of awe, fear, abuse, and hate, for the perpetrator, it was a feeling of power-dominance and pride.

While aggression and protection gain respect on the streets, those who pursue higher studies or advanced skill training, have a consistent job and share a good equation with the staff and management of the Residential Home, are well respected.

Educational aspirations took a new turn in the Residential Home after the boys completed High School and entered college. Zuben completed Junior College. He was now pursuing a career in pharmaceutical medicines. His friend, Jamil finished high school and was doing a bachelor's degree hoping to pursue a career as an electronics engineer later on. Afridi began pursuing a course in computers; he wanted to pursue animation.

The move to pursue new courses gave a new dimension to the educational aspirations of the children in the Home. More importantly, it gave great respect to the ones who pursued these new careers; they shed their street identity and stepped into the world of middle class aspirations and achievements. They became advisors to the other children voluntarily.

Resilience may be defined as "the ability to get through, get over, and thrive after trauma, trials and tribulations" (Siebert, 2000; quoted in Fernandes, D'Souza and Samuel 2002: 2). According to Wolin and Wolin (1993), it refers to the capacity to bounce back, to withstand hardship, and repair oneself. It is a kind of psychological strength, an inner resolve to survive, to construct a sense of "home" in a situation of homelessness, to make best use of scant resources, to make a network of relationships and sources to cope, to be resilient, however traumatic and abhorrent the situation is.

There is a certain system that is in place on the street—the street children go from shelter to shelter and avail themselves of the services of different institutions. There are several service providers who visit the same spots at different times or meet with the same boy or groups of boys after short intervals. In big cities, there is a plethora of service providers which gives the street child more options to choose from, for both his "peripheral needs" and his "core needs" such as protection, security, and "parental guidance." This can be either to his advantage or detrimental to his moving off the streets, for the decision not to enter or runaway is influenced either by a fear of losing "freedom" or by hearsay, that is, fear generated by what others have said about the institution.

When given situations wherein he is shown that he copes with life, earns, feeds, and looks after himself as compared to those children from families who need their families to look after them for those same needs, the street child feels a sense of high self-worth. Such thoughts are best shared with the street children in a controlled guided environment.

The street child has a peculiar relationship with stray animals, especially stray dogs, and tends to adopt them. The dog becomes his companion in most of his situations, gives him unconditional companionship, and does not judge him the way he is judged by human beings; the dog is his best friend. The street child may not have much to eat, but will feed the dog first or give him part of his own meal, *"We can at least earn, how can Kaliya (dog's name)?"* They play, sleep and live alongside the dog, as part of a close circle. Such unconditional acceptance enhances his sense of self-worth. *"I get* izzat *(respect) when I perform on the stage in the Residential Home, Rocky (dog's name) gives me respect and love even if I do not perform,"* says Umied. His relationship with the animal is one of mutual friendship.

LOOKING UPWARD

The transition from the street to a Home or an institution is often not very smooth. The rehabilitation process is again a struggle. Street children are not used to living within four walls, with strict rules and discipline. It is a gradual process of education, of leading with motivation and openness to let them make their decisions. Once their minds are made up, they are prepared to go through this difficult transition process. It makes the movement from home–street–home rational and the process, however difficult, manageable.

Street children especially the younger ones, have a strong urge to build emotional relationships, to touch, to feel close.

Your children at the Residential Home are so cute. They do not have any inhibitions, they just come and hug you—see Chotu (5 years) and Trikaya (7 years) they do not want to leave me.
— Italian visitor, July 2006

Initiating contacts with street boys is always a recurring exercise. Geeta Didi (outreach staff) says, *"I have to spend time with them, have a cup of tea with them, go watch a Bollywood scene being shot on the road, and basically show them that I am with them in most of their activities. This boosts their confidence in me."* This is an indicator that rapport building takes time. Only after protracted contact with them do they feel comfortable divulging among other things, the often-unpleasant truths and experiences in their lives.

The emotional bonding between a street child and an outreach staff depends largely on how the outreach enabler handles the relationship.

Ravi (17 years) belonged to the same South Indian state as Geeta "didi." She took a keen interest in Ravi's activities at the railway station and he in turn waited to have sweets or tea with her or just be with her. Ravi had run away from two vocational schools, once after stealing, and the other after a fight with a teacher; Geeta "didi" counseled him on managing his temper and on being honest, scolded him for bullying younger boys or using abusive language and saw that he did not get into any substance abuse. Finally, she managed to place him as a trainee with a small pavement mechanic's workshop in return for stay at the Residential Home, food, and a small stipend.

— Case File, Residential Home, June 2006

The street enabler used her bonding with Ravi to give him a sense of worth. Her relationship and care helped Ravi sustain his venture into mainstreaming.

The staff team plays a vital role here. At times, when street adolescents have been misguided by street enablers who promise them employment, training, or a residential home and have not been able to keep those promises, it has left the boys dejected and let down, "*Uncle only gives big talks*"; they do not approach the street enabler again and tell their friends of the street enabler's incapability to help them. The staff team constantly encourages the boys, gives them a platform to express themselves and focuses even on minor details. By spending time with them, giving them respect and talking to them and appreciating them, volunteers and visitors enhance the boys' sense of self-worth. On the streets, "*If people wanted us out of the way, they would just shout at us as though we were like dogs. Here they talk to us so nicely.*" Or "*I used to see Sulekha didi at CST station going to work. She never looked at me when I was in the station, but here in the Residential Home, she comes to play and talks to me; it feels so good.*" This is a major motivating factor to move off the streets.

On the streets, the boys tend to be governed by collective experience. These peers serve as support persons in case of problems, frustration, depression, and exercise a strong influence over the boys, particularly in their decision to go ahead with the detoxification process, stay on in the program or leave it. Peer influence in developing mindsets is very strong. They develop opinions, fears, defense mechanisms, and mindsets as per their peers' sharing of experiences. Nearly two-thirds relied on the stories and opinions of their peers on city life to make the decision to leave home, and 78 percent chose a trade because their peers had chosen it. Hence, research in peer influence is an important factor in understanding the street child and shaping his mindset.

In the streets as well as in the institutes, newcomers follow the same pattern; those who arrive together or come from the same area tend to band together as they already know each other. The duration of these dyadic bonds, even within institutes, are usually weak, since boys often relocate between the street and the institute.

Yusuf (22 years) and Suman (21 years) had been in the Residential Home for over 8–9 years. Yusuf had been driving the Residential Home's vehicle for the past four years. Since Suman could not learn any particular skill, we sent him to learn driving. Suman would drive the vehicle for short distances whenever Yusuf was busy. Yusuf got a full salary from the agency supporting the Residential Home, while Suman got a small stipend. In the sixth month, the agency increased the salaries of the staff. So we increased Yusuf's salary too. Suman felt that he should get the same salary as Yusuf. For his part, Yusuf was backing Suman, though they were not the best of friends. A whole delegation of boys came up and demanded that Suman be paid on par with Yusuf, because Suman had donned the role as their "peer supervisor."

— Residential Home, May 2003

It was interesting to notice the camaraderie of the boys. They refused to accept our explanation that we had kept Suman on just as an apprentice and were on the look out for a job for him. This peer support changed the way the boys perceived themselves, and helped them attain better self-worth.

Peer relations contribute substantially to both social and cognitive development and how effectively we function as adults. A childhood predictor of adult adaptation may not be school grades or classroom behavior, rather, the adequacy with which the child gets along with other children. Peer support derives from the willingness and ability to turn to their peers to discuss concerns, worries and problems, and this is particularly significant among street boys.

Regular and protracted contact with street enablers and other influencers such as health post workers, philanthropists, shopkeepers, concerned local authorities, provide an opportunity to the street child to enhance his awareness regarding the availability and accessibility of options, with regard to need fulfillment, vocational pursuits, future life, and goal-setting. Their feeling of self-worth is greatly influenced by the quantum of "street wisdom" or "networking knowledge" they possess and the ability they have to organize the same around their survival.

SELF-PORTRAITS

The respect and value that the public attaches to various occupations have considerable significance for the individual and for what he thinks of himself in relation to his work. A certain amount of self-worth is linked to the possession of skills that society considers important for "success." Street boys consider educational and vocational skills as hallmarks of self and societal recognition. Acquisition of new skills whether educational or vocational such as carpentry, tailoring, electrical work, driving, mechanics, welding, learning English, or computers promotes a sense of high self-worth and proves to the boys that they are capable of engaging in skilled work. This also stimulates them into building a vision for their future. Many street children avoid returning home till they attain their dream of a better life. They want to be known as a "success story." Living in the city gives them a chance to rub shoulders with the elite and they dream of becoming a part of that elite some day. Interestingly, a street boy's sense of identity is distinctly bound with being a part of a group; hence, sending him along with a group for educational or vocational training tends to reduce the chances of his dropping out of the program.

Rizwan was put to work as an apprentice earning a good wage in a factory just outside Pune; he was given boarding and lodging but he felt lonely and called up a member of my staff team in the rehabilitation program to say he wanted to leave the job that month itself. I spoke to Rizwan on the phone and realized that he was feeling lonely. I asked Joseph, the staff member, to send two more boys (who had already been prepared) for the apprentice training earlier than scheduled. Rizwan and the two other boys are still at the job after 14 months.

— Rehabilitation Program, Monthly Report, May 2006

Approbation from the peer group serves to bolster the self-worth of street children. Such approval reinforces the street boy's belief that he is worth a lot more than the rags he picks. When he moves to a new way of life, he is insecure about himself and his behavior and needs reassurance that he is capable of adapting to the new lifestyle.

In the absence of mature adult supervision, respect is inextricably entwined with role models on the street and the behavior displayed by them.

When three of the older boys appeared for the NIOS for the first time and passed, we gave them their certificates at the monthly "mela" where over 600 boys were present and then asked them to talk to the "mela" boys. They remarked how they had initially thought it was a distant dream, but were encouraged to give it a try as failure would not spell disaster. But now they felt they could achieve more, get a decent job, study further, obtain their ration/citizen card, be able to vote, feel like a normal youngster, may be even go to a regular college. They felt they had broken boundaries that they thought were not meant for them. One of them promised that after two years he would return to get his Junior College certificate and urged the rest of the boys to also try and pass their SSC through the NIOS system.

— Monthly "Mela" Report, Residential Home, August 1999

Immediately we had several boys making enquiries about appearing for the NIOS examinations—the cost, how much they would have to study, and the procedures involved. Subsequently, in the following year, we had 11 boys from the streets wanting to be admitted. Yogesh said, *"If Arun can, why not I? He also grew up with me and I am cleverer than he."* Over two-thirds said that the peer educators in the Rehabilitation Centre were their role models.

Role modeling is an educative tool which I have used with the boys and is an intrinsic part of my efforts to help the boys out of their difficult situations by placing before them the successful as well as the negative examples of their peers. Modeling and social approval are two processes that guide a street child's life—they either lead him into drug-taking or help him get "clean." At the rehabilitation program, when the new boys see that the older ones have completed their detoxification successfully and have acquired some skill, they feel emboldened to stay on and this becomes the basis of a new alternative. The role models from among their own peers are worth more than a number of counseling sessions with an animator. It helps them see that it is possible to break barriers, to *"let us try, it is possible, he has made it."*

After arriving on the street, the boys begin to behave in ways that are indicative of street culture. The new lifestyle is learned from those more experienced on the street and includes the formation of street groups, engaging in street activities, such as discovering places where they can obtain free food or places to earn some quick money, drug-taking, gambling, going to a video parlor to watch popular Bollywood or X-rated films, and hanging around with some friends.

I met Iqbal (13 years) at the main city railway station within the first 2–3 days of his arrival. He was a first time runaway, who had burnt two of his stepmother's saris in retaliation for ill treatment. It took him 9 days to arrive from Delhi to Mumbai (a normal train journey would take 16+ hrs). He had learnt to hop on and off the train and dodge whenever a ticket inspector came into the compartment, eat the leftovers thrown away by the passengers and catch the next train to Mumbai.

I asked him if he would like to come to the Residential Home, but he was very frightened. I introduced him to some of the boys of his age who had been living at CST station for a couple of years, to "teach him the ropes" of life on the streets.

Four months later, I met Iqbal again at our monthly "mela"; he looked confident, had another set of clothes, got on well with the other set of boys and was taking drugs. He told me he went to pick scrap around the office area of Colaba at 5.00 am and if his friends did not wake up on time, then he would go to eat "vardi" (free food) at a hotel.

— Residential Home Report, 2001

Iqbal had learnt the "ways" of the street just as "a normal" street boy would. It is a norm to be inducted into street life by the more experienced boys on the street and imitate their lifestyles.

Some boys come to the realization that living in institutions enhances their chances for improving their lives besides providing security. These boys illustrate a desire to change their situation and exhibit a determination to engage proactively in a different lifestyle in order to succeed. The mindset change that emerges from their new value system prompts them to move off the streets, pushes them to attain higher goals and to acquire new skills.

After living at the Residential Home, the boys exhibit a certain sense of urgency in their desire to become productive and contributory citizens. This new image means that they no longer wish to be labeled as street children. There has been a movement in the history of my organization, of the boys wanting to be accorded the same status as middle class youngsters. They did not like the slogan, *Sadak Chapp Zindabad*.[5] It was the first in many steps to move towards this newfound concept of self and demand for dignity that found its culmination in the boys' demand at the centenary celebrations of my organization's presence in the country: *Do not introduce us as street children, we are children of a home* .

REFLECTIONS

I have understood that street children like to be looked upon humanely, be treated with dignity, and gain recognition. Their situation often demands that they dress shabbily to avoid being abused. They do not get opportunities to showcase their talents or the self-reflection to discover their self-worth. They have circumstances that make them feel unwanted, despised, abused, exploited, and accept these situations as part of their destiny in conformity with the negative labels that the society gives them. Once they get caught up in such a mindset, programs and interventions meant to enhance their talents, skills, and qualifications always fall short.

The giving up of the typical street child's occupations of scrap collection, "*wadi kaam,*" "*coolie*" or street habits of gambling, drugs, video parlor visits, and moving on to academic pursuits in mainstream institutions, to speaking English, to learning vocational certificate courses, to attaining white collar or stable blue collar jobs, to owning a bank account, to independent living, all add up to the "dignity process" that enhances the child's self-worth.

My experience of success and failure has taught me that our programmatic interventions should first work on their mindsets, on their belief in their own dignity, in understanding that they are worth something, and that they can contribute too. Facing and overcoming difficulties is part of the "dignity building process." For this they need the help of organizations and/or persons (enablers) that help them to reflect and realize their self-worth and potential.

---

[5] *Sadak Chapp Zindabad*—Long live street life/street persons.

3

Defining Images

PERSONAL OWNERSHIP

Children are not just victims of experience, they can also be resilient authors of experience. (Gilligan, 2003)

Children are active players in the search for their own destiny. They help shape the relationships they have with the people around them. Hence, the participation of children in their own development cannot be overlooked. With regard to street children, it is they who are the major stakeholders in their decision-making process.

Piaget outlined several principles for building cognitive structures. During all development stages, the child experiences his or her environment using whatever mental maps he or she has constructed so far. If the experience is a repeated one, it fits easily or is assimilated into the child's cognitive structure so that he or she maintains mental "equilibrium." If the experience is different or new, the child loses equilibrium, and alters his or her cognitive structure to accommodate the new conditions. This way, the child erects more and more adequate cognitive structures (Piaget, 1995).

The concept of personal ownership is an iterative process for the street boys and may be regarded as including elements such as freedom, personal autonomy, money, materials owned, space, preferences, decisions, attitude towards and relationships with friends, employers, staff team, management as well as street culture and possessions. It is an attempt to take responsibility for one's own actions.

This study views "personal ownership" as taking an independent decision to live either on or off the street. For instance, when the street adolescent is faced with the unpleasant consequences of his decisions, he resigns himself to living with them and getting on. How does the adolescent condition himself to this?

Ten year old Arun and his fourteen year old brother Ashok, stole their father's pay packet and ran away from Latur in Maharashtra (India) to Bangalore. Two days later, they heard that an earthquake had destroyed much of Latur, and that theirs was one of the 19 villages reported to have been "swallowed into the ground." No survivors were reported from those villages. Arun and Ashok were in tears, but they said, "Now what's the use? God punished us by taking away our parents and making us orphans. We have to live like this now."

— Case File, Residential Home, Mumbai, 1996

I asked Arun what he felt after seeing the earthquake on television. He said, *"What to do? God punished us. I have to live with the punishment."*

The thought process is not reached through conscious analysis. These children do not understand the magnitude of their decision or the consequences of their action. After the boy runs away from the Residential Home, has no food, and is in search of a place to sleep, he repents. However, he does not return as he considers it part of the consequences he has to bear and takes it in his stride. My study of the initial experiences of a street adolescent's feelings and thoughts just after leaving home (2002) revealed that 38 percent took responsibility for their action and continued with their choice, however difficult or undesirable, despite a very real sense of insecurity and fear about their future.

FREEDOM ON THE STREETS

"Freedom" ranks high among the key motivations for boys to go on to the street and tends to hold them there. Initially, they imagine the street to be a free and fun-filled place, where resources for survival are apparently easy to find. The opportunity to live among other boys and girls, to hang out with youngsters of the opposite sex, to consume legal and illegal drugs, to be the master of his own life, all without adult supervision, holds tremendous attraction for the street boy in his "honeymoon period" on the street.

Personal freedom is highly valued by the street boys and viewed as a form of escape from adult restrictions and reprimands. "*We can do as we like to do with our money, go to the movies when we wish, eat what we like, go to places we enjoy. No one can say anything to us,*" said fourteen year old Quasim about his understanding of four months of freedom on the streets.

Street boys have ambivalent views on the world of the streets. Some revel in their unconstrained freedom away from the rigors of discipline of parents, elders, and teachers, while those who have been on the street realize the pitfalls, dangers, and unsheltered harshness. Some apparently are satisfied with the conditions on the street. They fall into a "gotten used to" pattern of living. For the smaller boys, though, it is a case of "getting used to" style of living. This "getting used to" phenomenon is about going through what the bigger boys had gone through, who have earned sufficient money and who have the freedom to spend it as they wish to, and who have managed to cope with the negative aspects of living on the streets. However, it is just for a period of time; when they do begin to think of their future, they revise their opinions. This is what 26-year-old Radhe, who spent 14 years on the street, had to say,

No one understands how difficult it is to live on the streets. You have to take the beatings of the police, go without food and work for days together; no institution wants to help you as you have grown up. Where can we go, there is no future, these streets are like a prison, once trapped you cannot get out of it.

— Outreach Report, September 2002

This shows the transition from the "honeymoon period" of street life when the street adolescent's mind and thoughts are of a "carefree" life to one of "a degenerative period" in which the streets are perceived to be a prison that has not given him the opportunity to move ahead.

MINE FOR A DAY?

CONCEPT OF PERSONAL POSSESSIONS

Street children are icons of destitution in both a figurative and literal sense (Gigengack, 2006). Every street child has his own peculiarities, which he can seldom shake off in an alienating social environment. The street child is often unaware of these characteristics, and survives with these negative traits in an oppressive social environment. However, it is incorrect to assume that they possess nothing apart from the clothes they wear. Their attributes may include their drugs paraphernalia, items required for survival on the streets, personal belongings and other consumption articles. Their attitudes and peculiar characteristics are blighted by their situation and poverty.

The street adolescent's material possessions are utilitarian. They often carry small personal items such as a comb, a pack of cards and some money. If they are ragpickers, they carry a sack under their arm. A few of the older boys may carry photographs of either a favorite film actress or of a girl they desire. The street boys' drugs paraphernalia may include inhalant substances (glue, paint thinner, a piece of cloth, or a pipe to smoke pot), while among older boys, survival items may include a sharp pointed instrument like a blade. These personal belongings not only help to express the street boys' identity, but also serve to highlight his individuality. Thus, their material possessions are either for survival, to enhance their self-worth, or are indicative of their lifestyle and of having made the street their comfort zone.

Money Ills

Money is a bane especially if it is in the hands of little children who are not guided, have too many options, and only themselves to act as judges as to the utilization of money. Hence desires, wishes, and feelings have a major role to play in their decisions and choices on how to spend the money.

A 5–6 year old having cash in hand normally thinks of the food it will buy him to satiate his immediate hunger. Once that is fulfilled, he uses his judgment to spend money on what "others" are using it for; for example, gambling, drugs, or giving *vasuli* to the bigger bully. Once his sexual desires develop (often at the early age of 13–14 years, being exposed to it much of the time), he starts visiting commercial sex workers. I was conducting a session with the bigger boys (15–17 years) on the negative elements on the streets. One of the many elements mentioned was "money." I asked them, "Why do you put it in the negative column?" They said that from an early age of five or six, they have money which corrupts them. They have to spend it as their friends tell them to on food, drugs, gambling, and also sex. "*It is the reason why we stay on the streets; it gives us the opportunity to enjoy something that is usually forbidden which is not good in the long run."* After this session, the very boys who were giving a lucid explanation and understanding of the "ills" of having money on the streets said that they wanted to leave the Centre and return to the streets. Each had a different excuse, to meet a friend, to collect some money, their clothes or just to go with the other companions since they would feel "bored at the Centre" without these friends.

Reflecting back with those who stayed back, I realized that it was the recalling of the enjoyment they had on the streets that brought back the passion and desire to go for it one more time. They began missing what they had experienced, especially the visit to the red-light district, the good food, the high of the drugs, and paramount was the fact that they could do as they wished. This prompted them to leave. On our outreach rounds in the following month, two of the boys met my staff saying it was a mistake, *"I should not have left but now what to do? It is my fault, forget it!"*

The problem with money is the options it brings with it and the freedom on the streets with no guidance. It enhances his "live for the day" concept; his idea of enjoyment and fun is related to money. Hence, it is one of the root factors that keeps him away from reflecting, working on consequences, and keeps him firmly grounded in the world of the "here and now—tomorrow will take care of itself." I think money is one of the key factors that needs to be worked on as a concept in any therapeutic rehabilitation program for children on the streets.

However, the street child sometimes goes beyond the "street child image" and adopts the identity of a "normal" adolescent. Much of the salary that a street boy receives from the *wadi mukkadam* (wedding work supervisor) is spent on buying new sets of clothes, shoes, mobile phones, handheld music gadgets, movies, and good food for a few days. This behavior is indicative of the fact that street boys like to be regarded as "normal consumers" and not as symbols of poverty and destitution. This is their way of overcoming the prejudices they suffer in their daily lives and an attempt to acquire goods and status valued by society.

CONCEPT OF PERSONAL INCLINATIONS

Street children have their personal preferences. Prolonged life on the streets makes them more prone to acquire certain behaviors at an early age. As the ones being protected by their "protector," they run errands for their seniors aiding them in many anti-social activities, but soon start doing things on their own. The streets can be considered a school for the street child, an "institution" of learning, where his habits and behavior are determined by individual experiences.

Sixteen year old Ravi would often steal or snatch away the earnings of the small boys at the central station. When he was caught stealing a man's bag, he caught the man's legs tightly and begged for forgiveness. When the small boys complained to their bigger boy "protectors," Ravi would hold the feet of the "protector" and beg for forgiveness so that he would either be forgiven or get less beatings. The boys in the central station area called him "the leg catcher."

The street child's mindset in dealing with his situation is peculiar to his learnt behavior. Like Ravi, several children develop behavior patterns to respond to situations. This preference to cope with situations of stress in a particular way is their way of owning responsibility for their actions. As Ravi grew up to be a 19–20 year old, he changed his habit of stealing and snatching money from the younger boys and started threatening the newer boys, demanding *vasuli* (protection money) from those who were not "protected." Ravi found this an easy option; when caught by a bigger bully, he would not hold his feet, but would hit back to show that he was not afraid and that he was the local toughie. His physical growth gave him self-confidence, a power to threaten as well as challenge. His shift in inclination from snatching and stealing to demanding and threatening changed his mindset. This shift was from begging for mercy to challenging those who questioned his authority.

WHICH GROUP AM I IN?

CONCEPT OF GROUP COHESIVENESS

Peer influence is very high amongst street children; they believe in their friends but this friendship is more need-based. They make friends for protection, security, and survival. Strong friendships are frequently cited by those who have lived together on the streets for years. In some instances, friendship can be traced back to the village and it plays a role in the boy's initiation to the streets. Those who are close tend to band together in small groups, but at night, they seek protection from bigger bullies or the police in the form of larger groups. Friendships on the street are transient and lack elements of durability and permanence due to the mobile nature of this group and because these friendships are not founded on trust, but evolve in terms of their ability to fulfill basic needs.

Ghanshyam was upset that Raghu, his friend of four years, had betrayed him and robbed him of his money at night. Raghu lied to him and told him that the other boys sleeping with them had robbed his money. Actually, Raghu had met his village friend and had decided to go with him to Delhi. He needed money and so stole from Ghanshyam. Ghanshyam did not want to do anything with Raghu anymore. Ghanshyam said, "On the streets, it is like this, you cannot say who your true friend is."

Thus the term "friend" on the streets is functional and fulfills the needs of protection and survival. There is an inherent irony underlying this "friendship"; street boys go out of their way to help a sick or hungry companion or leave an institution with a secure future for the sake of this friend(s) but if there is a greater benefit to be obtained from another, then he would not hesitate to betray him.

Although grouping can be seen as a defence strategy on the streets, relations within the group may get strained at times. Arguments and fights between group members can force an individual member out of the group; also an element of distrust within street groups raises the possibility of betrayal. It is then that the boy may think of seeking help in an institution or seeks alternatives to change his lifestyle. His group cohesiveness changes as per his changing situation or lifestyle and, thus, his mindset may be one of constant adaptation to the changing environment. This is what is included in his "survival strategy kit."[1] He takes responsibility for his actions however detrimental they may be to him. His "here and now" survival takes precedence.

---

[1] Survival strategy kit: The boy uses different coping mechanisms to deal with his situation on the streets. To survive on the streets he uses behaviors that may be detrimental to his future, body or value system. But survival here and now takes priority.

HOW DO I KNOW WHAT IS MINE?

FACTORS IN PERSONAL OWNERSHIP

A multiplicity of emotional, situational and psychosocial factors plays a role in shaping the mindset of a street child.

Emotions and fears

Youngsters recount that on the streets, night time is the most threatening period; the period when they are most vulnerable to many forms of violence. I have been making street contact, often late at night. In my study, I have observed that 85–90 percent of the children abuse inhalants or smoke marijuana at night.[2] Invisible by day, they come out at night when the offices and shops shut down, but their personal freedom is always counterbalanced by fear. It is at night that they are abused, violated, or bullied by other street persons or by the police.

Their mindset is one of constant suspicion of bigger bullies, of the police, and fear of the unknown at night. On my night street contact rounds, when I approach a group of boys who are new or whom I have not come in contact with before, they tend to run away thinking I am either a police personnel or that I have come to beat them up.

I saw three groups of boys huddled in a railway yard, inhaling drugs in an abandoned area meant only for the parking of the trains. I approached the groups; they ran away immediately, only three boys who were not consuming drugs stayed back. They asked me to get out of that place and advanced threateningly. I said I wanted to meet Abdul (I made up this name to win their confidence) because he had told me that he wanted help to get off drugs. Immediately, the boy shouted to the others, "It is ok, he is not a policeman, he is a doctor. Sir, forget about Abdul, help me. See, I cannot get out of this habit." Subsequently, I had a group of 11 boys seeking help to join the program.

— Outreach, April 1993

---

[2] Outreach by Night, July 2006.

Perceptions and misperceptions

The boys feel that their freedom is curtailed at the Residential Home. A number of boys feel that shelters or homes are "like prisons." After experiencing the "freedom of the streets," they cannot adjust to the regimented lifestyle at the shelter which reminds them of the constraints they faced at home. Often a street boy views life at a shelter as a threat to his only possession—his freedom. It is one of the factors that time and again attract him back to the streets, and the reason why many boys cannot sustain a prolonged stay at a shelter.

During the Orientation Camp, we had a Focus Group Discussion with 14 boys who had gone back to the streets and who wanted to rejoin the Rehabilitation Program. When asked what was so attractive about the streets to cause them to leave the program, they enumerated several reasons: they missed their friends, they were not able to be as mobile as they were on the streets, there was no money, they missed the freedom to do as they pleased—the movies, the non-vegetarian food, the opportunities to gamble, and to take drugs. In general, it was a restraining life at the Residential Home as compared to the carefree life on the streets.
— Ex-boys' Orientation Camp, Rehabilitation Phase 2, June 2003

Need fulfillment

The street offers a refuge for those who want to get away from family breakdown and turbulence at home. Family and community support bases sometimes prove to be inadequate to meet the ever-increasing needs and demands of the boy and hence he may turn to the streets. The quality of parenting exercises a dominating influence in a child's life. Parents are his role models with whom he identifies himself. In the absence of adequate role modeling and the caring touch of a parent, the child finds his home hostile and threatening. He wants to escape and run away from it at the first available opportunity (Agrawal, 1999). The fields of influence at home and those on the street exert different pressures, often at odds with each other.

Allure of the streets

One of the strongest factors that tie the child to the streets is the "freedom" and "independence" it offers. On the street, they make their own rules which are often antithetical to those of the society that rejects them. The boys have the freedom to exercise their choice in terms of food, friendships, mobility, avenues of entertainment, and expenditure. A staff team member observed *"street life is sheer enjoyment—roaming around, movies, sexual satisfaction, and addiction."* It is viewed as a permissive space allowing personal "freedom," a lifestyle which the street adolescent finds difficult to give up. These "moments of enjoyment" are treasured by the children and they offer a cover to the harsh realities that are present on the streets.

Some of the boys want to continue earning their living on the street. They do not like to do the unpaid work of cleaning the Residential Home. *"We can earn at the railway station simply by sweeping the place and then spend it as we like."* The money they make is spent on "instant gratification." They do not keep money for fear of its being stolen. Often, they spend on drugs rather than on food, under the misconception that the consumption of drugs keeps their hunger pangs away. Others say that they use drugs to self-medicate fear and depression, to provide strength to live in difficult circumstances, or as indications of a pathological need for immediate gratification. There have been instances where street children inhaling glue still maintain their ability to cope with the demands of work on crowded streets.

Peer influence

Street boys invariably mention the joy and security they experience in the company of their peers who serve as psychological supports during times of depression, frustration, illness, and police arrests. With the lack of parental or other adult supervision, these peers become role models and exert an overwhelming influence on the street boys' behavior and attitudes; the only relation boys cherish while on the street is a friend. They yearn for emotional warmth and security. One of the reasons they survive on the street is because of this friend who plays multiple roles within his emotional context. On the other hand, they tend to have limited working relationships with *"need fulfilling friends,"* that is, the group of friends to sleep within a secure place, or to fulfill a particular need. Befriending paraprofessionals and social workers does not take much time, but this relationship is of a receiving nature and a top to down one. Hence, it cannot be termed as a friendship with an enabler, but a guide or teacher–pupil relationship.

For a majority of the boys, socialization takes place on the streets with peers. However, there are also those instances where group affirmation can be nonbeneficial, where one boy leaves the Residential Home and takes two or three more with him back to the street.

Charu (12 years) kept repeating this pattern of behavior. Over a period of two years, he came four times to the Residential Home with a request to stay and go to school, but within 2–4 months, he would run away and take two or three boys with him. He would then return alone to the Residential Home, only to repeat the same behavior.

— Case File, Residential Home, Mumbai, 1998

Therefore, the longer the boy remains on the street, the greater the likelihood of his getting into deviant behavior. Key processes of peer influence include: friends modeling drug use, friends making drugs immediately available, and peers creating norms and expectations that support or encourage alcohol and other drug use.

Asif (14 year) had been doing well in his studies. He was sent for a computer course. Yet every now and then Asif would leave the Residential Home to meet his friend Mohammed (14 years), who was still on the streets. Mohammed would try to convince Asif to come back to live with him on the streets. Asif would come back very disturbed each time, trying to decide if he should go back to the streets or stay in the Residential Home. Twice Asif tried the inhalant Mohammed was using at that time, as Mohammed forced him to do so. On both occasions Asif returned to the Centre after a couple of days. He had been with Mohammed for 8 months on the streets prior to coming to the Residential Home three years ago. Yet he still had a strong attachment to Mohammed. He would go especially to tell him of the upcoming events and celebrations at the Residential Home and invite him to join. Mohammed did not want to join, he was into drugs and lived with a group of boys who were considered trouble makers at that railway station.

— Case File, Residential Home, Mumbai, 1999

Asif was very protective of his relationship with Mohammed and would often secretly take blankets, plates, and some food for Mohammed, whenever he went to visit him. This put me in an ethical dilemma. When should I, as a guardian take control of the situation and ban Asif from meeting with Mohammed? One day he would influence Asif to leave his progressive academic life and force him into drug dependence and back to the streets. I would sit with Asif each time he got back and counsel him on keeping his mind focused. I worked with him on his thinking, over not letting his emotions or his friendship with Mohammed take over his future plans.

Thus, strong impressionable relationships are often established even if for a relatively short period. Yet it is these very friendships that can prove a hindrance to a street inhalant's decision to join a rehabilitation program or to leave it. The mindset of Asif is that of a typical street child who has maintained a strong bond with a friend on the streets so that he (Asif) can continue to still "experience by proxy"[3] life on the streets. Asif, in his mind, has not yet given up the streets and is experiencing the same through Mohammed. His choice to do a computer course was clear, yet his feelings for street life had not changed. He knew it was bad, yet he enjoyed the "no controls freedom" it gave him. Now Asif lives independently in a rented room and has set up a computer software partnership business on the outskirts of the city. Though he was lured to street life, he did not succumb to it.

Often, the foremost criterion in the street inhalants' decision to leave the streets is the fact that they would need to quit drugs or leave a close younger or older companion with whom they have been sharing a relationship of protection, provision (of food and other types of help), and sexual gratification. These types of companions are "utility-boys."[4] They fulfill mutual psychological and emotional needs and their relationship is one of "abuser and the abused." Such relationships cause a regression of growth for both, causing psychological damage to the abused. The boys are trapped in a vicious circle when they are on the streets. Often their desire to escape is strong, but the "addiction to the streets" and the fear of the "protector" restrains them. They are aware of solutions to their lifestyle-related problems and agree that unless they get out of these types of bonds and off the streets, qualitative life improvement is not attainable.

The "protector–utility boy"[5] topic is taboo among the children. Only if the two boys involved are of a similar age or a couple of years older or younger will the others talk about them. These relationships

---

[3] Experience by proxy: Wish to experience what the other is doing, so take joy, relive or listen/go to meet the other person who has been undergoing that experience.

[4] "Utility-boys" is also used in the same sense as "protector–utility boys."

[5] Protector–utility boys: Big boys who use the younger boys for sexual pleasure and to run small errands, whilst protecting them from other bullies on the streets.

are kept outside their everyday conversations with their peers. In a focus group discussion with the boys of Phase III, none mentioned their own experiences, but kept talking in general that the boys have a protector to whom they give their earnings. The protector looks after the utility boy when he is in need. When asked about this "need," they said it could be medicines, food, or being saved from the beatings or threats of another boy. Further investigation about abusive behavior met with silence. Only one boy said, "*It is about those who want to take drugs or do other 'wrong things' with them.*" After the focus group discussion (FGD), three boys came up to me individually, and said that the protector gets the utility boy addicted to drugs, instills so much fear in him that he is afraid to go on his own to any other place to live. The protector would come to know of it from the other boys and he would get a beating. Most of the protectors sexually abuse their utility boys regularly. "*It is something one cannot escape,*" they said. "*It is part of living on the street.*" I had followed up on Guddu who was the utility boy for Kishore.

Guddu (11 years) had come to the mela *(July1997). I had asked him if he would like to stay in the Residential Home. He liked it but when it was time for the rest of the boys to leave and for him to join the 14 boys who were staying, he wanted to walk out. I asked him why he had changed his mind. He gave a few excuses that he had left some money which he had to pick up from the kiosk vendor. His peer of the same area said, "He will not stay, Kishore has warned him against it." I called Kishore (22 years) who was standing outside the gate a little distance away. I asked him if it was a problem to keep Guddu, he was young and could be sent to school and his future could be taken care of. Kishore said, "Yes, he can come after six months, he has to pay my money back." I offered to give whatever money Guddu owed him. He said, "No he can come after six months, I want to send him home." I offered to send Guddu home too, but Kishore just said no, did not give any more explanations, and walked away giving Guddu a threatening look.*

Guddu stopped coming to the melas*. I would see him occasionally at the central station on my outreach rounds, but he avoided me. In August 2006, Guddu came to the* mela*. I recognized him and noticed he was grown up and was now "protecting" Rinku, a nine year old. I offered to keep Rinku in the Residential Home. Guddu had pre-empted this by already warning Rinku that I would ask him to stay back and had warned Rinku with dire consequences. As soon as I began talking to Rinku, he came behind me, made a few threatening gestures to Rinku and walked away. Rinku did not want to speak to me from then on. He and Guddu left the* mela *within the next 15 minutes.*

— Mela, July 1997 and Mela, August 2006

The abused often becomes the abuser in later life. It is a cyclic process. The utility boy becomes the protector, as in the case of Guddu. Unless they are helped to heal in their abused–abuser situation, the cycle perpetuates.

The bonding that their relationships bring is one that is functional and utilitarian. Once in an institution, these relationships do not perpetuate if the utility boy manages to get out of the "protection" of his protector. Then the relationship equation changes into trying to get the maximum benefit from the system, giving rise to another type of functional utilitarianism that is more "dependency laden." The exit is the most difficult part of their relationship with the institution. This situation creates a mindset of being comfortable in a system and fearful of stepping out of it.

STREET CULTURE

After arriving on the streets, the boys begin to behave in ways that are indicative of a "street culture." These patterns are learned from those more experienced on the street and include the formation of street groups, engaging in work activities and sometimes in drug-taking and petty theft, and sleeping in large groups at night.

Vulnerability, insecurity, fear, and marginalization are constant on the street. Being on the street is inevitably associated with a high degree of mobility. Many children keep wandering because of their constant search for identity, need satisfaction, adventure, or because of disputes with other children. Once they have found an area where their survival seems secure, they maintain those particular areas as points of reference, mark their identity and tend to remain within this region—though it might be necessary to move for economic reasons to a place where it is easier to obtain resources or for reasons of personal safety.

Behavioral patterns among street inhalants may be seen as a manifestation on a continuum of emotion ranging from vulnerability through fear to bravado and aggression.

- A typical pattern of behavior of street children is that they feel hurt and lonely if spoken to rudely at the institution/shelter. They say, "*What is the difference between the street and the institution, if we have to listen to rude things?*" They like to consider being in the institution as a sign of upward mobility and gaining self-respect.

- They tend to stay in specific areas/groups. The younger street children prefer to stay in groups because of their fear of older children. Group life affords them protection from the dangers on the street.

- Street boys tend to play upon, exaggerate and re-create the harsh realities in which they live. They have an immense capacity to create chaos and their actions often combine creativity with destructiveness. For example, a toy does not last its life span with these children, it is always ripped apart after a while, broken or roughly used. All these actions display a self-destructive streak, an expression of their inner feelings.

- A few boys display aggression. A tendency to act on impulse is an inextricable part of their survival repertoire on the streets. It takes a long time for them to control their aggression and learn to manage their anger. Street children, who have not received proper care, attention, and guidance from their parents, may not learn to manage their anger and hence develop distorted personalities. Suppressed anger or violent expression of anger in the childhood in the absence of proper training may turn them into "criminal adults."

- Externally, they put on a show of bravado and give the impression of being independent and not needing anybody. However, they are afraid of leaving themselves open to exploitation.

- Most boys have a low attention span and are unable to sit in one place for long. Their minds are not trained to self-discipline and are in a constant fluid state. Hence, activities and exercises to expand their attention are an essential element of their rehabilitation.

- They exhibit no future planning or thinking and do not show interest in developing themselves. This is reminiscent of their philosophy of living for the day and of wanting instant gratification.

- The boys do not like being constrained by rules and regulations and initially resist these. They often runaway due to this inability to adjust.

The boys are well aware of the detrimental effects of substance abuse; how it harms their health, happiness, and general ability to function well. But their "self-destructive agency" is responsible for the importance they attribute to inhalants, their overwhelming desire to obtain them at all costs, and their willingness to act accordingly.

Street children continue to abuse drugs despite seemingly having every reason and knowledge to avoid them. Drug usage is one of the forms of risk-taking behavior. A study of 218 boys on high-risk behavior of street children highlighted that sexual behavior, gambling, and not caring for the consequences on their future and on their health characterized their risk taking behavior. The major reasons cited for such risky behavior included pleasure, excitement or arousal, desire, feeling of depression or boredom and seeking relief from hunger, fear, pain, and uncertainty. A high level of awareness does not necessarily mean logical action as in this case; it does not prohibit the use of drugs by street children. This raises questions about "informed choice."

The children have knowledge of actions harmful to them, yet they give in to its detrimental consequences. I think it is for this reason that working on their thought processes and mindset is essential to help informed choice. The mindset of the children needs to be changed from "instant gratification," "live for the day," and spur of the moment decision-making to a well thought out cognitive approach.

THE CAREGIVERS

A comprehensive orientation by the staff team about choices in terms of expectations, activities, results, and outcomes is essential, particularly with regard to education, training, enrollment in a de-addiction program, or going back home. The staff team plays a specific role in providing a helpful environment. It may not be the counseling or the specific awareness program that has its effect on the street inhalant, but the conducive atmosphere—the conditions prepared for him to make or sustain his decision. Respecting his choice despite the misgivings and apprehensions of the enabler, yet guiding it and providing a more suitable avenue, reflects the effectiveness of the enabler in the decision-making process.

At a staff meeting, one of the team members put forward the problem that the boys were too small to make a decision on their own. "We know it is a wrong choice, but they are often adamant. What do we do?" I put forward to them the ethical dilemma that I have been facing in my experience with the children. When can I say, "Let the boy make his choice" and when can I say, "I have the duty as his guardian to guide him away from that decision?"

— Staff Meeting, May 2006

The question arises that if he were my child at home, would I say "do as you wish"; would I not guide him or at times be firm with him? There is no general principle for us to follow, but a principle specific to each individual's characteristics and psyche. Accordingly, the enabler needs to be firm, guiding or leading the young child to an informed choice.

Gupta (16 years) decided to pursue a cooking course when he witnessed how it had helped change his friend Ejaz. Ejaz was now earning a good salary, looked smart, lived in the training centre, and was respected. A staff member, Dinesh, tried sending Gupta to help out in the kitchen, but saw that Gupta avoided cutting vegetables and washing vessels and did not like the heat of the stove. He did not seem to have an aptitude for cooking. However, he showed a natural interest in plumbing, so during his apprenticeship, Dinesh put Gupta with the cook part time and with the local plumber part time. Gupta enjoyed working with his tools and managing the Residential Home's plumbing maintenance work. Thus, by showing Gupta an avenue which encouraged his natural abilities, coupled with counseling, Dinesh managed to get Gupta to change his initial decision on pursuing the cooking course and instead enroll for a course in plumbing.

— Case File, Therapeutic Program, 2001

When the boys encounter the staff team on outreach, their responses range from curiosity to interest born out of their survival instincts for self-improvement. If they feel that the information/services are important enough for them to seek further help, and they are convinced that the staff is interested in their well-being—by taking care of their immediate medical needs, sharing a cup of tea with them, and giving them appropriate care in situations of difficulty—they start bonding with the individual street enabler.[6]

---

[6] Street enabler: A staff team member who goes on outreach contact on the field to enable the street child with services for his well-being.

In the initial stage of entry into the Residential Home, the children are wary that the staff team might report their whereabouts to the family or the police and, therefore, often hide their true identities. With time, the boys slowly accept the staff, build trust, and their relationships get cemented. They become more receptive to suggestions from staff regarding education, training, and their future. However, despite being used to the hardships and vagaries of street life, the boys do not like strict discipline or punitive measures. While some of the older boys tend to retort or abuse the staff if they get agitated, on the whole, the boys resent the staff team taking sides, reprimanding them in front of their peers or taking a moral stand.

Once a bond of trust is established, many children seem to flourish and develop a desire to learn and better themselves. The benefit is that these children are welcomed, most for the first time in their lives, into a loving family lifestyle. Siraj (24 years), a former resident at the Residential Home, came with his wife and said, "*Give your blessings to your daughter-in-law.*" Babloo (23 years) came to visit us at the Residential Home with his new born son and wife telling us, "*You are the grandparents of my child.*" This denotes their bonding as well as their desire to assign labels which are typical of a "normal" family. Siraj and Babloo could not trace their biological families and so transferred the labels of family ties on to us. Their use of labels as "Dad," "Mummy," and "Grandfather" is in keeping with their need for normal family recognition.

THE WORLD WITHOUT

External forces sometimes threaten to fragment the group and may encourage its members to think of change. For instance, when the government decides to "clean the streets" for a dignitary's visit, the boys are rounded up and put in remand homes or are imprisoned. They tend to run away from those areas of the city where the police are clamping down on them or seek to get into shelters and thus change their lifestyle. Correspondingly, when an older boy comes for help to the Residential Home, 70–80 percent of the time he is seeking a way of getting out of a difficult situation on the streets. Very often it would be one of not being able to pay back loan/protection money; or that he has beaten up someone, robbed someone, or has not done what he was told to do by a more powerful street stakeholder; and/or is being pursued by the police or the protector/bigger bully. Circumstances "force" him to make decisions; the choices he makes are the ones that he takes responsibility for and he accepts the consequences of his choice. He chooses an option that he is comfortable with and where he still has control over his life.

LIMITING FACTORS

The process of transition from the streets to a shelter and living within four walls is gradual and involves adjustment and considerable change. Leaving the street to stay in an institution bound by rules and time-tables is not easy and the restrictions which seem to contravene the freedom enjoyed on the street often prevent them from making this decision. The lure of the freedom of the streets, the temporary comfort of "known" bonds, and their reservations about their future with their "new mentors" hinder the exercise of personal ownership.

On the streets, relationships are functional, a matter of who helps him to "learn the ropes" and does not exploit him; in a shelter, where basic needs are met, trust is a reflection of their belief that the staff team would not try sending them back to abusive homes without their consent and would not reveal their information to the police or their parents or relatives. Trust is placed once a comfort level is reached after confidence has been built, but even this can be transitory.

The transitory nature of the trust and relationships that these street children establish reflects not only their life, but also their mindset. What is intriguing is why the children love the streets even after being abused and exploited. They sometimes spoke of their problems, but more often spoke of the times they were having fun and the instances of how they could do as they pleased.

I had organized a picnic for eight boys. When we had assembled at Mumbai Central Station, I asked, "You know the problems you go through and the difficulties. You know if you leave the streets you will have a brighter future to establish yourselves and ensure your happiness. Why don't you go when field workers invite you to their institutions?"

The boys said, "We would like to go, but it is difficult to follow a disciplined lifestyle. Many of us know it is the best for our future, but for now we want to live here, maybe later we will go."
— MSW Course, College of Social Work, Mumbai, 1987–89

That "later time" is often too late. Of the 54 NGOs in the CCVC forum in the city, only three NGOs have institutional care for children above the age of 16. Therefore, it is often too late to help when they get serious about their future. Despite their awareness about the exploitative nature of the streets, the street children preferred to re-live the few moments of joy when compared to the harsh realities, a clear indicator that they were overcome by the instant gratification phenomenon, with little thought for the future. Their mindset is of the "here and now." They seldom indulge in reflection, for it brings back past unpleasant memories. Reflective sessions were held during the camps of outreach boys,[7] and they had difficulties. It was the first time that they were reflecting and they were either nostalgic or repentant: "*We should not have left home," "the street is not the best place to be," "this is not what I wanted to do*," and thoughts such as these. For some, these reflection sessions help change their mindset, while for others, the fear of discipline and loss of freedom prompt them to drop out of the program.

MIDWAY EXITS

Every program of rehabilitation has to contend with the issue of drop-outs. The reasons for leaving could vary from individual problems with the environment, not meeting material needs, to problems with the staff team, to an inability to "fit-in" due to an impulsive decision, lack of motivation, inadequate preparedness or being unfit for one particular model of rehabilitation. The reasons for dropping out may include personal, familial, interpersonal, and socioeconomic factors—anathema to discipline and unpaid work at the Residential Home, differences of opinion with the staff or peers, feelings of inadequacy and inability to cope, the separation

---

[7] Outreach boys' camp: A group of 20 plus boys are taken from the streets for 3 days to a beach residence for an orientation program to the De-addiction Centre and returned to the streets if they choose to go back.

from all that is familiar, loneliness, influence of unfounded rumors, and lack of a support system.

Samad (14 years) had been spreading rumors about the Rehabilitation Program at the central station. He said that the staff beat up the boys and locked them up and that the food contained worms. There was only manual work given all the time to the boys. After listening to Samad's experience, many boys were hesitant to join the program. Ajay (staff team member) met Samad and asked him whether all the rumors that he was spreading were true. Samad accepted that they were false. Then why was he spreading these rumors? Samad said he was angry with one of the staff members, who he felt was partial to the bigger boys and was always threatening the smaller boys.

— Case File, Rehabilitation Home, Phases 2 and 3, 2004

In the third phase of Rehabilitation, the drop-outs reduced as they began to realize and appreciate the changes that they were undergoing, the self-respect they started getting, and the fact that they could make a worthwhile contribution in society. Most importantly, their thought processes and mindsets were being worked on in this phase—"a mending of their brokenness." They began to think constructively about their future. Yet not all their street patterns were unlearnt immediately and there were drop-outs occasionally in the first couple of months of the third phase.

Each time a boy ran away from the third phase, I asked my staff to introspect, to learn how to avoid such situations, how to perceive neglect, how to cultivate the ability to read the boy's body language, and to pre-empt future recurrences.

Mahadev had run away at the third phase of the program as he was given the job of cutting the other boys' hair. He was upset when the other boys teased him, calling him "Hajaam" (barber) in a derogatory sense.

Staff suggestions in this case included refraining from casteist statements, a talk by a reputed local hair stylist, paying Mahadev a small stipend, and asking him to teach a couple of boys who were interested in this profession.

In the training phase, the boy may run away if he is not allowed to make his own choice regarding training, or because of development of a new interest, relationship problems with the instructor or the roommates, inability to cope with the language or with the work, lack of confidence in his ability to do the job, being threatened or verbally abused by the employer, not being paid on time, reprimanded for coming late, unsafe environment, exploitation, non-availability of friends, or even just the day-to-day routine to relax.

Those who return to the streets have been repeaters of the program, who on their return to the third phase, trouble the staff and are therefore sent prematurely for their training without adequate psychological preparation. This perpetuates the movement to and from the streets.

REFLECTIONS

Although there is a common perception of the street as being devoid of morals and values, it has been found that street boys uphold the same values as society in general: being respected, having their own homes, work, families, and study as a form of social mobility. When most street inhalants contemplate a course of action which they know to be "negative" or "undesirable" (such as running away and returning to the streets), they require support and affirmation from their group. However, when they take a decision to return alone to a shelter, is this help-seeking behavior a reflection of their sheer need for self-preservation in the face of their inability to cope with the vagaries of the street? The principle of survival makes them consider their own self-interest first; altruism is not considered a virtue, survival is.

Although boys who live on the streets are consumed with maintaining their immediate survival and security, they also harness a set of values and strategies to establish their self-worth. They dream of overcoming the prejudices against them; by acquiring goods and status valued by society; by the way they dress, eat, and conduct; their affective relations; and in their dreams for their future.

During a group session at the Therapeutic Centre (Phase III), I asked the children to represent their reflections pictorially. All their drawings depicted more abuse and exploitation than moments of enjoyment. This reiterates my assertion in this research that working on the mindset, the thinking and thought process is a key factor in the street child's understanding of his future and the beginning of his process of rehabilitation.

Each boy has his own history of family trauma, abuse on the streets, and his own inward brokenness. This experience has made me understand that to deal with the group, I need to deal with the individual in the group. To achieve a balance between the two, I felt that rather than trying to act as if I knew what was good for them and imposing it on them and the staff, it would be worthwhile to get everyone involved in the planning of their syllabus, activities, and taking certain decisions which would have implications for their future. For instance, the boys at the Therapeutic Centre decided on the outdoor games to be played, the music and television programs that they would like to watch, the choice of vocational training, and their returning home.

I have tried to question the decisions of the children, their taking onus for these decisions, and whether there is a cognitive approach in their decision-making process. In cases where there has been an abusive situation at home causing him to run away, he does not blame the perpetrators of the abusive situation but takes ownership for his decision. My understanding is that he needs to go back to that harsh situation mentally, and then reflect, analyse, and understand it. The psychological mending of his brokenness lies therein. He has blocked those past harsh realities out, hence he believes that his decisions and actions are based on *karma* or fate and the feeling that "*I have to accept it; I cannot do anything about it.*" For instance, when he decides to leave an institution, he assumes responsibility for his action, saying, "I have to bear the consequences of what I have done. Let it be for now. When a *didi*/uncle approaches me, then I will see." Research and analysis of this type of mindset is significant in understanding personal ownership of the street adolescent.

4

In Transition

MOVING OFF THE STREET

"The decision to move off the streets becomes realistic when the children receive the motivation and assistance in reconstructing their broken lives."

Moving off the street is a process which involves spatial relocation and a decision to move out from a state of homelessness. Theirs is a struggle to break away from street culture and lifestyle. The foremost consideration about leaving the street is about individual choice and changing identity, behavior away from street activities, reducing ties with street culture and street friends, and reconstructing relations with mainstream society. Reaching this stage entails a major transformation in thinking, and a change in mindset from identifying with the streets and its culture to a transition in identifying with mainstream society. A change in identity means making the right decisions and choices of "giving up" certain immediate pleasures/behaviors, places of "comfort" for long-term gain which is not always seen as desirable or logical for the street child. It is a process of reflection, thinking, understanding his situation vis-à-vis his future, and a change in his mindset that prompts him to act towards a change in his identity and to move off the streets.

After living on the streets for years, many boys have conflicting feelings about their homelessness. On the one hand, they are confident of their abilities to survive on the streets, but when they see the older street adults at the *Dargah*[1] waiting for alms, their situation and physical state deteriorating over the years, they become depressed and fatalistic about their situation.

The transition into a non-street world is set into place when the boys are motivated to take an active step towards an independent, productive, and violence-free life through employment and/or job training and educational activities. Thus, moving off the streets involves all the features of habilitation into mainstream society; it is what I term spatio-tempero-behavior (STB). STB is a planned gradual movement that may go through institutional care, training, and a period of independent living to a settled life. On the street they are mobile, yet rooted to a place/space which is their comfort zone. They move off the streets to a place/space that signifies their movement into a new location (spatio). The period in transition (tempero) is when they have alternate living arrangements and recourse to education and acquisition of skills. This entails unlearning the habits and behavior learnt on the streets and acquiring socially accepted mainstream ways of behavior. We experimented with our *Bal Samiti* (Children's Parliament) at one of our camps, which set the tone for our future program.

There was a value education camp[2] in May 1997 in which 45 of the big boys participated. Instead of conducting the normal sessions on family life, sex education, and relationships, we decided to let the bigger boys decide the process of upward mobility of the new boys entering the Residential Home. They discussed charting the stay, syllabus of the children in the Residential Home, and the exit policy. They came up with a plan for the new boys below the age of 12–13.

— *All of them should go to school to learn the three Rs—reading, writing and arithmetic.*
— *Only if they are not capable or are over the age limit, should they go into skill training.*

---

[1] *Dargah*: A mosque; a place of prayer and alms giving. Many street children and beggars congregate outside the dargah to get charity food. Most of the older street adults who have no hope of change pass their time outside the dargah begging for alms.

[2] Value Education Camp: Held for a group of boys of the Residential Home during vacations at a sea side locale for 3 days, wherein intense sessions on personality development, abuse, sex education, budgeting, and relationships are conducted. It has one main theme on which the entire group and trainers focus. At the end of the camp, decisions are taken by the group for their betterment.

Our staff team was present; they accepted this mandate from the boys of the Camp of 1997 and to date this principle has been followed in the Residential Home.

—Value Education Camp Report, May 1997

The boys from the Bal Samitis of the Residential Home often undertake activities that will enable them to make decisions with the management that will directly affect their lives.

After deciding for the younger boys, we asked them to think about themselves. The big boys argued logically that once the new boys grew older, they would follow their example and introspect, "How long can we be totally dependent and stay in a Residential Home? We have to move on." They realized that they had to be stable and have a steady income to live away from the streets.
They decided:

— *To form groups of 3–4 boys who got along well.*
— *To leave the Residential Home in the next 12 to 18 months.*
— *To live in a rented room and divide their household responsibilities.*
— *To request the Residential Home to help them with the rental deposit.*

The Residential Home decided to give them an allowance to buy their bathroom equipment and kitchen utensils.

—Value Education Camp Report, May 1997

The movement off the streets is an educative process learnt over a period of time. It is a process of attempts, failures, and learning from experience that makes the individual understand the need to get off the streets for his future. This understanding comes after reflection, analysis of his situation and rational thinking which leads to a mindset change.

STREET MOVEMENTS

Life on the street is transient for many, with the exception of a few who remain immersed in street culture and grow up to be street adults.

Usman (29 years) had been coming for the Residential Home melas since he was 12–13 years of age. He did not want to join the Residential Home as he

*was enjoying his "freedom." At the age of 20, he became a heroin addict and
headed a group of younger children, who would give him part of their earnings
as "protection money." However in 5–6 years, he lost his hold over the group.
Those boys gave him some money out of pity for his condition. He lived outside
the dargah, on alms, charity, loans, or theft to support his drug habit.*

For most boys, their movements are patterned by their thoughts of
home and their levels of self-worth on the streets. Some boys begin to
miss home and the presence of the family—both symbols of security and
support. Despite the material deprivation at home, the abusive or disruptive
family situation, they often think of returning to their families. Sixty-two
percent wanted to return home after 3–5 weeks on the streets; what kept
them back was the fear of reprisal for running away. Even though many
stay on the streets for extended periods of time in order to avoid conflict
at home, most boys express a desire to return home after they have earned
a substantial amount of money.

The alteration between street and home is a common phenomenon
among street children. The frequency of the movement varies according
to the situation in which the child finds himself. It is important in two
situations: one when the child comes back home for utilitarian reasons,
has no major problems in the street, and for whom returning home is
part of a routine; the second instance is that of the child for whom the
street has become a dead end and who looks for an alternative. The child's
return to his home stems not from utilitarian intent, but from a hope to
be able to stay at home. This involves the restoration of confidence in the
relationship with his mother or his parents.

Sanjay (14 years), a regular visitor to the monthly mela, *shuttled between the
streets and the Residential Home. At every Hindu festival, he would get agitated.
He had a home, parents, a sister, a brother, and property in his village. When
he was small, he had lost his way home and only remembered that he landed in
the Remand Home after being picked up by an official. I sat with him on several
occasions trying to trigger his memory about his village, its location, names of
people or places, gave him a book to write/draw anything that he could remember.
One day a new boy came to the Residential Home who said that his surname was
"Yellappa" a typical South Indian name. Sanjay at once said that it was his father's
name. We contacted a Street Children's Home in Andhra Pradesh, India, and
finally managed to locate his family.*

—Sanjay Case File, Residential Home, 1998

Sanjay's case reiterates my view that once a street child has focus, determination, and a goal, he like any other "normal" human being will be driven by it. He changes his behavior, lifestyle, and most importantly, his thinking and mindset.

For the child on the street, the street is his only comfort zone. He has an apprehension about participating in conventional mainstream society. Some street children have become used to living by their own rules and structures and do not wish to forfeit their independence.

Santosh (12 years), who had just come to the streets two months ago, had this to say of his happiness on the streets, "I imagine the street to be everything. I can walk around freely and get things easily. I have a lot of friends, money, and above all, my freedom."

— Santosh Case File, 2004

The very thought of leaving the streets behind engenders fear in the hearts of street children. Rational thinking and analysis is not part of their reflective understanding; therefore, fear of the unknown is related with lack of effort. Orientation camps for 2–3 days are organized for these boys to take away their fears. Much of their fears are based on hearsay and stories made up by boys who have left the camp often due to their own inadequacies.

"I heard from Sandeep," says Jaggu, "that in the Rehabilitation Program, they beat you up, the rice has worms and also there is no training, they only make you work without pay."

The seeing and experiencing in the orientation camp changes their mindset and fears of the unknown, or of the negative impressions they have about the program.

In my experience with the children, I have often seen that once they have made up their mind on an issue, no amount of counseling worked. Shambu (18 years) said,

The one in-charge asked me to do the NIOS. I did not want to do it. Because he told me, I had to. I would prefer to get a job rather than study.

This reiterates that participation of the children in their own development/decisions is essential. The desire to move away from street life arises from a number of reasons such as lack of security, poor health, exploitation, need to hide from the law or from a problem, to control a drug habit, a desire to find companionship or get married, or a need to find their home.

Lucchini (1997) distinguishes three types of exit from the street: an *active exit*, an *exit because of the depletion of resources* or due to inertia, and a *forced exit* because of removal or expulsion. Active exit entails a conscious choice by a youngster to leave the street and take an alternative course; it derives from the path his life has taken on the street. When the exit stems from an exhaustion of resources or inertia, a dead end has been reached on the street where resources for survival, mobility, and sociability have been depleted. This form of exit differs from an active exit since the youngster does not have a viable alternative to the street. This kind of exit is, therefore, marked by its instability and by sporadic returns to the street. The third form of exit occurs because of forced removal, such as prolonged institutionalization (in a remand home) or imprisonment, and it is as such, no real exit but only a temporary break.

This summarizes the types of movement the child makes off the streets. His active exit is the ideal. He thinks of this future and is focused; he has a plan and accordingly goes through the difficult process of learning a new behavior and unlearning street patterns. This movement is generally a successful one, leading into a settled form of living. He has changed his mindset to understanding the importance of moving off the streets.

STREET STRESSORS

Life on the street is rife with tensions and uncertainties. The discrepancy between what is normal for their age and what they are compelled to do by circumstances is a source of enormous stress. Very often one may view the street child as an independent adult in a child's garb. There are several stressors on the street which work on the individual either singly or in combination. Street boys undergo stress and anxiety when they have to look for food, security, health care, protection, and drugs. This is accentuated especially when they run out of money and when they fall ill. On the streets, they are insecure, vulnerable, and subject to exploitation from various sources. Several individuals or gangs use these children and exploit them to achieve their own ends. They regard these children as "cheap labor" or "easily expendable." Being on the streets also means that the boys are deprived of facilities such as nutrition, health, recreation, and education.

Biku says, "Yes, there is a lot of stress on the streets. We have no tension when we have sufficient money to buy drugs. We get tensed when we do not get to take drugs as the addiction grips us from inside in such a way that it becomes necessary for us to have the drug at any cost."

Life on the streets is symptomatic of a state of temporariness, which induces stress in street boys. Accidents, illness, financial difficulties, change in relationships, change in frequency or nature of sexual experiences, inability to have influence over the same young people, loss of physical strength, police crackdowns, losing money and belongings, and fights with friends are some of the life changes associated with stress on the streets. These stresses promote thoughts of lifestyle change.

Different sets of factors help us to understand why some boys move off the street. These movements could be either temporary or permanent. These factors can be grouped into the following categories:

THERE IS LITTLE ON THEIR PLATES...

The street child faces the uncertainty of finding food and this leads to a heavy reliance on junk, stale, and discarded food or competing for free food distributed at temples, mosques, and hotels or even scavenging in dustbins. Invariably, children fall prey to stomach-related disorders and malnourishment. Most street boys are employed in jobs that require hard manual labor. Often the food that they obtain fails to satisfy their calorific requirements, rendering them easily tired and listless.

Rashid (after he had run away from the Residential Home) told Vikas (staff out-reach team member), "On the streets we get good food such as Chinese, biryani, mutton, chicken, and fish. In the institutions, it is only on Sundays that we get some non-vegetarian food." When Rashid had come for the monthly mela, I asked him, "How many times a week do you have all the non-vegetarian food that you like?" "When I have the money and I feel like eating it." "How often is that?"

I asked him. He replied, "Sometimes once or twice a month; depends on the scrap I pick or the 'wadi' salary I get."

The street child while in an institution/home, fantasizes about the good moments he had enjoyed while on the street. This attitude is an underpinning of his philosophy, "live for the day." I think it is this incongruence of thought between the recollected past and the lived reality that pulls the child back to the streets. However, the street child has his own sense of dignity when it comes to food, and a fine line of distinction exists between a street child and a beggar.

Sirshat (staff outreach team member) said, *"All the new boys we meet on the streets are coming into the city hungry; the first thing they ask us is for food."* These new boys are confident that the institutions will provide timely food if not other facilities. Food, therefore, could compel new, sick, handicapped, and very young boys to seek the help of an NGO or other service providers. Yet, this may not necessarily be a sufficient reason to retain them over a long period.

Food is a major preoccupation of the street child, especially for the small and new boys, and the stress related to it often prompts a mind-set change in them—to move out of the streets into institutions or alternative care situations. This alternative care situation could be, not running away but accepting the abuse of the protector in return for food and security.

The child on the streets has to take what he gets. He has to contend with long hours of work, irregular payments, an appalling work environment, and physical and sexual abuse.

Street children identify themselves in terms of a primary work activity closely linked not only to a preference for a particular mode of income generation, but also to one that reflects their preferred social and cultural networks. Choices made by street boys about how to earn money are socially patterned and related to both background and situational characteristics, and this affects their ability to gain and maintain employment in the organized sector. They engage in patterns of work/income generation that are characterized by instability and diversity. This flexibility of work strategies is their response to an inherently unstable lifestyle. Work is essential for survival and once enough has been earned for the day's needs, it is time to turn to recreation.

The abilities of the street boy remain limited to doing petty jobs for earning his daily bread. There is little scope for developing specialized skills. Most street boys are engaged in hazardous occupations such as scavenging for resalable scrap in garbage bins; heavy manual labor such as carrying luggage for travelers; loading and unloading material from trucks at godowns; hopping on and off running trains while selling water bottles or trinkets; weaving and *zari* work that renders them vulnerable to injury, abuse, infection, and deterioration of eyesight; working at small restaurants for long hours; heavy *wadikaam*, peddling drugs, or working as masseurs by night that leaves them vulnerable to sexual abuse.

Their lack of skill and being underage force them into employment in the unorganized sector which does not give them labor law rights. Their labor is valued for the day. They get hired and fired regularly. Procuring regular jobs is difficult because they do not have a guarantor, and the owners of workshops tend to believe that they are unreliable, irregular, and untrustworthy.

Work demands are one of the factors that push boys out of their homes onto the streets. The same reason is also a factor in boys wanting to leave the streets temporarily and joining an institution. This can be attributed to the economic exclusion of many street boys and their consequent sense of insecurity and risk in the current scenario of market societies. This instigates the youth to strive to achieve conventional goals such as home, family, and a job.

There Is Little in Their Pockets...

Boys on the street are involved in odd jobs in order to earn a living, but most often the income they earn is insufficient to secure even the most basic needs. Since they have no fixed income, inadequacy of money, unfair practices by their employers, and long hours of work push them to resort to unfair means to have that cash in hand.

They wish to have won the lottery or gamble and win all the money possible to help achieve their desires. Money has its connotation of "freedom of the streets" for the street child, and when they do not have the money to fulfill their momentary "desires," it prompts them to run away from the institution/program.

Rafique (15 years) had saved ₹900 over a period of two months. He demanded the money as he wanted to buy a walkman. I tried to convince him about the need to keep his savings for other purposes. He would not take that advice. He had a long pending desire to own a walkman and now wanted to fulfill it.

In many cases, street children who are employed are paid at the whims of the employer, and often they do not get paid for long periods of time. New children are commonly picked up when they just arrive and are sold to small restaurants.[3] They work for 12 to 14 hours delivering tea, food parcels, cleaning tables, serving, or washing dishes and cups in the scullery. Rohit said, "*I was getting just one meal of rice and dal at 4 pm and in the morning, a slice of bread and tea as my payment, so I ran away after two months.*"

The seasonal nature of their occupation has no avenue for saving money. For example, *wadi*[4] work, which employs street boys in large numbers, is limited to the "marriage seasons"[5] only. The fear of not having money to buy food, clothes or drugs is an insecurity that they have to live with constantly. Impoverishment may not necessarily be the central reason why children opt from moving off the streets but it is one of the most common reasons that compel boys to seek an alternative. Some find themselves helpless with regard to the exploitation of the employers. Some think it is sensible to get a regular job that gives them a constant salary and dignity.

Kishore (19 years) was an ex-addict who had completed the Therapeutic Program. He was now employed with us as a peer educator and had taken an ice-breaker session—songs and games with the orientation camp group of street addicts. He showed them his bank book that had a savings of ₹12,000 in two years. He was earning ₹800 a month (his boarding and lodging was being taken care of).
— Orientation Camp, Lonavala, March 2004

The boys pointed out that Kishore had more confidence compared to those peers who had no savings. He also had the respect of the street boys,

---

[3] New children are commonly sold to small restaurants. A type of "mafia agent" who waits on the platform identifies runaway children, picks them up under the lure of offering them food and a job. He sells them to a small restaurant for a fee. The child gets just a meal and place to sleep, with no other remuneration.

[4] *Wadi*: Working at marriage parties—helping in cooking, as porters, as waiters, and other odd jobs.

[5] Marriage seasons: According to the Hindu religion, certain periods in the calendar are considered auspicious to marry.

staff, and visitors. Now with money came a dignity and an ambition to save. Kishore was proud to show off his bank book; he became a role model. Some of them wanted to become peer educators like Kishore.

THERE ARE NO APPLES TO KEEP THE DOCTOR AWAY...

Street life has a destructive influence on health. The poor and unhygienic living conditions of the streets intensified by poor city planning in terms of congestion and pollution has a detrimental effect on the health of the boys living on the street. The evident damage on health due to poor quality and quantity of food is exemplified in their case. What compounds the problem for the street children is the lack of easy access to health care.

Street children are a subgroup of vulnerable children who are at high risk due to the vulnerable settings they live in. They are at a high risk because of their lifestyle, lack of knowledge of preventive measures or just do not bother about it. There is increased prevalence of high-risk behavior and susceptibility to AIDS and STD amongst this group of children. Nearly 78 percent agreed that consumption of drugs had an adverse impact on health. About 66 percent knew about the harmful effects of unprotected sex, but did not take the trouble to practice. It reiterates my view that they live more on the emotive, feeling level of the moment rather than the thinking level.

Access to health facilities are often beyond the reach of these children not because they are unavailable, but because their situation and circumstances make it so.

Ramesh (16 years) had a cut on his hand above the elbow while scavenging for scrap in a garbage dump. He did not know what to apply, could not meet the outreach worker "uncle" who carried medicine. After a month the cut had swollen and festered, he had temperature and could not use his right hand. He decided to go to the general hospital where medical aid was free.

At the hospital, he went through the labyrinthine process of going from counter to counter for nearly two hours. He was scolded for being smelly and dirty and for not treating his wound earlier. He was miserable about his experience and thought it would be better to die with the illness than go through the formalities at the hospital.

— Outreach Report, 1997

Street children face serious health problems ranging from malnourishment to lack of sleep and health care, exposure to risk and work related hazards. About 60 percent of street children are victims of sleep disorders—a result of stress or anxiety, lack of proper place to sleep, fear of sexual abuse, and fear of being robbed. Excessive drug use also tells upon their health; 60 percent of the children up to the age of 14 who were taking "solution"[6] had contracted tuberculosis. Their high-risk sexual behavior, their exploitation, and prostitution causes many of them to be infected by HIV and other STDs. Often victims of street violence, street fights, and accidents these boys have little access to medical facilities. Faced with constant ill-health and chronic disorders and infections, boys seek the help of NGOs, the street outreach worker, drop-in centers, and residential homes. This movement into an institution may not always lead to permanent residence there, as some boys return to the street after recovery and medical treatment.

Akbar (16 years) came to the Residential Home after he met with an accident. He felt better in a week and left. He came back when his infection turned septic. He had left the Residential Home a second time before he had completed his course of medication. He came back for the treatment, discontinued it again in less than a week as he felt better and was back again a third time at the Residential Home, when the infection started spreading.

My experience with children like Akbar has led me to believe that while I should make available the service, the child should also be made accountable. Helping the child understand the consequences of leaving his medication midway and participating in his own healing procedure is my educative responsibility.

The Big Brothers Are Watching ...

Age specificity is an important component of street life and this differentiation is also observed in terms of the tensions and anxieties experienced by the streets boys. The younger boys in the age group 9–12 years are chiefly concerned with survival on the street. Anxiety about

---

[6] Solution: Type-writing correcting fluid. It has an acetone base and its components are toxic. It is commonly inhaled on a piece of cloth by young street addicts. It is highly addictive and is a commonly sought drug.

acquiring food, clothing, and a safe place to sleep predominate their actions and behaviors. At times, older boys lure the younger boys in the guise of being their "protector" to continue the abusive relationship. Some smaller boys prefer the company of older boys in spite of being sexually abused by them as they need to be protected on the streets by them, thus getting into a "protector–utility boy" relationship.

After living on the streets for years, many boys have conflicting feelings about their homelessness; they are confident of their abilities to survive on the streets and of their experiences of travel, but soon are depressed to see "the end point of street life." They become fatalistic about their situation.

Yaseen was almost 40 years old. While I was on outreach at the Mahim Dargah area, he asked me, "Can you take me with you? Is there any hope for me now? I have tried to give up street life, but where do I go for support now? I had a family, but they threw me out years ago because of this addiction of mine. Is there any possibility at this age? I do not want to die like the rest of these people around."
—Outreach, Mahim, Mumbai, 1999

Homeless youth experience social exclusion and operate on the economic margins of society. Yaseen's case is common for the street child who has grown into an adult on the streets. Those boys who have left home at an early age lack educational qualifications for certain courses, and hence they lack skills to sustain them in the labor market. Nagesh says, "*Once we are old, we cannot do the heavy jobs of the wadi and we do not get employed by the mukkadam[7] anymore.*"

Their reflection on their present life vis-à-vis their future is often a trigger to move off the streets. The toughest task is to get them to think and reflect.

THERE ARE NO SHELTERS, ONLY OPEN SKIES COME RAIN, HAIL, OR SHINE...

Street boys have no protection from inclement weather. They live and work on the roads, with inadequate protection, if at all. Often the rainy season is the most difficult part of the year for them.

---

[7] *Mukkadam*: The supervisor/employer for street boys at wedding parties (*Wadi*).

Mr Mota (regular Residential Home donor) brought Babajhan with his three grandsons who were found begging at the central railway station, cold and wet. Babajhan had come to the city in May 1995 due to his inability to repay some loans in his village. He did not have a place to stay or means to feed the children. He made them beg and stayed on the platform, braving the rough elements of the streets. The two younger boys had pneumonia and the baby had maggots in the wound on his head. The doctors gave the two younger boys 15 days to one month to live. Mr Mota asked us to keep them in the Residential Home so that they would have a warm dry place to die in peace. We were ready to keep the three boys but not the grandfather. He was waiting for the rains to subside to leave for his village in Uttar Pradesh.

— Residential Home Monthly Report, July 1995

Every rainy season, over 220 children come in to stay in the Residential Home, about 40–50 more than the usual numbers. Those living in public places find their surroundings unfit to sleep in during the rains, and their susceptibility to water borne diseases and infections is high. Given the seasonal nature of their occupations, street boys look for alternatives. Most boys move into institutions during the monsoons. Thus their movement here is temporary; it is an exit due to the depletion of resources.

THERE ARE COPS ROUND THE CORNER, RUN, RUN, RUN...

About 88 percent of street boys refer to negative experiences with the beat constables. The most common complaint of street boys is that they are regularly rounded up, detained illegally, beaten, and tortured by the police. This they say is done in order to fill the "quota"[8] for their registers.

Ashok (17 years) told the staff team about the dynamics of protection payments on the local trains. Ashok's friend, Zuber introduced him to a popcorn maker, who gave him a big sack of popcorn at wholesale prices. While selling them on a local train, Ashok was caught by a constable and slapped for unlicensed vending. He was sent by the constable to meet Laxman (a middle man) who introduced him to Farzana a middle-aged woman who told him the rules. He had to pay her ₹30 every day to be "protected." She sent him with Laxman to the station officer whom he had to pay ₹50 every day. Only then could he sell his popcorn. Ashok had to

---

[8] Quota: A certain number of cases registered is the target set to monitor the duties of particular police stations.

make up the money for buying of the popcorn, keep some for his food, and also pay
₹80 as protection money. He gave up the job in two days. Zuber again introduced
him to a man who "took care of the protection" on the trains and Ashok had to sell
sandwiches for him.

— Ashok Case File, November 2005

This reveals the vulnerability of the child especially in his ability to trust
adults. His levels of trust are in friends/peers only. The lack of psychological
or sociological support systems further accentuates his mindset of fatalism.

Friends or Foes?

The peer group influences the child's conscience and he tends to comply
with the demands and mores of his peers. Forming close associations and
living in groups is an integral part of survival on the street. The group
often provides food, shelter, drugs, and most of all protection and a sense
of security to these boys. The group takes on the role of an extended family
and often boys are influenced and model their behavior on their peers.

Allauddin (14 years) had lived in the Residential Home for six years. For the past
five months he had been doing very well as a trainee apprentice in a two-wheeler
garage. One day, his friends Kamresh (14 years) and Paresh (15 years) were visited
by their mother who said that their father had to undergo an ear operation costing
₹20,000. She needed the two boys' help and so Paresh and Kamresh decided to
leave the Residential Home. Allauddin, too, decided to go with them. He said, "On
Rakshabandan day last month, their sister tied a Rakhee to me and she gave me
a meal." I tried telling Allauddin, "You are doing so well in the garage, you have a
bright future, you will be a good mechanic in 3–4 years time; you can start your
own small business if you like." He was adamant, "No, she is my sister and if she
has a problem, her father becomes my father and I have to look after him too." I
warned him that he would be on the streets in less than a month, but he said, "No,
my sister's family will look after me."

—Allauddin Case File, Residential Home, 2000

Allauddin was a typical example of the influence peers have on each
other. He had met her just once and her tying of the *Rakhee*[9] had influenced

---

[9] *Rakhee*: A band tied on the wrist of a boy by a girl on Rakshabandhan day (Hindu festival),
signifying that she is his sister and he as her brother will protect her for life.

his decision; his friends had become his brothers. The feeling that he had found a family and the emotional bonding he developed overtook him. Allauddin could not help his friends earn the ₹20,000. His "sister" and "mother" were upset that he was staying with them and felt he was a burden. In two weeks he was back on the streets and in a month so were Kamresh and Paresh. They were wary of coming back to the Residential Home or going to their former place of work.

In the absence of family relationships, friendship takes its place and is seen to influence a number of the street child's impulsive decisions. However, many boys undergo bad experiences with their friends on the streets. Some are robbed, forced or lured into taking drugs, or are physically and sexually abused. Betrayal and loss of friendship is a common factor in these children's lives. This factor makes them move, sometimes with another group or gang and at times even off the streets.

They Are Closing In, Closing In...

It is extremely difficult to survive on the streets alone, especially at a young age. Various groups are formed on the streets. *"Gang leaders are the ones who rule the streets,"* says Rahim.

In a hostile environment, the peer group/gang is an important defense mechanism. Furthermore, the street child views the solidarity with other children as a substitute for familial protection and warmth. Moreover, there is fun, excitement, and adventure. The gang develops its own value system and the children who no longer belong anywhere, once again belong to a community—the community of the street. They now have their own rules and laws and often even their own language.[10] Gangs have a monopoly on certain streets and they do not let any other gang enter their area. When this happens, fights usually result. Generally, there are older leaders who demand obedience in exchange for protection; the gang is organized in a hierarchical fashion and has a tough social environment. Many gangs use violent initiation rituals to recruit new members, and those who break the rules are punished. To avoid punishment for a mistake committed, individuals move off the streets.

---

[10] Own language—own slang.

MOVEMENTS WITHIN, MOVES WITHOUT

For many, the thought of leaving the streets induces fear; a move from something known, albeit difficult, to something poorly understood, which they feel they have little confidence to deal with. Thus this move is made with the utmost caution.

Figure 4.1 illustrates the various combinations that work for the street child in Repatriation, Relay (Lucchini, 1997), Relapse, Rehabilitation and the children working the system to their advantage.

(A) *Immediate problem solving/running away*: Owing to the abusive situation at home, the street child makes an impulsive decision,

Figure 4.1 The Home–Street–Institution—Independent Living Dynamic

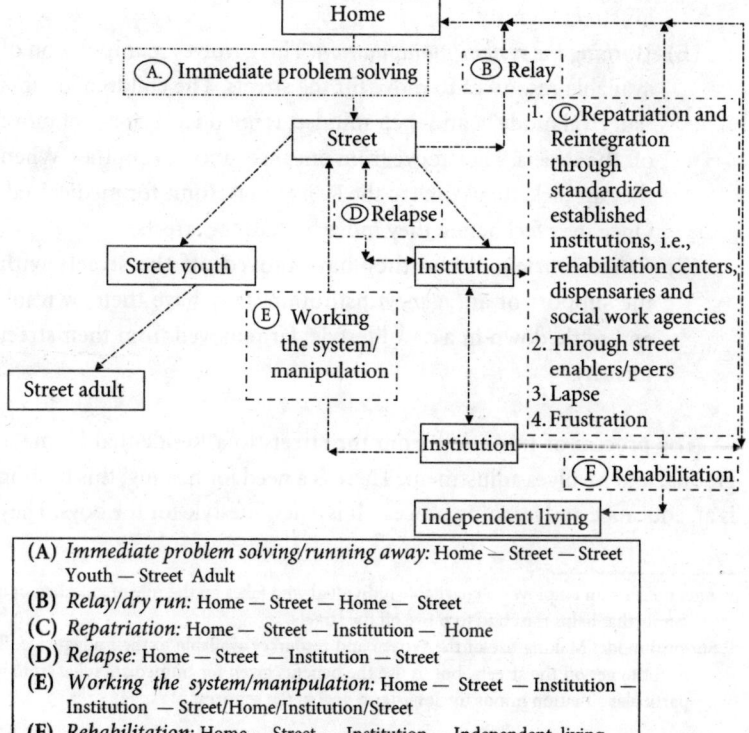

(A) *Immediate problem solving/running away*: Home — Street — Street Youth — Street Adult
(B) *Relay/dry run*: Home — Street — Home — Street
(C) *Repatriation*: Home — Street — Institution — Home
(D) *Relapse*: Home — Street — Institution — Street
(E) *Working the system/manipulation*: Home — Street — Institution — Institution — Street/Home/Institution/Street
(F) *Rehabilitation*: Home — Street — Institution — Independent living

the consequences of which he understands later. He may make several unsuccessful attempts at moving off the streets, but ends up in "the terminal situation."

(B) *The relay or dry run*: This generally goes hand in hand with his immediate problem solving situation. He runs away to known persons, like relatives or common friends, but gets back home either on his own or with his relatives.

(C) *Repatriation*: This movement off the streets and back home is guided by the institution. It is often a prepared move. It could involve his having acquired certification (academic or vocational) and earned a sum of money; above all, he is mentally prepared to face the challenges at home.

(D) *Relapse*: This is the situation when the child, after leaving home and being on the streets, tries moving off the streets with the help of an institution/agent[11] but fails because of his inability to shed his street identity.

(E) *Working the system/manipulation*: This involves manipulation of available resources to move off the streets. The children are in a "survival mode"[12] and their mindset is not on a permanent move off the streets. They move from one institution to another. When they are sick, they come to the Residential Home for medical aid. Once they feel better, they move back to the streets.

(F) *Rehabilitation*: When they have moved off the streets with the support of an agency/institution, they have their own job and settle down in a new lifestyle, far removed from their street identity.

The process of transition from the streets to a Residential Home is gradual and involves adjustment. There is a need for healing; this healing is an educative and learning process. It is a new lifestyle for the boys. They

---

[11] Agent: Either an employer, a charitable individual who takes on the role of guardian or a family that helps the child to move off the streets.

[12] Survival mode: Making use of the system and resources available to their advantage. It is not to get off the streets, but to use the benefits given for immediate relief from a particular situation minus the long-term goal of the services.

may dislike it initially but eventually grow to accept that this change is for the better. It is the initial acclimatization that is the most difficult period due to a lack of maturity to handle initial adjustments coupled with the habituation to instant gratification. Factors in this transition include:

1. *A desire to renounce street identity:* The thought process of the child may not always follow reasonable and logical cognitive processes of understanding to decision-making. There is no cognitive understanding or thinking of the consequences of the action. Habits occur unconsciously and habitual behaviors usually occur in chains, which are set off by "triggers" (stimulus events that bring them into mind and which reinforce their execution). Once a trigger sets a habit chain in motion, it is difficult to stop it. A trigger like the feeling/desire, the money, and the opportunity can effect an individual change but it also requires resilience, confidence in one's capabilities, a spatial change, and an ideological concept of having gone through street life. Life off the streets maybe viewed now as a movement out of a degenerative street life.

2. *Unlearning street lifestyle:* A prerequisite to moving off the streets is the mindset and thinking of the street child. He has formed his ideas and is "settled in" in his comfort zone on the streets. To get him to a new way of life would mean unlearning what he has already been habituated to and to learn new ways of survival. For this, he has to have a mindset that is conducive and open to change. In an institution, street children try to leave behind their past life and move ahead. They try controlling their degenerative habits (drugs, sex, abuse, and gambling), but they do not compromise when somebody uses bad language against them. Vikas (staff team) was upset with Rajesh for repeatedly stealing other boys' clothes. He told Rajesh, "*What is your status? You are a street person and you will always be so, you will never learn to behave, you will always be a thief.*" Rajesh felt insulted. He did not want to be called a street boy anymore as he felt he was out of that situation; he had already undergone an identity change in his mind.

3. *Reflecting on their past to build a future*: Once street adolescents are part of a residential home, they start understanding the implications of their actions. They start thinking and preparing for their future and show a willingness to make compromises. This represents the first step towards mature and acceptable behavior. Being aware and reflecting on this type of lifestyle, analysing how to cope with the new type of life, seeing that others from a similar background have made it successfully, helps to change their mindset.

THE THOUGHT PROCESS OF THE STREET CHILD

This figure illustrates that there are certain *triggers* in his feelings or desires that are largely propelled by his philosophy of "live for the day" or of "instant gratification." What further encourages this type of thought is the *money* that he has/earns and the *opportunities* he has to spend it on a variety of choices he can make based on his *feelings* and *desires*. Since he does not have a cognitive approach to act at this level, his choices are governed by his *impulsive actions*. These impulsive actions are generally *deviant behavior*, for which he has *late realization* and whose consequences he has to bear. He has *fear of facing* those consequences and hence decides to carry on in his status quo situation on the streets (see Figure 4.2).

Institutionalization and taking boys off the streets require utmost prudence and systematic child-focused nurturing and care. This means an enabling environment for people to enjoy a long and healthy life, to acquire knowledge, and to have access to resources needed for a decent standard of living. The ultimate goal of many child-focused organizations is to reintegrate these youth into mainstream society. If street boys are to get off the street and stay off the street, they need to join the non-street culture/society as a potentially employable person. If they are not employable, then they need to become part of a support system which caters to both their survival and developmental needs.

Figure 4.2 The Thought Process of the Street Child

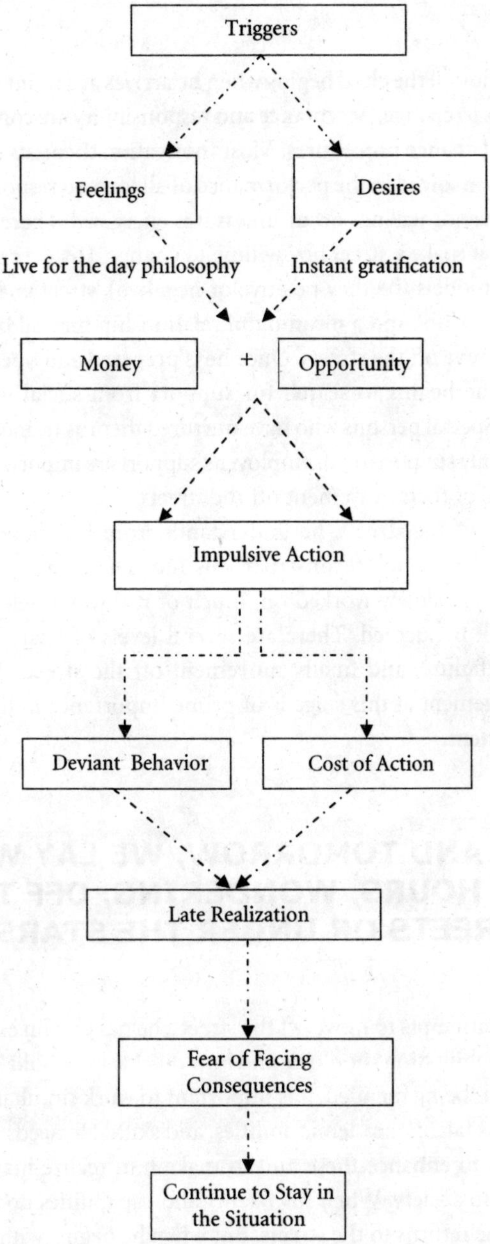

```
                    ┌─────────────┐
                    │  Triggers   │
                    └─────────────┘
             ┌───────────┴───────────┐
             ▼                       ▼
      ┌─────────────┐         ┌─────────────┐
      │  Feelings   │         │   Desires   │
      └─────────────┘         └─────────────┘

 Live for the day philosophy    Instant gratification

      ┌─────────────┐         ┌─────────────┐
      │   Money     │    +    │ Opportunity │
      └─────────────┘         └─────────────┘

                 ┌────────────────────┐
                 │  Impulsive Action  │
                 └────────────────────┘

      ┌───────────────────┐   ┌─────────────────┐
      │ Deviant Behavior  │   │  Cost of Action │
      └───────────────────┘   └─────────────────┘

                 ┌────────────────────┐
                 │  Late Realization  │
                 └────────────────────┘

                 ┌────────────────────┐
                 │  Fear of Facing    │
                 │   Consequences     │
                 └────────────────────┘

                 ┌────────────────────┐
                 │ Continue to Stay in│
                 │   the Situation    │
                 └────────────────────┘
```

TOWARDS SELF-DEVELOPMENT

The preparation of the child begins when he arrives at a point of openness and readiness to change. Acceptance and responsibility are components of psychological change procedures. Most motivation theorists assume that motivation is involved in the performance of all learned responses; that is, a learned behavior will not occur unless it is energized. There are various influences that make a street boy willing to change. His peer group, close friends, role models (be they positive or negative), street enablers/social workers, counselors, and a meaningful relationship may all help prepare his mind to move off the streets. Once he is prepared and open to change his lifestyle, he begins to search for support from social workers and institutions. Special persons who have nurtured them as trainees, servants, their own family support, or an employer's support are important elements in the process of their movement off the streets.

To move off the streets, he understands from his friends or social workers that he has to "reconstruct" his life. The areas of habituated deterioration are slowly worked on, much of it through self-denial and a resolute will to succeed. There are several levels of trial, followed by preparation, failure, and finally movement off the streets. Motivation and encouragement at this stage is of prime importance in his quest for self-development.

TODAY AND TOMORROW, WE LAY WASTE OUR HOURS, WONDERING, OFF THE STREETS OR UNDER THE STARS?

When a child attempts to move off the streets, he has certain expectations of how his rehabilitation should be and how quickly he should be reaching it. As his past is being mended, it is important to work simultaneously on his present, his talents, academic abilities, and skills. He needs to be given opportunities to enhance these and to make him realize his worth, his contribution to society. When his talents and capabilities do not match those ideals, he returns to the streets. But when he begins with attainable and realistic ideals, he is better prepared; his ideal matches his preparation for it.

Jai (16 years) has set his goal. He wants to work in a software firm. He is now studying for his HSC (Higher Secondary School Certificate), has been taking English classes, and has asked us to get someone to sponsor his computer language course. He studies early in the morning and late at night, practices what he learns in the computer room in the Residential Home when he gets back, and keeps talking to the staff and the volunteers in English. He wants to do well in his studies, get a good job in a computer firm, buy his own house, and live like a middle class youngster.

—Jai Case File, Residential Home, 2006

EDUCATION

The movement to self-development begins with steps towards educational attainment, academic qualifications and planning for future work. The street child understands that this is fundamental to his progress. There has been a marked difference in the Residential Home education program of the children over the past ten years.

In 1996, when we first admitted four children to the nearby Municipal school, we were under the impression that they would not be able to cope being in a school for six hours. The following year, 31 more boys asked to be admitted to school. For the next two years, admissions to primary school increased and a few opted for the High School Certificate course by correspondence. In the past four years, there has been a change in the pattern of education. The younger children now want to be in mainstream school right up to high school and college. This has prompted them to seek other avenues, too. They have begun looking for classes in English, learning computers and are no longer focused on blue collar jobs. Their educational capabilities are now focused upon getting into the white collar domain and moving into the middle class.

— Residential Home, 2006

The boys at the Residential Home are allowed to participate in their own development by making a choice from among a range of training options. Often, if a street adolescent is not able to enter a certificate course due to his inability to meet the institution's academic requirements, he goes in for training for which academics is not a prerequisite. There are several institutes that regularly take in boys of the Residential Home for training and tailor their course content accordingly. Several small local workshops have provided training to those boys who have not had the qualifications to enter formal training institutes. They often struggle to succeed and make full use of the opportunities they get, and these are the boys who are focused and eventually succeed in moving off the streets.

EMPLOYMENT

Having been trained in "mending the past" and obtaining certification, the street adolescent takes up a job in his process of movement off the streets.

Raju (19 years) had completed his training in an electrician's course. He could not find a job immediately. He decided to take up a house keeping job in a shopping mall in the interim. In seven months, Dinesh (staff team member) got him a job as an electrician's assistant. Raju gave up this job in less than two months. The electrician used to abuse him, keep him till late at night, get him to do all the difficult jobs, but not teach him anything. Raju went back to work at another mall. There, too, he had difficulty with the supervisor and left the job. He did not want to go back to the streets. He began searching for jobs himself and got one as a sales representative for a water purifier company.

It is in Phase V that the street adolescent often encounters problems with employers who are abusive, exploitative, and unreasonable. Yet once he has begun living independently, he develops resilience and if he does not manage to get along, goes on to find a new job or deals with his problems. The street child has worked on himself, his mindset and motivation, mended his past and availed himself of support structures. These are indicative of his permanent movement off the streets.

VISION FOR TOMORROW

Once their basic needs are attended to, these adolescents start developing a vision for their future. Many of the younger boys opt to study and continue with their schooling which has been disrupted. For the older boys, the Residential Home prepares them to face life and its challenges, to conduct relationships, and adopt socially acceptable ways of living.

A drama depicting street life was discussed at a meeting with the boys preparing for the Diwali *Mela*, 2006. Many in the group said, "*Do not mention the topic of street life and drugs, we have forgotten it and if you talk about it, we will think about our old ways again.*"

This implies they are keen to erase their past, but whenever reminded of it, they find it demeaning. At the Residential Home, therefore, there is a concerted attempt to focus less on the past and look more towards the future.

THE REHABILITATION PROCESS

The process of moving from dependence on the streets to survival in an institution marks the movement off the streets and the start of the rehabilitation process. When the street child decides to move off the streets, he develops a dependence on the institution.

THE SETTLEMENT PHASE

From the institution, once he becomes economically capable of living by himself, he moves into a home of his own. It could be either moving back to his family or sharing a house on rent with a group of friends. Moving off the streets is always linked to living under a roof. It means developing one's security and establishing a socially acceptable identity. A house gives that identity and sense of achievement to the child. He has a place to belong to, an address he can claim as his own.

When the bigger boys decided to move out of the Residential Home, the management gave them a refundable deposit of ₹10,000 each to pay for their new lodgings in a slum. Research over a three year period revealed that 25–30 percent of the boys found it difficult to get used to this new lifestyle of waking up at 3 am, standing in long queues to collect water, and doing other household chores without help. Some of these boys could not cope with the harsh realities of living in a slum, surrounded by the degenerative habits that they had tried to shed; they dropped out of the program and returned to the streets.

— Residential Home, 2004

When asked to reflect on their situation, they responded that the Residential Home was comfortable and that they did not have to do their daily chores. They also confessed their inability to handle their newfound freedom. We decided to experiment with renting small apartments in the suburbs which were affordable and offered a more supportive environment. There has been a marked difference; to date, there has not been a single drop-out from these apartments, indicating a 100 percent reintegration into society.

The transition process begins when the boys are able to generate enough capital to rent a room and participate in NGO training programs such as carpentry, tailoring, or various vocational and technical courses. Although a homeless existence may be a temporary stage in the children's life on the street, the difficulties they encounter do not disappear immediately when street life changes to community life. Many still engage in precarious day-to-day survival, while actively seeking ways of obtaining secure employment. These maybe considered as the ones who have gone through the process of understanding that life on the streets is degenerative and who have built up resilience and a determination not to go back to the streets.

Joshi (21 years) left the Residential Home to live in a group home. His was a story of tenacity in the face of a series of work-related disappointments—he lost his job in a small factory making noodles as the owner went bankrupt. He found a job after two months (until when he borrowed money to survive) as a courier boy, only to lose that job, too, as he made a few mistakes on his delivery rounds. He was out of earning for a while. After a two-month gap, he began selling toothbrushes on the local trains, often getting into conflict with the railway police. He failed to make a profit. Ultimately, he got a permanent job in a blood testing laboratory, carrying blood samples from people's homes to the laboratory.
— Joshi Case File, 2006

Joshi had understood that his identity was no longer that of a street boy. He built up resilience to combat his loss of jobs. Street children are resilient, creative, and ingenious. Given the needed opportunities and drawn into a situation, they are capable of bringing about some kind of personal transformation and behavioral changes. Resilience refers to positive patterns of functioning or development during or following exposure to adversity. The now rehabilitated youth tries different avenues of work to stay off the streets. A permanent residence has given him the identity and respectability to get jobs with responsible persons/concerns.

HOME REPATRIATION

This is not a mere relocation in geographical terms, but more a paradigmatic shift from a street culture to a family culture. It is rediscovering relationships and social networks. He may undertake this return himself or with the help of an organization. Organizations often help with the transition particularly if mistreatment or family conflict was the reason for the child's coming to the streets. The varying patterns of rearing and socialization along with the consistent lack of face-to-face supervision and communication affect parent–child relationships.

Qazi (17 years) left home at the age of twelve, when his father chastised him physically if he did not learn his lessons or chant the Koran properly. Qazi ran away, took to living on the streets and became a drug addict. He joined the Residential Program, learnt tailoring and finished his NIOS High School examination. This sense of achievement propelled him to want to return home. Anselm (staff social worker), took a keen interest in preparing him to understand the difference between life in the village and city. He was sent to the pre-training home situated in a rural environment for three months to understand the reality of a village and its dynamics. His parents were called and prepared and he rejoined them. For the last three years, he has been in touch with me on Id and Diwali.

— Qazi Case File, 2000

Qazi stayed on at home and adapted well. He said that though it was difficult at times to be scolded by his father, the attachment to his mother and sister was the reason/motivation for his staying on.

In 1995, I made a study of the 11 boys who had gone home to their villages from the Residential Home. Nine boys returned, saying that it was difficult to cope with the slow paced life in the village. They had to work hard for a little money. In the city, they collected scrap for an hour or more and earned what they would get in 2–3 weeks of heavy labor in their native village. They could not adapt to the controls on their freedom of movement, decisions being taken for them by the family members; hence they came back to the city.

— *Residential Home Samachar,*[13] No. 1, August 1995

There was not much preparation to go home. They thought they needed to earn and collect over ₹2,000 to override the initial familial

---

[13] *Residential Home Samachar*: Bimonthly newsletter of the Residential Home, publishing information and news regarding the happenings at the Home and its various projects.

acrimony over their past mistakes. They had not acquired any skills to find work in the village or nearby towns. Some of them were still addicted to inhalants and found it difficult to maintain their habit in their villages. The fact that the street adolescent is now far removed from his old lifestyle and used to his new lifestyle causes him to return to the streets. It is only when he begins to think reflectively about his situation on the streets and compares it to his life at his hometown, that his mindset changes.

This study and reflection on the boys' return from repatriation to the streets prompted the management to change the philosophy from "let them be" to "let them become." The "let them become" implied helping them to realize their potential, equip them with a skill that will enable them to stand on their own feet and get a job anywhere, help them with the preparation to go back home. "Repatriation at the Residential Home: A Study" (1998) found that of the 63 boys who returned home the previous year, only four returned to Mumbai, all due to family breakdown.

— *Residential Home Samachar,* No. 14, October 1998

In some instances, children exploit resettlement programs, using them for the purpose of "adventure" or for short visits to friends and relatives. This also indicates that the majority of homeless people desire to establish some form of permanence in their lives and move out of their nomadic existence.[14]

RELAPSE

However, resettlement is a difficult process and is not always successful. Some street children return to the streets in a "serial manner."[15] The child, who comes back to the street after a brief return home, speaks of the boredom and his longing for the diversified activities and friendly relationships on the street. Membership in a group and identification with a place such as a market square, park, crossroads, vacant lots, metro stations, or a big store stand in contrast to the lackluster, monotonous life

---

[14] Shelter Report, May 2003.
[15] Serial manner: Keeps on oscillating between the institution and streets.

at home. The children who have had a regular job for some time compare the constraints of this activity with the liberty they have experienced in the street. Resettlement may fail when the boy sees that conditions at home have not improved, or that he is unable to find regular, gainful employment in the village despite his skills and training. There are also instances when parents send the boy back to the city for enhanced income.

This demonstrates that movement out of street life must be voluntary, with children taking the initial decision; it cannot be forced. The movement has to be accompanied by intense preparation and simulation of the expected lifestyle in terms of family demands and responsibilities, adjustments, and compromises.

The oscillation of the street child between the states of addiction and periods of recovery are a constant. The stressors he faces on the streets combined with factors conducive to drug abuse and its habitual use sets his lifestyle in a cyclic pattern of stress–drug abuse–attempts at recovery–and back to the streets. He manages to break this cyclic pattern only through support systems that sustain his recovery period. His efforts, intentions and motivation constitute the first step but a support system in the form of external structures such as hospitals, supportive individuals, and non-governmental institutions helps translate this effort into a permanent movement off the streets. The loss of this support due to failures from either side causes a degenerative movement back to addiction. This process is explained in Back to the Addiction Cycle (Figure 4.3).

When the street children are initiated into a support structure like the Residential Home, they are very friendly and attached to the staff team. Once they settle in, they often react violently to small incidents and have several mood swings. Before bonding with new peers, they remember their friends on the streets and begin missing their street lifestyle. If they are addicted to it, they often go through a phase of craving to return to the streets, the drugs/tobacco, and the freedom from discipline.

Not being able to resist the craving to get back to the streets and without a justified reason to leave the institution, the street adolescents try to make lame excuses, *"I have my clothes in the laundry, I will pick them up and come back"* or *"I have my money saved with the shopkeeper, I will get it and return."* On occasions when the staff has accompanied them, they give the staff the slip. This is because their mindset is still that of the streets, and they have

Figure 4.3 Back to the Addiction Cycle

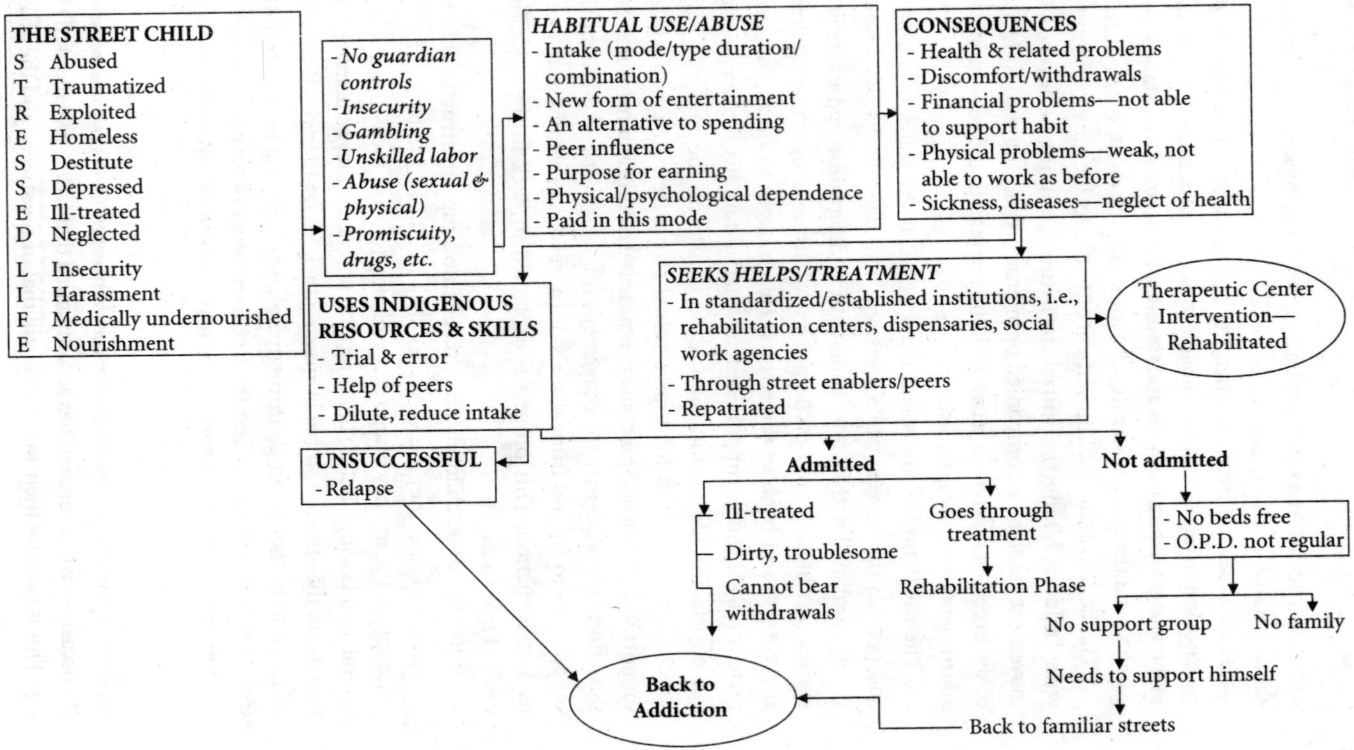

THE STREET CHILD
S Abused
T Traumatized
R Exploited
E Homeless
S Destitute
S Depressed
E Ill-treated
D Neglected
L Insecurity
I Harassment
F Medically undernourished
E Nourishment
- No guardian controls
- Insecurity
- Gambling
- Unskilled labor
- Abuse (sexual & physical)
- Promiscuity, drugs, etc.
HABITUAL USE/ABUSE
- Intake (mode/type duration/ combination)
- New form of entertainment
- An alternative to spending
- Peer influence
- Purpose for earning
- Physical/psychological dependence
- Paid in this mode
CONSEQUENCES
- Health & related problems
- Discomfort/withdrawals
- Financial problems—not able to support habit
- Physical problems—weak, not able to work as before
- Sickness, diseases—neglect of health
USES INDIGENOUS RESOURCES & SKILLS
- Trial & error
- Help of peers
- Dilute, reduce intake
SEEKS HELPS/TREATMENT
- In standardized/established institutions, i.e., rehabilitation centers, dispensaries, social work agencies
- Through street enablers/peers
- Repatriated
Therapeutic Center Intervention— Rehabilitated
UNSUCCESSFUL
- Relapse
Admitted
Ill-treated
Dirty, troublesome
Cannot bear withdrawals
Goes through treatment
Rehabilitation Phase
Not admitted
- No beds free
- O.P.D. not regular
No support group
No family
Needs to support himself
Back to familiar streets
Back to Addiction

come to try out the Residential Home experience because of any of these reasons: a friend has come along, to move out of an undesirable situation on the streets or to see and experience for themselves, and fantasize about a middle class lifestyle.

Once the boys have come to this stage of wanting to leave the program, the staff identifies it and tries to help counsel the boy and ask his peers to counsel him too. Yet, 80 percent of such cases leave. This raised several questions, should one let the boy take the decision, especially in cases when he was only 7 or 8 years old, or even just 12 or 13; as guardian or a "father" should I not let the boy know what was best for him? I consider them my children. This led to the dilemma about the fine line to be drawn between ethical leanings and professional distance.

Those who have dropped out of the program are often the ones who influence the other children's opinion on the streets about institutional care. They are in a transitory mindset, often at fault for not having adhered to the principles of rehabilitation that the institution has laid down and with no focus. In those cases wherein the child is focused, has thought about his future, he overcomes the demands of rehabilitation.

Zakir had been in the Residential Home for five months, but disliked waking up at 7 am and avoided doing the jobs given to the "Don Boys' group"[16] and would get angry with the staff who insisted on his being clean and doing his duties. One day, when a staff team member pulled him up and asked him to finish his jobs before going to play, he quietly slipped away from the Residential Home. Back on the streets, he told the outreach staff, "There the food is very bad, there are lots of stones in the rice and they do not give you a full meal. The one in charge of the Don Group beats us a lot, he hit me very badly so I ran away."
—Zakir Case File, Residential Home, 2002

Zakir is a typical example of how boys react to leaving an institution. To cover up for their mistakes, they make up a story about the services of the institution. The common reasons are that the food is either not good or insufficient (48 percent), that the authorities are very strict and beat you up, or that the other boys are bullies (34 percent), and negligence

---

[16] Don Boys' Group: Formed in Residential Home for those who were being prepared for schooling, training, or for work. It entailed imbibing a certain routine, discipline, responsibilities, values, and work ethics.

(28 percent) on the part of the NGOs. They do not convey the positive aspects of rehabilitation services in education, home placement, and skills learning. Their peers develop opinions about that institution based largely on the narrations of the drop-outs. These negative opinions cause a deep impression and form most of the street child's opinion about institutional care.

Thus the forces, dynamics, and characteristics on the streets keep pulling the child back. To move away from it, he needs a replacing support system that is attractive and sustaining. The first step in moving into a new support structure is a change in mindset which lends a new meaning, a new focus, and less chances of the child going back to the streets.

AT HOME—REWARDS AND REPERCUSSIONS

Institutionalization is not the only strategy to deal with the problem of street boys unless it has an enabling atmosphere that closely approximates positive familial conditions. The long years in the field has made me realize that there is no one right method of care to get the children off the streets or help them get off drugs. We have to consider the fact that we are dealing with human beings with differing needs and experiences. The one method I strongly propose is to help the child reflect, to set him thinking about his future. There also needs to be a well-planned movement for each child, which covers not only his stay in the institution but also goes well beyond it in the form of a meticulous follow-up plan to sustain him off the streets (see Figure 4.4).

The "dependency" factor has been a common phenomenon in all institutions. Rootless and marginalized children tend to be dependent on institutions for long-term support (4 to 10+ years). A well-planned Exit Policy needs to be framed with the participation of all three agents (beneficiaries, staff, and management), with definite time schedules, monitoring, and evaluation. A majority of institutions face difficulties once the dependents move out of their immediate care. Hence an integrated follow-up plan for sustainability is imperative.

Figure 4.4 Movement to and from the Institution

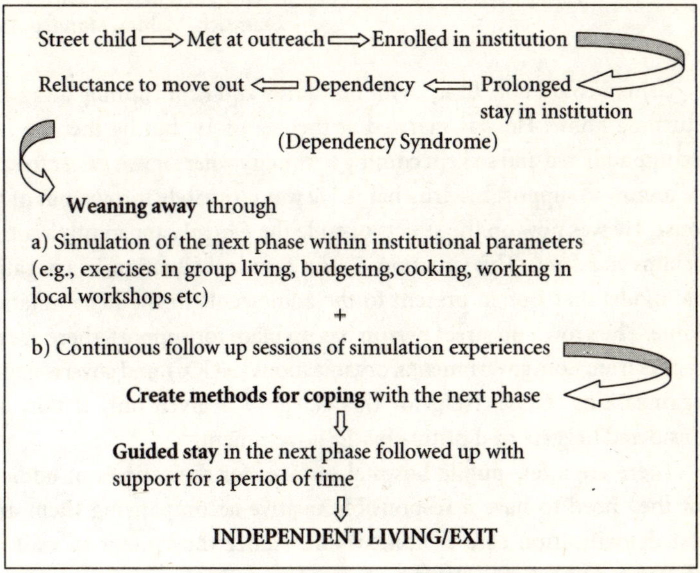

Street child ⟹ Met at outreach ⟹ Enrolled in institution ⟹

Reluctance to move out ⟸ Dependency ⟸ Prolonged ⟸
stay in institution
(Dependency Syndrome)

Weaning away through

a) Simulation of the next phase within institutional parameters
(e.g., exercises in group living, budgeting, cooking, working in
local workshops etc)

+

b) Continuous follow up sessions of simulation experiences ⟹

Create methods for coping with the next phase ⟸
⇩
Guided stay in the next phase followed up with
support for a period of time
⇩
INDEPENDENT LIVING/EXIT

Some of the boys, who had left the Residential Home, when asked what
had prompted them to go back to the streets, identified the following reasons:

*Dorai had been avoiding the issue of moving out of the Residential Home and
settling with his friends who had taken up rented rooms. He kept saying, "I will
never leave the Residential Home." Dorai, who had been working in a cycle shop,
moved briefly out of the Residential Home only to spend his entire savings on
alcohol and "solution." He was unable to "manage" his money.*
— Dorai Case File, Residential Home, 1998

Dorai was unable to shake off his dependency on the Residential
Home and could not handle an independent life; his mindset had not
changed. There is an element of forced movement, be it peer pressure or
institutional exit policy.

The movement off the streets, if not adequately prepared for, makes
the transition from street to institution to rehabilitation difficult, with
possibilities of repeated failure.

*Usman, nearly 32 years old, was one of my first experiences of trying to work with
street addicts in 1986. I had met him on my outreach rounds, and yet after thirteen*

*years, he pleaded, "Please give me one more chance! I will not repeat my mistake.
I have tried to give up street life. But where do I go? Please take me with you!"*

— Outreach, Mahim, Mumbai, 1999

Usman could not "fit in" with his family and kept running away and returning home. He was married at the age of 19, but by then he had become addicted and so kept coming to the city where it was easier to earn the money to support his drug habit. He was ultimately thrown out of his house. He was now on the streets outside the *Dargah*, apparently waiting for alms and drugs. This situation is "The Terminal Situation,"[17] a negative role model that I often present to the adolescents in the Rehabilitation Home. The grown up street person has no place for support, there are no services from non-governmental organizations (NGOs), and governmental organizations (GOs). Help for this category is given only if they are considered beggars or destitute by the government.

There are a few public hospital services for these types of addicts, but they need to have a responsible relative accompanying them and post detoxification care is nonexistent. Hence they prefer to wait on the streets until death. Having no options, no help, and no avenues to pursue an alternative way of life, these street children are in a situation of hopelessness, causing them to relapse into addiction. The question asked of them is, "Would you like to end up like Usman?" This question was put to many of the older boys who came to the *mela*, who were gently but firmly reminded about age catching up with them and the NGO sector not having services for them. This was meant to prompt them into analysing their situation, giving some time for reflection and thought for the future.

REFLECTIONS

Each child has to be considered individually and guided to make the best decision for himself. I have tried to consider each street adolescent differently and used my judgment in helping the child to arrive at a decision that is best for him—if he were confused, vulnerable to deterioration, or

---

[17] The Terminal Situation: A situation wherein a street child has lived out his childhood on the streets and is now a grown up adult. He is heavily addicted to substances, unable to work and earn, lives on charity, outside charitable institutions (on the streets). He does not have a fruitful future, no agency to support him—he is staring at a difficult death situation on the streets.

was attached to one of the team members, I would persuade him to stay on at the Residential Home and give it another try. On the other hand, if I observed in him a determination to leave (run away), my experience has taught me that no amount of persuasion or counseling would change his mindset. In such instances, I made it known to him that he is welcome to come back, and that it would be a good idea to keep in touch with our outreach staff, visit the Drop-in Centre, or come for the *melas*.

For those who stay in the program, despite their initial wariness, resistance to discipline, and hygiene, all a carryover from their street life, they find coping strategies—in their newfound peer bonding based on similarity of interests and shared experience and in an increase in self-expression and self-confidence by taking part in group social functions. For those who undergo the pain of withdrawal symptoms during detoxification, accompanied by a craving to get back to the streets, the presence of an "enabler" works both as a deterrent to running away and as a source of assurance to complete the program. They "enable" the child to come out of the "meditative pause" when he swerves from violent mood swings and shunning all company to making that crucial mindset change to a new focus and a goal. This increases the adolescent youth inhalants' adaptability and determination to move off the streets. A major motivational exercise to boost their rehabilitation is the bi-weekly Progress Chart (refer Appendix 2 Boys' Feedback Form) where both the staff and the children themselves participate.

The mindset change needs a constant boost and indicators that re-assure his focus and thinking. The initial period of Phases IV and V is crucial in his permanent movement off the streets when he begins to move slowly out of institutional/agency support and starts learning to cope with issues and challenges by himself. His success at managing these challenges further encourages him and marks his movement off the streets permanently.

In my experience, I have observed that moving off the streets is a positive method for a child to progress and be a contributory citizen. The street child cannot do so living on the streets. The "terminal situation" explains the end point of street life. The movement from street child to street youth and subsequently to street adult is a terminal and dehumanizing situation. Movement off the streets is the solution to this terminal situation. Support structures have a particular role to enable him in this process. However, it is the individual's mindset change, his choice and effort that makes the movement off the streets possible.

5

Shifting Frontiers

ORGANIZATIONAL ISSUES

"Strategies adopted in street-based interventions require to be reviewed, reexamined and reframed ..."

Deep within each child is the yearning to belong to a "normal" family. It is during childhood that an individual's personality starts taking definite shape. Once it has grown in an undesired direction and taken root, it cannot be brought back to the natural course. It is very important that society take sufficient measures to ensure that its future citizens have ample opportunities for right growth. All policies, programs, and interventions must be guided by certain basic tenets and premises so that they are child-focused and rights-based. Programs that provide sporadic or seasonal assistance only serve to attract boys on the street, leading to seasonal increase in their numbers. During the monsoon, for instance, the weather conditions and lack of earning opportunities lead them to seek shelter.

During the rains, we would get over a thousand boys staying overnight at the Residential Home (at the monthly mela *from 1988 to 1996–97). The space was limited and about 300 odd could be decently accommodated; the boys would sleep at night huddled up or sit on the staircase, in the hall, and in the tiny corridor of the Residential Home. In 1997, we decided to take in only children below the age of 14. With this, the numbers attending the monthly* mela *reduced drastically, there was more space and the activities conducted were more effective.*
           — *Residential Home Annual Report*, Mumbai, December 1998

Organizations provide a range of benefits and services that aim to address the immediate needs of street children such as education, family repatriation, medical care, psychological counseling, and recreation among others. For the program to be effective, the environment in the institution must be enabling, culturally sensitive, and should closely approximate appropriate familial conditions, keeping in mind the child's emotional, physical, vocational, and psychological needs. By understanding the child's background, the organization works toward the goal of integrating him into a structured family "space."

ORGANIZATIONS AS PRIMARY CAREGIVERS

Assistance programs ensure stability, care, predictability, and protection. Children without the guidance and protection of their primary caregivers are often more vulnerable and at risk of becoming victims of violence, exploitation, trafficking, discrimination, or other abuses (UNICEF, 2007). Organizations working with children in street situations have their own mandate, vision, and mission. Keeping in mind the vast geographical area that the children come from and their consequent politico-socio-psycho-economic problems, one realizes that these mandates are largely unidimensional and fall short of treating the macro problems involved in the street children's experience. The common concern is an attempt to focus the issue at various fora, enhance the child's coping mechanisms on the streets, or move them off the streets towards repatriation and rehabilitation. Working with their mindsets and thinking is not their primary focus. Therefore, the role they play in the macro dynamics of street children is need-specific, not comprehensive. This entails government policies, village units, families, and agencies that help contain the street children phenomenon.[1]

---

[1] New roles for non-governmental organizations in development cooperation, Ministry of Foreign Affairs. Available at http://www.regjeringen.no/en/dep/ud/Documents/Reports-programs-of-action-and-plans/Reports/2006/New-roles-for-non-governmental-organisations-in-development-cooperation/4.html?id=420467 (retrieved on 1 June 2007).

Another problem is that of services overlapping due to the mushrooming of NGOs which are independent, non-profit institutions. Their services and interventions have remained largely fragmented and, unless integrated, do not have long-term positive consequences. Each NGO works within its own milieu and fails to establish common grounds of collaboration and networking. Concerted efforts at networking can bring about major policy changes with the government and achieve the desired social change.

Provision of assistance serves as a pull factor affecting the visibility and presence of boys on the street. Taking the boys out of the streets is not the only solution; post-care and follow-up strategies are necessary to reduce and prevent the street–shelter–street cycle that may also develop into a street–shelter–home–street–shelter cycle experienced by most who take to the streets.

SPECTRUM OF SERVICE PROVISION

Organizations catering to street boys usually provide a multiplicity of services, often in combination. Primarily, these services are health and nutrition, educational development, skills training, residential care, residential/temporary shelter (drop-in facility), crisis intervention and counseling, income generation, and family repatriation, all part of a preventive approach. The adoption of a preventive approach means that issues of poverty and family-related factors have to be addressed, as all these are crucial for the transformation of the adolescent and his views of the street. The sheer diversity of these services call for personnel, especially qualified and skilled, social workers, peer educators, field staff, psychiatrists, and medical professionals.

The Residential Home began in 1987 with just the management, who were social workers. The outreach staff consisted of peer educators; medical care and other routine services were managed by an employed social worker with the help of the older boys. As the programs developed, the various needs of the boys could not be met by the skeletal staff, and skilled personnel from various professions were employed. It made the program more effective.

Organizations that have multiplied in the past eight to ten years in the city have started with a paucity of resources, thus compromising quality care. When there is no code of conduct in the beginning and no supervision by a regulatory body, then the administration of child care institutes becomes ad hoc and standards and quality decline. The emphasis is on numbers and services provided are not always child-centered.

ADMISSION AND EXCLUSION CONCERNS

Institutions offer a multitude of services to the child. The street child makes his decision not to enter an institution when he is afraid that his "needs of instant desire" (addressed arbitrarily and without apparent rationality) will not be met, when there is fear generated over what others have said about their stay in institutions or when there is fear of losing "freedom." On the other hand, he would want to join an institution for short-term or long-term benefits.

The dilemma faced by most organizations is when to restrict the entry of children in street situations and those with problems, at what point one should accept them, what strategy should be employed, and what treatment should be extended to these children.

The phenomenon of children in street situations does not confine itself to just that group of "rootless and roofless" children who live on the streets day and night. The definition is inclusive of various categories of children who live or may not live all the time on the streets, or earn or return to it for economic survival (Lucchini, 1997). The definition could include pavement/slum children, children having problems with parents such as commercial sex workers, children of prisoners, and street drug addicts. It is difficult to draw lines of demarcation between these groups.

Organizations have to make tough decisions in taking care of specific groups and draw up admission policies for these categories stating their area of focus as well as their limitations. They take on these groups under labels of preventive measures (pavement, slum, and migrant children's education programs), treatment measures (residential homes, night shelters, and drop-in centers), campaigning responses (advocacy, publications, and research units), and what I term as "knee jerk" responses (one time/seasonal activities in response to an immediate event).

These measures and terms are often conceptualized in a "holistic program." The focus of the organization tends to get diverted under this label of a holistic program, particularly in view of the fluidity of the term and manageability of the groups.

There are certain criteria that a shelter may specify regarding the admission of boys. Each child has his own story, his handicaps, health problems, background, and several characteristics that render him unique and, therefore, he has to be treated as an individual case for consideration for admission into an institution. Since organizations have a mandate and focus for their services, the criteria for admitting children in street situations have to be in place.

An *age criterion* for admission helps to keep the group homogenous. The Residential Home had for its first eight years, street youth (180 children) approximately in the age groups of 18+ (45 percent), 15–17 (30 percent), 12–14 (15 percent), and below 11 (10 percent). Thus the group was not homogenous. There were problems of abuse, violence, bullying, and stealing from each other. Staffing was too minimal to take care of the problems of the different age groups. The oldest boys took on much of the routine jobs, including the problems of younger children, for which they had no formal training. It was after a self-evaluation in 1995 that the organization changed its policy of admission, restricting it to only those below the age of 14. An exit policy was framed by the older boys and they moved into group homes. Thereafter, there have been two homogenous groups of those above 14 years and those below 14.

The homogeneity of a marginalized group in terms of age is an important factor in therapy. Homes with children of varying ages with wide age gaps tend to have separate spaces for the different groups, who come together for common programs like food and recreation.

My experience has shown that those who grow out of the adolescent age group and move into adulthood with "untreated behavioral problems" demonstrate acute adult behavior issues that often find expression in criminal activities and conflict with the law.

Sharad (21 years) was constantly stealing other children's clothes, stationery and money from their lockers. He was sent away from the Residential Home to a

branch of the organization in a rural place, often considered a punishment by the
Residential Home boys. After two months he returned without therapy; he began
stealing again and was asked to leave in a month. After a year, he was readmitted
to the Residential Home (he was in another home in the interim period but was
asked to leave due to his stealing). Once again, he began stealing and was asked to
leave. A year later, he was brought back to the Residential Home by the police in
handcuffs for breaking into a house with another companion.

— Sharad Case File, Residential Home, 2005

Organizations are the last stage for help for children with behavioral problems. If they do not help them, where will these children go? They are left with their problems which only become more acute in the oppressive environment of the streets. It is important for organizations to focus on their admission policies and on the dilemma of numbers vis-à-vis their vision and mission. Devoting special attention to problems of individuals will help avoid escalation of behavioral disorders in their adult life.

PROBLEM BEHAVIOR

Behavioral problems in adolescents are a manifestation of their child-hood situations of trauma, neglect, abuse, family discord, and other forms of psychological problems. The "psychological baggage" they carry extends to their later life. In the case of children in street situations, the problems are compounded by the fact that the environment is not an educative one. Their peers tend to view these issues not as problems to be treated but as amusing incidents. When these adolescents enter an institution which has smaller numbers, the individual attention given often helps to identify and treat the problem at an early stage. In those institutions with large numbers, problems tend to remain unaddressed, except those that are particularly outstanding.

Those boys who have a history of thieving, have a criminal background or have sexually abused boys, or exhibit problematic behavior tend to be barred from entry. I think the problem of not "treating" these children, is more in the "dilemma of numbers."[2] Another consequent dilemma is

---

[2] Dilemma of numbers: The organizations concentrate on larger numbers and as a consequence, have to compromise on the quality of care.

that the behavior of the abuser/thief may be a result of his problematic psychological past. Owing to the problem of numbers, he is not "treated" but asked to leave the institution. The institution is the last stop wherein he can get help; his being sent back on the streets is going to make the problem more acute. When the law finally catches up with him, he faces punitive and coercive rather than corrective measures and this compounds his problematic behavior.

Rajesh (20 years) was a handicapped boy. Eleven years before coming to the Residential Home, he used to beg on the road. He is now the leader of the boys at the Residential Home. He was given a stipend to look after the routine work of the home and care for "on the ground problems" of the children. Rajesh was well respected by the staff and the children. One day he was reported to have sexually abused a small boy. A couple of European volunteers demanded that we throw him out of the Home since he had betrayed the trust the children reposed in him.
— Case File, Residential Home, 2002

We asked the volunteers as to where he should go. He had no skill; he would have to go back to the streets, back to begging. The mindset of the volunteers did not consider treating the problem of the abuser but thought only of punitive measures such as removing the source of the problem. When institutions eject these "trouble makers," they perpetuate the problems for the abuser. This raises the question of whether the institution should take care of the children that they reach out to on the streets. It depends, I think, on the stand that the organization takes.

Special Needs

Children with special needs require special attention. Organizations that deal with large numbers and insufficient caregivers refer such cases to other agencies and often the interim period has a negative effect. The move to a referral center is not always immediate—finding the right place, meeting the admission criteria of that organization, and finding time with the caregiver, all take time.

Rinku (11 years) had polio in both legs. He was a pleasant, nice looking boy, much liked by the outreach staff. He began taking 4–5 bottles of "solution" a day. His begging earned him lots of pity from passers-by as well as money and friends. At one of the melas, *Dinesh (staff team member) requested me to keep Rinku in the Residential Home after his detoxification. I asked Dinesh what to do with Rinku thereafter. What happens to him 5–8 years from now? We do not have specialized care, school, and facilities to take care of him. At that time, Dinesh was upset that I was not admitting Rinku. He argued that Rinku was vulnerable, that he was getting into a detrimental living pattern and needed quick attention. We had a discussion with the rest of the outreach staff on this issue. Rinku had to be given immediate attention, they suggested. We were not capable of taking care of his special needs; we had to refer him to the Spastic Society as soon as possible. He had to wait for eight months in the Residential Home, till we could find a vacancy and meet the admission criteria with an organization ready to take him. In that interim period, he went away twice from the Residential Home. He was frustrated and spread the word around that the Residential Home was not a good place to go to, as they did not do anything to help children in difficulties.*

— Rinku Case File, Residential Home, 2000

Children with special needs are referred to organizations which have the resources to deal with them. The period of waiting is often crucial to the children in question, particularly when the child is mentally handicapped. He feels that he is the odd one out in the group and finds it difficult to adjust as he does not have a curriculum to follow or the same capacities as those in the organization. This prompts the question whether organizations should admit children with special difficulties when they are not equipped to give them adequate care.

The ideal situation is when there is already a networking mechanism in place, wherein this interim period is not long and placements are immediate. Yet in my experience, each special needs situation is different. The mentally challenged of varying degrees, physically challenged of varying capacities, those with serious contagious or terminal sicknesses, and those abused and with special behavioral problems are a diverse group met by the staff on their outreach and who come into a street children's home. To give each of them special attention is difficult. Herein, there should be clarity of focus of the target group and its definition is necessary for an organization.

Restriction of entry should be based on the limitation of the institution's ability to handle specific problems of children, like the special needs of a handicapped child, speech defects, or terminal illnesses such as cancer and HIV.

REGULATING ENTRY...

The staff team is of the opinion that when boys are not admitted into the shelter, they usually form negative opinions about the organization. As a measure of retaliation, they try and prevent other boys from approaching the Residential Home and availing themselves of its facilities by informing them that the program is a waste of time; that the food is bad and that there is abuse, physical chastisement, and too much work to do; and that it takes a long time to show results. They abuse staff members, talk ill of them, and also try to persuade other children on the street not to pay attention to the outreach team. Thus they form opinions about the Residential Home and its staff, which are often exaggerated and not true.

In my opinion, there is need to define and clarify the terms used as criteria for admission. The defining limits of behavior should be set, and deviations from acceptable norms should be specified. For instance, "criminal behavior" is too strong a term, particularly when applied to street boys who are not yet adults. A more appropriate term to describe their behavior would be "delinquent or anti-social." However, restricting the entry of boys on grounds of "delinquent behavior" may negate any chance that the boys have of rehabilitation under the guidance of trained personnel.

There should be an in-house debate on the issue of expelling those who have sexually abused children and not admitting those known to have a history of sexual abuse. The institution is the "final frontier" of emotional and psychological help for the child. If a child is expelled, where does he go for help? He goes back to the streets, leading to more acute manifestations of such behavior. It would be ideal to have a place away from the Residential Home, wherein an expert could help. Our study on "High Risk Behavior among Street Children" (D'Souza, 2008c) states that 65 percent of the boys on the streets have faced some form of sexual abuse on the streets. This behavior is found to prevail in residential homes, too, though to a lesser degree. Therefore, a support therapy program should be part of the caregiving package for the children in and from street situations.

ORIENTATION OF STREET ADOLESCENTS

The process of orientation plays a pivotal role in motivating the boys to join a program. Such orientation is generally given on the street by the outreach staff team who are the first points of contact with regard to institutional intervention. During the orientation, the staff team attempts to convey a comprehensive and balanced picture of the program, explaining what it entails, its expected outcome and results, its restrictions on drinking, smoking and use of drugs within the shelter, types of activities organized, skill training involved, and the prevalent code of conduct. Such information conveys a clear picture of every phase of the program and any discrepancy leads to boys leaving the program.

Street children are very mobile; they move from one place to another. Before reaching one place, they form a certain image of that place and how their life would be there. If this does not coincide with their expectations, they run away. It is necessary for the management, staff, and boys to be prepared. The emphasis should be to achieve quality care. An innovative program capable of sustaining the children's interest and providing them with emotional and psychological support is helpful in preventing drop-outs.

An ethical dilemma crops up at the time of admission, whether it is the street child's need to join a program or the need of the institution to have the numbers to sustain their existence. Perhaps, it could also be put down to an altruistic motive to play a role in helping to reduce the street children phenomenon. A fine line of demarcation should be drawn as to when the institution can allow the child to decide to join its program without "pressure." While the institution's mission is unquestioned, the execution of its objectives by the staff can assume different dimensions.

Vikas (staff team member) was upset with Sanju from another NGO. Sanju was picking up street boys at the central terminus station and referring them to his NGO residential home. Vikas said, "These boys are in my group, I have been preparing them for the past few months. You should not take them without my permission. I have given them a date for taking them to my NGO." Vikas was underperforming and was pulled up by the management for it. He wanted to show results and confronted Sanju.

— Outreach Centre Report, 1999

The members of the staff compete amongst themselves as to who gets the greater numbers, an indicator of their productivity at the outreach. This reflects that the competition among NGOs, instead of being healthy, is riddled with "the problem of numbers."

ORIENTATION AT THE OUTREACH

The street boy's basic need is to have a sense of belonging, to regain his identity, and mend his psychological brokenness. The outreach team faces several obstacles while counseling the boys into leaving the streets. The first step is to build a strong rapport with the boys. This is mainly accomplished by regular visits and being present while they are engaged in different activities—playing, eating, working, leisure, or at times, when they are under the influence of drugs. Pruneeta, a staff team member says, *"If I do not visit the boys at the station for a few days, I miss out on what is new—the new boys coming in, those who are experiencing problems with the police and with bigger bullies, new dynamics, and incidence of thefts. Some begin to distance themselves from me; I have to be in constant touch with them."* The boys will look to satisfy some need; if their needs are not met by those persons who interact with them, they do not respond to them.

The follow-up with the boys who visit the Outreach Centre needs to be effective. During this phase, it is ideal to take boys of the same age group for an orientation camp, but often a mixed group of varying ages come together. On the streets, the older boys abuse and intimidate the younger boys, and the same is repeated during this phase. Therefore, care is exercised to see that older boys do not influence the younger ones negatively, but serve as their mentors.

ORIENTATION AT THE RESIDENTIAL HOME

The boys who are referred by the outreach staff team usually join the Residential Program with expectations of their own. The staff team tries to equip the boys with information pertaining to both the short-term and long-term benefits of the program, about the rules and regulations that govern their stay at the Residential Home. The orientation camps serve as a tool to help the boys understand the program and make their choice accordingly. The boys are informed about the daily sessions and activities (both mental and physical) that they would be expected to participate in. Their living arrangements at the Residential Home, the discipline to be maintained, the types of interaction patterns, communication and language, and duties and responsibilities are made clear to them. At the same time, there is an effort by the staff team to understand what the boys expect from their stay at the shelter, what needs they hope to fulfill and then try to achieve some congruence between the two. When there is significant discrepancy between the boys' expectations and the reality of life at the Residential Home, the chances of dropping out are high.

Any pressures or forms of coercion are unacceptable to the boys. Authoritarianism, at times, can cause children and students to adopt rebellious positions, defiant of any limit, discipline, or authority. But it will also lead to apathy, excessive obedience, uncritical conformity, lack of resistance against authoritarian discourse, self-abnegation, and fear of freedom.

The orientation in the Residential Home is based on helping the adolescent develop a mindset to move off the streets. It is an essential element to "trigger" his mindset into change, to move off the streets. It is an opportunity to shed street patterns of living and to learn acceptable behavior.

ORIENTATION TOWARD DETOXIFICATION

This phase involves stay in a hospital; blood, urine, chest, and other screening tests; possible separation from friends; and the possibility of being alone in the room and interacting with persons who are unfamiliar. Jagdish, one of the boys in the program said of the hospital period, "*I am very scared of the walls, the shadows are scary too. I do not like to stay in a closed room.*" The difficulties associated with the process of detoxification are exemplified by the high drop-out rate during this phase (Figure 5.1).

As shown in Figure 5.1, out of 679 street adolescent addicts who were part of the therapeutic program from 1999–2009, nearly one-fourth went through the education program and more than a third completed

Figure 5.1 Movement of Boys in the Therapeutic Program (1999–2009)

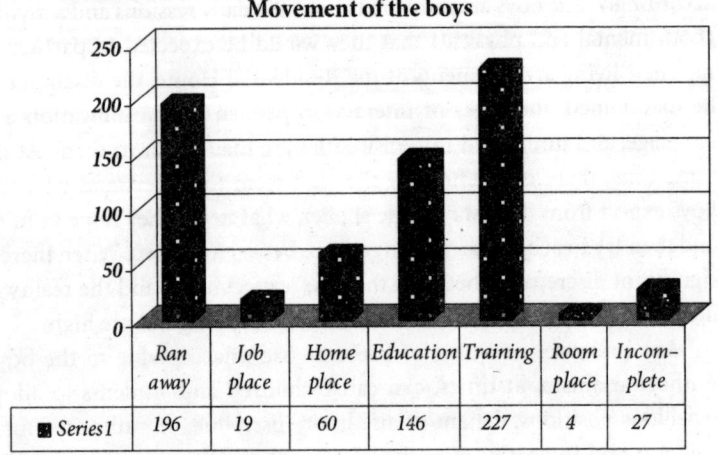

Movement of the boys

	Ran away	Job place	Home place	Education	Training	Room place	Incom-plete
▩ Series 1	196	19	60	146	227	4	27

Source: Evaluation of the Therapeutic Program—from 1999 to 2009 (an unpublished internal study undertaken by the organization).

their training (Phase IV) successfully. About 28 percent ran away for reasons such as fear of injections or the pain of withdrawal symptoms, boredom, lack of companionship, lack of understanding the orientation process, misconceptions about the program, inconsiderate treatment by the staff, and inadequate follow-up. All or some of these factors can precipitate the boys into running away. Therefore, it is essential that the staff provide them a thorough orientation, try to identify the boys' fears, counsel them, and help them manage their fears. It is also necessary for the staff team to orient the medical staff accordingly, making them alive to the boys' background, and their apprehensions and fears.

Organizations that do not have detoxification facilities on campus depend largely on public hospitals for this phase of treatment. The requirement in all such hospitals is that the patients have a 24-hour adult attendee. Typically, detoxification camps have over 15 to 20 boys awaiting treatment. Public hospitals have limited availability of beds which means that the other children are sent to more than one hospital simultaneously. There is, therefore, a requirement of three attendees for a shift of eight hours each. With three hospitals taking care of the detoxification simultaneously, there is need for nine attendees along with three staff members who have to be present for the tests and the doctor's consultation. The staff team then needs to be available for counseling. Beds/admissions are limited and, therefore, the detoxification period for the entire group may last for more than a month. The attendees are generally ex-addicts awaiting the commencement of their skill training/academic program. They often get frustrated on these hospital rounds and are not equipped to look after the recovering addicts; at times, they drop out of the program during this waiting period. The Residential Home was facing such problems during the camp period (1999–2004). Subsequently, the camp system was abolished. Now those children who are prepared and ready on the streets are sent immediately for detoxification and there is no waiting period. This has eased the pressure on the staff, the hospital and the ex-addicts taking care during this phase.

Is it right for an organization to keep ex-addicts as attendees? They come across as positive role models who have gone through the process; they are therefore better equipped to understand the finer nuances of the recovering patient. Before getting into their own training, this was an opportunity to contribute to their fellow street addicts—to be educated in the altruistic motive of giving even while receiving. Not all can play the role of attendees. There has to be follow-up, and they have to be prepared, and counseled to be effective and not lose their own motivation.[3]

ORIENTATION TOWARD TRAINING

Problems commonly identified during the training phase of the program are primarily those of choice. Their choices are often influenced by their companions. The boys have few vocational options to choose from due to their lack of qualifications or inadequate NGO networking. After this they are sent for the requisite skill training for a stipulated time period. Often they are unable to appreciate the skills taught. "*I did not know I had to keep banging metal pieces the whole day long to become a welder*," said Mukesh. Often, being street boys where instant gratification is the norm, they expect instant results from the training and when that does not happen, they lose interest. The interests of many boys alter midway through the program, making it difficult to help them change their trade. This again precipitates

---

[3] "Effectiveness of the Rehabilitation Program," 2003 (internal, unpublished report).

drop-outs. If the training is not consistent with the skills and aptitude of the boys, it poses problems. Work ethics may not be sufficiently ingrained in the boys; they have problems adhering to work discipline. Problems of interaction with batchmates also lead to drop-outs. This is largely due to the adolescents not being adequately prepared in their thinking and mindset.

The staff team's reflection was that the adolescents be first sent to local workshops (on the streets) for a period of 2–3 months to learn the trade of their choice. Some returned during this learning phase as the training did not come up to their expectations. It was then easier to help them try a different trade and thus prevent dropping out of the program.[4]

With academic qualifications being limited for many street children, not all have the ability or inclination to enroll for technical trades. Institutions have a misconception that if the adolescent is not academically inclined, he would automatically not be fit for a technical trade. When the adolescent fails at these technical trades, he is pushed to drop out or else feel like a misfit. In the past four years, trades such as delivery jobs, housekeeping, salesmen, and other service related jobs have opened new avenues for boys who lack technical abilities. These service-related jobs are easily obtained and do not require lengthy periods of training.

As a result, a majority of the boys have begun seeking such jobs and do not take the trouble to learn a trade. Even if they have been in an institution for a number of years, they prefer to choose the short-cut, in keeping with their need for instant gratification. One cannot blame it on a lack of preparation or counseling of the adolescent by the organization.

It is the mindset of the adolescent that has not shifted; his thought process has not helped him make a rational, focused, and determined choice.

ORIENTATION TOWARD INDEPENDENT LIVING/REPATRIATION

When a boy expresses a desire to go home, it is a decision he must be guided to take and be prepared for. The repatriation process involves the child, his family, his immediate social environment (school, job market, and relationships) at home, the staff team, and management. The initial

---

[4] Annual Report, Rehabilitation Home, 2000.

process is often to ensure that the family is prepared to take the boy back and also that the conditions at home are conducive to his return. Care is taken to ensure that a boy is not sent back to a home that is abusive or where the family members themselves are likely to send him back to the streets to earn for them. Once home, the follow-up of the boy over a period of time is crucial, as there are several instances of the boys returning to the streets after a few days. In 1995, our study revealed that nine out of twelve boys who were repatriated from the Residential Home returned to the streets.

In case the boy is reluctant to go home or is old enough to stay independently with a group, then he has the option of a group home, wherein 4–5 boys who have successfully completed the program and are of similar age, stay under the care of a supervisor. The supervisor ensures that the boys are able to manage the household chores, take care of the monthly rent and other expenses, and go to work regularly. The supervisor also identifies any problems that the boys may have with the living arrangements, with relationships at work, the neighborhood, or any other issue.

Most service providers working with street children have repatriation or rehabilitation in independent living as their ultimate objective; hence most of their activities are geared towards this end. This objective should have a concurrent agenda to work on the mindset of the adolescents. When the mindset change takes place, the orientation and preparation make the transition from the streets to off it much smoother and quicker.

EXIT POLICY

Residential homes providing education often face a problem of dependency. The "dependency" factor has been a common phenomenon among all institutions. Rootless and marginalized children tend to be dependent on institutions for long-term support (4 to 10+ years). A well planned exit policy needs to be framed which could be broken up into phases for the child's growth, development, and transformation into independent living. A specific plan with definite time schedules, monitoring, and evaluation has to be put in place with the participation of the children, staff, and management. A majority of the institutions face difficulties once the dependents move out of their immediate care. Hence an integrated follow-up plan for sustainability is imperative.

Along with the staff team, we decided that the boys be oriented at the beginning of each camp of the rehabilitation program to move from one phase to the next, their movement into the next phase being contingent upon their progress and performance in the present phase. This realization makes the boys impatient to move to the next phase—they gauge their progress and demand to move into the next phase. On the other hand, the children at the Residential Home become dependent on the institution and delay their moving out of the organization.

Samad (19 years) was living in the Residential Home for over 11 years. He was upset and kept grumbling, "What have they done for me? Where will I go? How much will they give me? The management here is very harsh, they want us to move out; they should give us a house and a job if they want us to do so. I will not go out."

— Samad Case File, Residential Home, 2004

This reveals that the organization should plan in partnership with the child, for only then can the child focus on his future. The exit is a transition and a transformation of the individual. Exit policies are educative as it helps the adolescent plan, focus, and think for himself. For the organization, it is a useful tool to evaluate, measure, and understand its productivity.

MULTIPLICITY OF NGOs ON THE STREETS

The outreach team faces stiff competition from other organizations in the city working with street children. In 1987, there were just six full time NGOs dedicated to working with street children. There are now over 60 NGOs working for street children in the city. Several factors have contributed to this "mushrooming" of NGOs dealing with street children. The number of street children in the city in ratio to the service providers in the 1970s/1980s was minimal. The government recognized the problem in its policies, world bodies like the UNICEF began giving special attention to the problem, and world-renowned individuals extended their patronage;

the attention also brought along strategies and funding dynamics with it in the 1970s/1980s.

While awareness has grown, there has been a simultaneous growth of service providers in smaller cities and towns which has arrested the "supply" of runaway children from the rural areas to the four major metropolitan cities of India. Rural India too has its share of NGOs. The sustainability of these NGOs depends on their financial viability and effectiveness with the target population. The children make use of the situation to "shop" for their needs with different NGOs. This scenario is not the best for the child's rehabilitation as the rehabilitation process becomes piecemeal, taking only those elements that are immediately beneficial but not the long-term benefits such as formal education, vocational training leading to regular employment, and societal integration.

ORGANIZATIONAL DILEMMAS

Service providers are often confronted with the dilemma of addressing the problems of poverty and survival on the one hand, and of providing a nurturing environment on the other. This is particularly true of those dealing with adolescents whose development stage revolves around self-expression, autonomy, and development of self-identity.

Rahim (15 years) has been habitually jumping from one organization to the other. When he feels the "uncles" are not listening to his request for training or not sending him for NIOS, he says, "I will go to the other organization which will give me what I want." Once he finds it difficult to cope with the demands made in that organization, he moves on to another organization. He asked to be sent home (he was sent home thrice but stayed only for a few months). When he was told that this was not a solution, he went to another organization and asked them to send him home.

— Rahim Case File, Residential Home, 2006

This pattern of behavior can be termed in different ways—resilience, survival strategy, or taking advantage of the system or "NGO shopping." The vulnerability of these children should be kept in mind here. While service providers are available to cover the child's vulnerability, his choice is limited as to whom to get services from.

QUANTITY VERSUS QUALITY: NUMBERS OR SPECIALIZED CARE?

The Indian Family and Child Social Welfare Board has passed a mandatory regulation effective since 2003 that all child care institutions should adhere to specific requirements as regards space, number of staff, rights of the children, and other measures for the benefit of child care.

However, those services which house staff and boys at over a ratio of 1:4/5 boys cater more to the group than to the individual. The emphasis is on numbers rather than on individual quality of service. A recurring dilemma in regions with a high proportion of street children and in institutions that have a walk-in admission policy is where to draw the line, how many children to cater to, and when to stop fresh admissions. The compromise is of quality versus quantity, individual neglect versus group care. The rehabilitation process in these institutions becomes that much longer or more difficult for the individual child.

Ravi (14 years) had been complaining of a toothache for two weeks. The medical person concerned said that her hands were full, as she had more urgent matters to treat; the detoxification of 8 boys was ongoing, there were another 7 boys waiting in the wings for detoxification, 2 boys were diagnosed with tuberculosis and required treatment at another hospital. In addition, there was a sharp rise in scabies among 14 small boys at the same time. She had some help from two peer educators, but for the moment, Ravi's dental problems were put on the backburner.
— Residential Home, May 2002

The above example highlights an instance of the inability of an institution to cater to individual needs. When preoccupied with too many individual cases, the institution first provides for an immediate response to pressing problems. Those that are not of an "emergency" nature are left unattended for a long period of time. Often due to such neglect the child runs away; the case gets worse or it is a case of "let it be till it gets to the emergency stage." Hence, the question—should institutions cater to smaller numbers and be effective to that population or rope in bigger numbers on the assumption that some form of care is better than no care? It is a case of "safer in the institution" rather than on the "mean streets," and there is at least some care for larger numbers.

HOLISTIC VERSUS INDIVIDUAL CARE

A constant debate rages over whether the type of services provided should be general or specific. There are certain services that the "safety of the institution" provides which attend to the vulnerability of the child. Yet it is those services that go beyond addressing that vulnerability, which focus on psychological needs more than economic or moral development, that require urgent attention. Nearly 74 percent of the marginalized adolescents have psychological issues as their primary developmental need. Thus, it depends on the stand that an organization takes in its treatment of the street children phenomenon.

Many harbor the notion that catering to specific needs is limiting and not feasible in terms of the sheer numbers involved. There is an ever-increasing list of categories, needs, and demands. This dilemma often results in the organization losing out on individualized caregiving. On the other hand, those institutions that have smaller numbers in residential care tend to have more specialized care that focuses on the individual. Care is imparted keeping in mind the holistic development of the individual—professionally skilled personnel are appointed; the numbers being smaller, resources are more intense; programs (branches) are not expanded but activities for the individuals are. This type of care is more common to countries that have sound economies and a significantly lower population of children who spend only a few hours on the streets and do not live and earn off it all day, all year.

STAFF CONCERNS

A core issue which is the driving force behind any NGO is its staff. In today's fast changing world, with its scientific and technological advancements, there is a pressing need for professional, trained staff sensitive to the pressures on the street. Social workers need to be trained as planners, trainers, evaluators, advocates, and organizers. This type of job requires relationships to be built, understanding individual children, the group, and the philosophy of the organization, for which experience and time has no substitute. The acquisition of skills, wages, effective training, constant monitoring and documentation, a healthy environment for personal and career growth, all affect the program and staff performance.

Professionally trained persons have high expectations in terms of salaries, status, and opportunities for growth. This poses problems particularly for recently set up organizations which are run on a shoe-string budget and do not have access to training resources at the local level. In the past eight to ten years, we at the organization have had 90 percent of our skilled employees gaining experience and moving within less than two years to corporate houses that offer higher wages. This movement affects the children who have created a bond with them as well as the organization which invests in training the staff.

Another area of concern is that there is often an overlap and lack of clarity of the respective roles and functions of the staff. Role clarity plays a critical role in explaining employee perceptions of service quality. Feedback, participation, and team support significantly influence role clarity. Non-clarity of job definitions and role specifications is another reason for lack of effectiveness of the program. Unresolved conflicts among co-workers create feelings of alienation and frustration and often translate into miscommunication and other related problems which ultimately reduces the efficacy of the program.

Staff meetings have been a time of reflection and sharing of concerns—how to identify potential runaways, how to handle the frustrations of slow learners, problems of sexual abuse, and how to make sessions more interesting for the children. These short training programs have helped build the capacities of the staff in child care. A psychiatrist has been appointed to address the concerns of the children and the staff.

Ashfaq (14 years) had come to the Residential Home for the third time. He had been reprimanded on two previous occasions for beating up the smaller boys. Gambadhi suggested that we throw him out of the Residential Home and not take him back as he was a repeated offender.

— Residential Home, 2006

The case was put before the staff. The staff was divided in their opinions. Some thought he should be asked to go away, while others felt that he should be given one more opportunity along with a strict warning. Some suggested punitive measures. The thought that Ashfaq needed therapy did not occur to them. This called for reflection—had they come across similar cases, and if so, what was the treatment given? They suggested they needed training in how to deal with these types of delinquency.

Often, the management keeps back certain information from the staff. Finance, volunteer acceptance, new staff recruitment policies, programs, and acceptance of new projects are well guarded domains of the management. This lack of coordination has frequently resulted in problems of overlapping, duplication, breakdown in communication, misinformation, new staff not being adequately trained in the philosophy of the organization, and consequent problems. Organizational communication is the key to the effective working of any organization. Effective communication is based upon the knowledge of the five Ws: When, Who, Where, Why, and What. In smaller NGOs, the organizational structure is hierarchical. This results in less sharing of responsibilities, transparency, and communication with the different levels of staff.

MONITORING AND EVALUATION

Monitoring and evaluation are tools to motivate, reorganize, and set goals for the staff. Organizations involved in field activities tend to ignore these aspects, making them less effective and causing burn out among the staff. Monitoring and evaluation sets targets and achievable goals for the staff and brings a sense of accountability to the organization.

Jerome (staff outreach coordinator) said, "Sometimes we at the Outreach Centre feel that no one in the management is interested in what we are doing. You only go by hearsay or by the lack of responses from the children. It is good when you have these evaluation sessions; it gives us an opportunity to showcase our work to the management. We feel good when you appreciate us at the end of it all."
— Evaluation, Outreach Centre, 2002

STAFF BURN OUT

If social workers do not have their goals redesigned after a period of time, they tend to stagnate professionally. Burn out results in selective job termination, mental and physical health concerns, relationship problems, and other issues. Stress among social workers is caused by job insecurity, poor pay, work overload, and lack of autonomy. Work-related violence is a major concern for the profession. For the first two to three years, social workers give their optimum service; thereafter if they have not been "looked after" and sent for ongoing formation courses, or if their roles and job description have not been reinvented, if timely appreciation is not given, they tend to go on a downward slide. Burn out not only affects the individual and his output and caregiving, but can also affect others around him. Routine sets into their handling of different cases, making their responses stereotyped and often detrimental to the progress of the child.

SYMBIOTIC RELATIONSHIPS— STAFF AND BENEFICIARIES

The significance of staff is especially noteworthy in view of the fact that provision of assistance/services by several NGOs to the boys on the streets is often seen to foster dependency among the boys.

Gowri didi (staff outreach member) has been visiting the dargah *near the railway station for the past six years. Sonu, Shayam, and Wahid have been living around the* dargah *for the past nine years. They make it a routine to have* chai *(tea) with Gowri didi, sometimes go for a movie with her or just spend time with her. If she goes on leave they get agitated and come to the Outreach Centre. They do not want to leave the* dargah *area, they do not want to miss out on Gowri didi's friendship nor do they want to take her advice and move off the streets.*

— Outreach Centre Report, 2001

It is often a mutual satisfaction of emotional needs that creates this dependency. Gowri *didi* has been having emotional problems on her home front. She insists that the children call her "mummy." The lack of professionalism in her dealings is to the detriment of the adolescents; they do not want to leave the *dargah* area, as they know they will not meet their "mummy" everyday. The dependency factor is largely due to an emotional attachment that is irrational and an impediment to a positive movement. Yet, it has also worked in the opposite way, when the adolescent has moved off the streets because his "uncle" or "didi" advised him to do so.

MANAGEMENT CONCERNS

Since NGO management is a relatively new field in the country, management processes are still being developed and a few recognized solutions to the problem of how to organize large amounts of resources effectively for development are being formulated. NGO staff often work with considerable latitude, using their own judgment and reasoning and hence organizational policies are not always followed in practice. Many organizations go through initial struggles; some manage to overcome them, while a few carry on with the given limitations.

NGOs AS AGENTS OF DEVELOPMENT

NGOs are a critical sector of civil society committed to social development. They attempt to create an environment which is conducive to all members of that society, by developing and utilizing the potential of all the members. However, NGOs for street children tend to direct their initiatives towards immediate needs like food, clothing, health, education, and skill training. These strategies are relief and welfare strategies. The responses are to situations and can be classified as follows:

KNEE-JERK RESPONSES

NGOs invariably respond to the immediate needs of a situation, citing its urgency with respect to vulnerable children.

Shantanu (9 years) had polio, was fair skinned, and looked cute. The older boys abused him sexually and he developed STD. He needed immediate hospital attention. After treating him at the local hospital, the outreach staff brought him to the Residential Home. He stayed on, with no specialized care and he has been there for the past four years.

— Shantanu Case File, Residential Home, 2001

These responses, though immediate, seldom cater to the long-term needs of the child.

SYMPTOMATIC RESPONSES

These have been made to address some of the issues on the streets where the boys tend to congregate and include the provision of a drop-in center, wherein the child's temporary needs of shelter, food, medical assistance, or counseling are satisfied. Those children seeking long-term facilities are accommodated at open houses, which also cater to their education and vocational training, besides their basic needs. Monthly *melas* give the children an opportunity to enjoy, recreate, and obtain information on diverse issues. Statistics indicated an alarming incidence of drug addiction among street children in response to which a drug rehabilitation program was started in 1999.

CONSEQUENTIAL RESPONSES

Studies have indicated that many street children are at risk of dropping out of school due to the lure of earning easy money and also an inability to keep up with the academic syllabus. Among the most valued programs offered by NGOs are the educational programs for formal schooling and alternative education. Street education through pavement classes is an attempt to bring together the otherwise mobile and restless children for educational sessions on the streets. They help prepare children adequately for school and, by providing requisite academic support and adult supervision, act as a measure to reduce potential drop-outs. Such education also enables the street children to know about their rights, improve their skills in facing and managing crisis, receive value education, and deal with street risks.

CAMPAIGNING RESPONSES

Addressing the well-being of street children requires a multipronged and multisectoral approach since their social reality is complex. Experiences with program operations and implementation bear testimony to the fact that partnership and collaboration are critical to the success of any program. In this regard, membership in common fora, such as the Coordinating Committee for Vulnerable Children (CCVC), serves to promote the interests of street children. Women's groups, judicial branches of the government, law enforcement agencies, youth organizations, and others require to be mobilized. Documentation of experiences with diverse groups of marginalized children can be the foundation for publications, which constitutes another platform for networking. Media coverage (print and broadcast) of events like the Diwali *mela* gives greater visibility to the problem of street children and promotes public awareness and consciousness about this issue.

ROOT CAUSE RESPONSES

Problems can be tackled at their roots with the emphasis being more on prevention than on cure. Unevenness of economic growth has led to large-scale migration, with a consequent increase in the numbers of street children who come to the streets in the absence of adequate supervision. This means that poverty and family-related factors must be addressed. This is best exemplified in the rural community development project, where a sustained facilitating effort has been made to reduce the incidence of alcoholism in the villages, through interventions in the form of equipping the villagers with educational and vocational opportunities within their village itself, thereby arresting potential migration and its concomitant problems, while at the same time enabling them to enhance their standard of living.

Most organizations "make responses" to needs arising from the field. These responses seem to be logically coherent, yet the element of specialized care is occasionally compromised. Expansion into new areas at the organizational level may be indicative of progress, yet the human element of dealing with individuals with problems unique to their situation tends to get lost. Reflective analysis would make the organization more proactive and creative.

VOLUNTEER WORK

Volunteers come to the organization to achieve a sense of fulfillment and to fulfill a requirement for study or an academic course. Their motives are often altruistic. Local volunteers fit in well with the culture, while foreign volunteers take time to adjust and have to overcome difficulties of language, dress code, food, and finding a role to play in the organization. When the organization is not prepared to receive a volunteer, the orientation and preparation is not done systematically and in advance, causing grave concerns within the organization. A volunteer coordinator eases the process. Volunteers bring in a special dimension of care by helping to procure finances, reflect on its policies and caregiving structures and their questions and suggestions help the organization in its reflective analysis.

Funding Pressures

Funding agencies as well as governmental, national, and international charitable trusts provide a substantial proportion of funds to NGOs. Often tightly specified project proposals are a precondition to providing funds. There is a need for workers to consider their approach to practice and how this may impact on the assessment, intervention, and evaluation of their work with service users. A clear focus on skills, social work processes, and the suitability of different methods enable the application of a theoretical framework to practical situations.

Individual donors also give money to NGOs based on their brand, supported by sophisticated marketing techniques or publicity. This creates pressures to present messages which grab attention and are simple, rather than messages that recognize the difficulty and uncertainty of the developmental challenge. It also has implications for measuring success. NGOs are accountable to funding agencies and expend a great deal of energy on quantitative aspects of interventions such as causality, measurement, and comparability which have hindered progress.

An organization that has more than one program activity has more than one funding resource and has to comply to meet its demands. A semigovernment organization requested us to take care of a part of its HIV awareness campaign for street children for a period of three years. This was in keeping with our "holistic approach" ideology. We had to give up the project in two years as we were not in a position to meet the demands of those who tested positive or obtain referrals for them.

Most of the voluntary organizations suffer from paucity and uncertainty of funds and even when the funds are allocated, they are not revised to meet the current inflationary trends, further complicating the organization's financial position and rendering them incapable of providing quality services.

RECOMMENDATIONS

A skilled professional in the helping profession needs to be someone who has a strong respect for persons, a steady regard for the autonomy and reality of others. In addition, she/he needs to be capable of insight, understanding, and compassion without losing boundaries; to be exceptionally reliable, trustworthy, and discreet; to be able to put her/his own interests and concerns aside in the presence of clients (patients and parishioners); and at bottom have some affection for fellow human beings (Strickling, 1998).

Staff Induction and Training

Working with street boys who have a history of substance abuse requires a trained staff who can deal with their particular psyche. Thus, capacity building and on-the-job training are essential to deal with the treatment and habilitation of the boys.

- Induction involves orienting the staff towards motivating the boys into the program: daily scheduling, follow-up, report-writing, reflection and analysis of recurring issues, education, and training.
- Regular training of the staff for improved communication patterns, team building, and stress management are addressed at monthly meetings. However, the staff dealing primarily with addicted boys need more specialized training on areas

such as guidance and counseling, drug addiction, child development, psychological testing, sex education, research, and reflection.

• Regular staff visits to other specialized centers aid in building up their knowledge of current field practices as well as networking as a long-term goal.

• Early identification of symptoms of behavioral problems of children, tailoring their sessions to meet these needs and foresight in planning, and encouraging the children by the staff are essential for an effective staff and program.

STAFF EXPECTATIONS

• Like any other helping profession, the staff dealing with street inhalants experience frequent burn out and need the services of a counselor.

• Constant research and evaluation is irrelevant if there is no prompt implementation.

• Healthy remuneration is vital for any staff and is a concern and an expectation.

• Common methods should be adopted by the staff in working on problems relating to children. Coordination among the staff members is necessary to stop children from taking advantage of the situation.

• Specialized training specific to their responsibility and goal-setting will help the staff to creatively reconstruct their roles.

• Staff safety is an important concern as the staff deal with local communities, street children and are highly prone to infection and disease. Thus there is a need to have risk incentives and medical assistance incentives.

• Each staff member needs to have key areas for which they are responsible and accountable and should be evaluated as per their performance in those areas.

• Improved quality of basic amenities and a more interactive environment to work in results in mental satisfaction and provides adequate outlets for recreation and entertainment.

AUTONOMY

- Freedom to work and autonomy as well as participation in decision-making and its processes aid in developing the capacities of the staff.
- Regular training programs and information dissemination help in coordination and promote teamwork among staff.
- Sensitization of the staff towards the problems of the boys helps them cope effectively with the change process in the rehabilitation program.
- Encouraging staff initiative and responsibility to conduct programs on relevant issues increases their sense of belonging to the organization.
- Training-guided exit policies with the participation of all those involved helps avoid the "dependency factor."

PROGRAM PERFORMANCE

Several factors may contribute to the satisfactory performance of programs for street boys. Among these, the following may be mentioned:

- Availability of needed resources and services.
- Presence of highly committed street educators and program staff.
- Partnerships, networking, and institutional linkages of groups and organizations involved with street children.
- Regular staff development and capacity building sessions.
- Availability of information, education, and communications material useful for the continuing education of the boys as well as the staff.
- Regular meetings and assessment sessions among the program staff and institutional collaborating partners.

ADVOCACY AND POLICY

Strategies that are effective in attaining the goals and objectives of street children programs include the use of street education approaches, networking, advocacy, community organization, regional and national level conventions/conferences among street boys and the caregivers, well-coordinated referral systems, participation from program beneficiaries, and empowerment of children. The adoption of these strategies serve to reach more street boys needing assistance and protection, enhance their access to basic social services and develop responsibility of other sectors of society towards the concerns of street boys and promote wider collaboration in meeting their needs.

All interventions and action plans to address the well-being of street boys must be guided by a rights-based policy. Their well-being should be viewed as a shared responsibility of the society, families, communities, private organizations, children, and all sectors of society such as media, government, and social work agencies. Providing street boys with the necessary opportunities helps realize their potential and promote their integration into mainstream society. Service provision must be carried out in a manner that fosters independence, self-determination, and self-reliance.

Regular assessment also helps identify the most vulnerable targets, facilitate exchange of experiences and lessons learnt, and ascertain the strategy that works best in the situation. Advocacy and affirmative action in favor of street boys must also be worked out through development of ordinances and strict enforcement of national and local laws.

The mindset of the organization determines the intensity and efficacy of the program. It needs to move out of its "quantitative" mindset and concentrate on quality care. The element of competition among organizations should be replaced with closer collaboration in the field, sharing of information, and skills for the child to move off the streets. Once the family fails in looking after the child, organizations become the main service providers and take on the role of family. The organizations' staff, structure, networks, plans, and policies are key elements in the life of a street child. If they too fail, he does not have a support mechanism to help him off the streets. The child cannot wait.

6

The Resurgent Self—
The A-ha Experience

MINDSETS

Our mindset is not a minor personality quirk: it creates our whole mental world. (Dweck, 2006)

IMAGING THE MINDSET

A mindset refers to a set of assumptions, methods, or notations held by one or more people or groups of people which is so established that it creates a powerful incentive within these people or groups to continue to adopt or accept prior behaviors, choices, or tools. Our mindset explains how we become optimistic or pessimistic, and how we shape our goals and attitude toward work and relationships, ultimately predicting whether or not we will fulfill our potential. This phenomenon of cognitive bias is also sometimes referred to as mental inertia, "groupthink" or a "paradigm" and it is often difficult to counteract its effects upon analysis and decision-making processes.

The Mindset Theory (Gollwitzer, 1990, 2003) suggests a set of circumstances, when a window to realism opens up. Successful goal pursuit involves solving four consecutive tasks (circumstances): choosing between potential goals, planning the implementation of a chosen goal, acting on the chosen goal, and evaluating what has been achieved. When people get involved in these tasks, different cognitive procedures are activated (different mindsets) which make it easier for them to live up to the respective task demands. The cases of boys like Mohammed, Asif, Shailesh, and Rahim who completed the program successfully, despite setbacks, illustrate this mindset.

Mohammed had dropped out in Phase IV due to an instantaneous decision. When he got back to the streets, he saw some of his older companions in "a terminal situation" and he began thinking of the sessions he had undergone in the Rehabilitation Home. I observed that these sessions were absorbed into his thinking patterns, leading to changes in behavior.

His return to the program can be attributed to a change in mindset.

Everyone has one of two basic mindsets. A *fixed* mindset leads one to believe that his talents and abilities cannot be changed; either you have them or you do not. This is the path of stagnation and is common to many of the street adolescents. Kumar (a drop-out from Phase IV) has been coming regularly for the *mela*s at the Residential Home. He said,

It is no use trying to leave drugs; the past has kept its grip on me. I have to pay for my mistake of running away from Home.

This attitude often explained why the street adolescents left services that made tough demands on them; it explained their repeated failure to get off the streets. Once the boys made up their mind that it was not possible to change, it was difficult to get them to reason in a few sessions of counseling or within the group. This required a step-by-step guidance to educate their thought processes into a *growth mindset*. The fixed mindset creates an internal monologue that is focused on judging: "This means I'm a loser"; "I cannot change what I have been destined for." Those with a growth mindset are also constantly monitoring what is going on, but their internal monologue is not about judging themselves in this way. They are sensitive to positive and negative information, but they are attuned to its implications for learning and constructive action. Interpreting challenges, setbacks, and criticism in a learning attitude was important for those boys who successfully completed the program.

Rahim, Asif, and Shailesh had similar explanations for completing the program successfully.

"I saw no future on the streets" or *"I saw my older friends on the streets, I do not want to end up like them, waiting to die like worms"* or *"The best thing that happened to me, is the vocational training course I completed, now I am confident that even if I lose this job I can get a job anywhere."*

Shailesh and Rahim lost their jobs twice, yet they lived off their savings while job hunting and felt that their life (mindset) was not meant to be on the streets. Situations arose wherein they felt that waking up at 3 am daily to fill water for storage, going back to bed, and waking again at 5.30 am to cook breakfast and lunch was difficult, while they saw their companions on the streets having a comparatively easier time. Yet their long-term goal of establishing their lives, gaining respect, contributing to society, and not having a degenerative lifestyle, typifying their "growth mindset," kept them going. This growth mindset brought about consistent modification in behavior.

Behavior modification is an expected outcome of changing mindsets. This is an approach that seeks to replace undesirable behaviors with more desirable ones through positive or negative reinforcement. Raju, another street adolescent who left during Phase III but later returned said,

The respect and applause I received when performing in the Rehabilitation Home made me feel good.

The principles of positive reinforcement have proved to be effective for use by practitioners involved in the fields of psychology, education, counseling, social work, nursing, and allied health. The "ABCs" of behavior modification include:

- *Antecedents*—things that initiate or precede "behaviors."
- *Behaviors*—undesirable "behaviors."
- *Consequences*—things that occur as a result of "behavior."

In applying the "ABCs" to the adolescents, one observes a link between the psychological brokenness they face in the wake of family breakdown or oppressive street situation and their coping strategies that produce undesirable behavior with detrimental consequences. This led us to focus upon mending their psychological brokenness, proposing role models, tools, and activities for behavior modification.

Mohammed (who returned after he had dropped out of Phase IV) said,

I felt I did not belong to my old railway platform anymore. Guru, our gang leader who was my hero earlier was no more my hero, but Kiran (ex-street boy, who was married and working in an NGO) was what I felt I should be.

Behavior modification techniques for pre-teens and adolescents comprise a number of therapeutic interventions designed to address specific behavioral problems and provide them tools to change those negative behaviors. These techniques tend to be highly effective in children and teenagers, primarily because of their youth and the fact that they, unlike adults, are not set in their ways. My experience with addicts told me that those above 25 years were difficult to mould; they found it tough to learn new courses or adapt to a new lifestyle and tended to leave the program as they could not cope with the demands of learning new behavior.

STREET LIFE AND CHANGING MINDSETS

Street youth do not choose to use drugs or engage in risky sexual practices in an environment of obvious answers or simple choices. They are constantly balancing the satisfaction of immediate needs and benefits of short-term coping strategies against the potential risks and future consequences of their actions and decisions. The "quick fix" mindset of street children is largely behind their problems of instant gratification—action without weighing the long-term consequences of their action. This type of a quick fix mindset needs to be guided through an educative thought process.

Babu (a drop-out of Phase II) did not like the fact that they were given only two pieces of chicken at the camp meal. He said,

I have more than four pieces of chicken when I eat, I do not want your miserly two pieces, I will go to my "adda."[1] I can afford and have more than what you can give me.

---

[1] *Adda:* Location of comfort, a familiar place where he knows he can obtain food, shelter, recreation, earning, and friends.

Babu's leaving the program was to fix his immediate desire. It is important to realize that the adolescents should want to change. Thus factors of *will* and *maturity* are important elements in ensuring change in behavior. This is done in an environment of self-analysis and critical reflection. Through a process of self-reflection, street adolescents learn to become more self-aware and establish self-esteem by taking charge of their thoughts. This self-analysis leads them to learn the self-discipline to attain their goals and aspirations.

Street adolescents harbor thoughts of attaining self-development/ fulfillment. The six adolescents who completed the Five Phase program were looked up to as role models by the boys at the monthly *mela*.

"I wish I can become like Asif or Rahim," said one of the mela *boys. "They have made their life."*

In the process of this research, along with the adolescents, we developed a step-by-step thought process to help guide a mindset that would enable attain this much desired self-development/fulfillment (see Figure 6.1).

Figure 6.1 The 13 Steps to Mindset Change

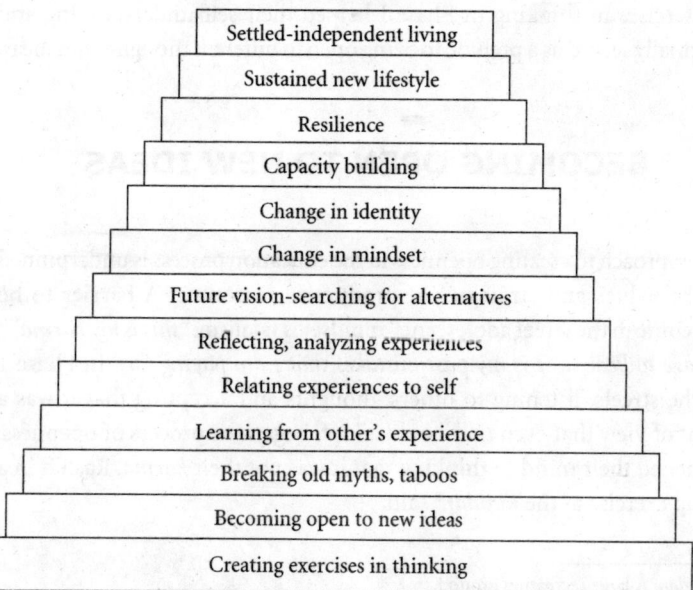

Settled-independent living

Sustained new lifestyle

Resilience

Capacity building

Change in identity

Change in mindset

Future vision-searching for alternatives

Reflecting, analyzing experiences

Relating experiences to self

Learning from other's experience

Breaking old myths, taboos

Becoming open to new ideas

Creating exercises in thinking

CREATING EXERCISES IN THINKING

How street children conceptualize issues is determined by their thought processes which are influenced by their life experiences. Street children "follow the crowd," because they feel secure. "Out of the box thinking" brings with it insecurity and possible undesired risks. My staff team and I created exercises through various techniques to make thinking more individual centered rather than "follow the crowd" or do what was always done by the group. During Phase I, we used various means of forming recreational groups on railway platforms or outreach points, or meeting individuals and instigating them to think individually. Several boys were asked what they thought about the movie running in the Capitol cinema (they frequented), why had the movie to end as it did? What would have been a better ending? Such questions brought forth their individual thoughts. While taking some rest from the game, questions were asked on some phenomena happening in the city, for example on the bomb blast that took place in July 2006. Such techniques were meant to stimulate their thinking and help them understand that they were capable of individual thought that was different and yet acceptable. This creation of exercises in thinking in Phase I helped their self-understanding and essentially served as a prelude to being open to different thoughts and ideas.

BECOMING OPEN TO NEW IDEAS

The approach to creating openness in the education process is underpinned by the values and strategies of productive reasoning. A barrier to be overcome in the street adolescents' mindset is fatalism: "*this is my karma*'"; "*I have to bear it, it is my past mistakes that I am paying for.*" In Phase 1 on the streets, listening to others' thoughts and accepting that it was a point of view that even they could adopt, began the process of openness. It opened their mind to thinking that it was not their *karma*. Rashid in a group exercise at the *maidan*[2] said,

---

[2] *Maidan*: A large recreation ground.

Allah gives us life, not curses of the past. Our life is a book on which we should write our own film lines (script).

It was a poignant remark, that we used often in other group sessions on the streets or to instigate similar remarks from other adolescents. It was a trigger to openness, to think beyond one's *karma*. In this approach to developing openness, the adolescents were asked to examine their own causal reasoning and to take responsibility for both detecting and correcting defensiveness if it existed. Facilitating such openness to learning new ideas set the stage for the adolescent street inhalants to confront their problems and move towards a solution through intense self-reflection.

The processes of learning and the transfer of learning are central to understanding how people develop important competencies to function in society. It is especially important to understand the kinds of learning experiences that lead to transfer, which can be defined as "[t]he ability to extend what has been learned in one context to new contexts" (Byrnes, 1996: 74).

Previous knowledge can help or hinder the understanding of new information. In the case of street children, their past harsh experiences often bias their understanding of new information. It is the openness to learn from other's thoughts and experiences that in a way overrides their own negative thoughts.

Ramu, a peer educator admitted,

I have learnt that the kind of life I had on the street should not be led by anyone else. That is why I have become a social worker on outreach. If I see anybody getting into drugs, I advise them not to do so. I have learnt to respect elders and women. Earlier, I used to abuse anybody without considering the person's age or status. Now, I give and also gain respect, from the children, the uncles, and didis of our NGO.

Thus, the openness to new ideas brings about productive reasoning and new learning for the street adolescent. The old myths, concepts, and taboos he had about life are slowly shed.

BREAKING OLD MYTHS/TABOOS

Myths were used to teach human beings behavior that helped people live in concert with one another. Children in Phase I on outreach have often said,

Going to an NGO means being imprisoned. There is no freedom—the NGO locks you up, the food is horrible, they beat you up, force you to wake up early, and do the cleaning for no pay.

Many of the street adolescents use these remarks to cover up their reasons for running away from the NGO, which are handed down as myths to other children. Ramiz typified this sort of myth although he had never been to an NGO.

You uncles promise to educate us and help us go home but actually you'll take us and lock us up and get your work done from us; I stay away from all such uncles and didis.

Listening to others' positive experiences and thoughts on NGOs, creating situations (post-recreation sessions) wherein they share thoughts guided by the outreach staff, cause the openness of mind to break such myths.

Street children have to fight for their own survival because the problems they seek to cope with are often *taboos* on the street. The issue of sexual abuse is virtually taboo among the street adolescents. Three out of five are sexually abused, yet strangely, their way of tackling such a question is changing the topic or avoiding it. Techniques of narration of critical incidents and exercises in drawing helped bring out their innermost feelings. Once their minds are open to new learning or to learning from other's experiences, they are prepared to break such myths and taboos. Counseling helps heal their past harsh experiences and clear their misconceptions.

LEARNING FROM OTHERS' EXPERIENCES

In terms of emotional health, the paucity of affection and care, of psychological nurture, or the lack of a close relationship with a caregiver, usually precipitates the choice or forced acceptance of street life. Once on the street, children adopt one another and other street people as models. Through this arrangement, cognitive and affective needs are met.

The "normal" course a street adolescent has is to look up to someone other than himself. He mixes his role models with his fantasy. Hence films

and their heroes play a large part of his virtual world. Bollywood films depicting rags to riches stories of film heroes are appealing. "Reality check" techniques such as drama and field visits to film shooting sites bring the children from their virtual world to the real world which has a huge impact on their thinking and leads to behavior change.

"I thought it was easy to be a hero, I did not know it had so much of 'politics.' It was my only dream. I think I have to be realistic and do something I can do in the condition that I am in," Salim said during our discussion following our visit to Film City, "My hero is still Salman, but I would like to be like Mark uncle (a social worker)."

Learning from their personal experiences and witnessing "dream role models," helps distinguish between fantasy and reality. At the *mela*, we used the technique of role modeling. Adolescents who had completed their High School, a certificate course, or possessed a bank pass book were called on stage, felicitated with certificates, and praised for their achievements. Such presentations give the boys a high sense of self-worth, relate to those on stage, and motivate some to do the same: *"If he can, why can't I?"*

RELATING EXPERIENCES TO SELF

Experience has a definite educative value, depending on the readiness of the individual to use it and on the importance of the experience itself. Children who work from an early age bypass some stages of vital psychological development, producing stunted maturation. Although they may learn to cope with everyday obligations, they have difficulty in thinking and planning beyond the present; the younger they are when they work, the worse the problem is likely to be. Rupesh (a drop-out in Phase III) started working in a *zari* embroidery workshop from the age of six. He worked 14–16 hours a day with no time for play or study. He came to the streets to escape the drudgery of his existence. However, he could not adjust to the Five Phase Program and dropped out. During the FGDs we had, he always expressed negative feelings about living in the Residential Home and of the social workers who were in charge.

The moral and psychological condition of working street children is characterized by severe personality disorders that shape their distinctive

value systems. Severance of normal social ties and abnormal socialization patterns inevitably affect personal attitudes and lead to skewed value orientations. The children's identity and behavior patterns are affected by street rules and customs, as well as weakened family bonds. Rupesh was sold by his parents to the agent, who gave them a sum of money and brought him to the city to work in the *zari* embroidery workshop. He hated his parents for selling him. Rupesh, like his companions, witnessed brutality, deceit, and violence and so learnt a lot about the vicious side of life.

Iqbal (a drop-out of Phase II) was the area "dada,"[3] feared by the smaller boys, who joined the program with five adolescents. When he found the situation not to his liking, he asked the others to quit with him, but just one agreed. Those who did not go back with Iqbal started reflecting on and analysing the experiences of those who had quit the program. They said that the experience of those who had returned to the same abusive and addictive situation of the streets was not what they wanted to experience again.

REFLECTING AND ANALYSING EXPERIENCES

The daily lives of many street children are unstructured and unstable. These children perceive the streets as productive or barren, friendly, or unfriendly at different times of the day or night. These aspects of their lives are put into perspective only through their own reflection and analysis of their situations, which invariably happens when they join a program. If this analytical and reflective process were guided while they were on the streets, their progressive movement would take place much quicker.

Magha successfully completed the five phases only when he compared himself to those whom he saw on the streets. A couple of years ago, he began reflecting on his past. He wanted to help and became a paraprofessional social worker.

I would do what my friends did, I did not think differently from them; I initially came to the program only because Rahim and Yusuf were coming. Now I want these boys to think for themselves.

---

[3] *Dada*: The local goon/toughie/bully/gang leader of the area.

Many educators consider Dewey (1933) as the modern day originator of the concept of reflection on experience, although he drew on the ideas of earlier educators such as Aristotle, Plato, and Confucius. He thought of reflection as a form of problem-solving that chained several ideas together by linking each idea with its predecessor in order to resolve an issue. To him, reflective thinking was:

> Active, persistent, and careful consideration of any belief or supposed form of knowledge in the light of the grounds that support it and the further conclusions to which it tends [that] includes a conscious and voluntary effort to establish belief upon a firm basis of evidence and rationality. (Dewey, 1933: 9)

Working on this principle, we used a technique of association. The adolescents were to link their experiences of the past with their present reactions. During reflection, they were trying to look for commonalities, differences, and their interrelations. The goal was to develop their thinking skills. As the practice became more familiar, the exercise helped better reflection. Raju (returned in the Phase III) linked his leaving the program to his anger at his trousers being stolen from the clothesline. He associated it with getting angry and upset six years ago when money was stolen from his pocket. He analysed that his anger was due to being cheated; the stealing of his trousers was a trigger to this anger. He felt that when he had come to the Residential Home for protection, how could he remain there once his trust was lost? His reaction was to run away. The analysis of what triggered his anger helped Ravi to cope when similar incidents recurred; for instance, when he subsequently lost his plate and his cricket ball, he controlled his anger and did not react the way he had earlier.

Critical Reflection involves thinking in such a manner that it challenges our beliefs, values, cultural practices, and social structures in order to assess their impact on our daily proceedings. Research by Hatton and Smith (1995) indicated that engaging with another person in a way that encourages talking with, questioning, or confronting, helped the reflective process by placing the learner in a safe environment in which self-revelation can take place. This needs an environment conducive to the boys' search for possible alternatives and solutions for a positive future.

FUTURE VISION—SEARCHING FOR ALTERNATIVES

The uncertain and volatile nature of a street child's life means that they tend to concentrate on those activities which will give them the best returns in the shortest possible time. The street child's disposition for instant gratification determines his choice of skill training, employment, and educational opportunities. As the street boys grow older, the mobile and uncertain nature of their existence tends to hold less fascination for them and they begin to harbor ideas of stability—of having a home and family.

An important part of my interaction was to engage the adolescents on the street, in Phase I, to think about their future (see Figure 6.2). This was facilitated through creative techniques such as drawing, dance, and drama.

The boys were asked to reflect on what they would like to be or do in the future. In the drawing shown in Figure 6.2, Arif (who completed five phases) depicts his ambition to become a computer graduate and work in an office. The staff encouraged him to learn computer basics in his spare time; he developed a liking for it and his first drawing was of the computer. His second drawing was that of an electrician. He was undergoing training

Figure 6.2 The Safety Net[4]

---

[4] Safety Net: Forming several alternative options that do not lead him back to the street.

as an electrician in a technical training hostel. This was his choice after Phase III. Once he realized that he could not manage mathmatics and the classes, he reflected on his own ability to perform and achieve. He saw his friend Bakshi, who was studying computer graphics, design the Diwali *mela* invitation and this made him want to achieve; he thought that becoming a computer graduate was possible but not for him. He decided to keep his options open, "*If not one, the other will work out,*" he said. Thus his drawing depicted his search for possibilities. Arif's thinking of alternatives to his electrician's course indicated that the street was not on his mind. He had made a mindset change.

CHANGE IN MINDSET

How do mindsets change? Mindsets do not necessarily change by dint of logic or persuasion. Even when things are not working satisfactorily, the first and often the only inclination is to look within the same paradigm, within the same mindset. When the adolescents were asked in Phase 1 what they would like to become, the reply invariably was "a film hero" or "a line *mukkadam*." However, others' experiences, both positive and negative, compel him to challenge his existing mindset, discover his capabilities, think of possibilities beyond his present paradigm, and take control of his own learning and his environment. Shailesh (who completed the Five Phase Program) was doing his NIOS and was also pursuing a course in the culinary arts. He decided that if he was not happy with a job as a cook, he would carry on his studies to become an accountant. It is this ability to think in terms of options outside the street "genre" that constitutes a mindset change.

The reason behind running away from services is that street children do not give themselves options, they do not think beyond what is within their purview. It is this inability to look for options that has prompted me to create a "safety net" of multiple options. Once this mindset is created, the adolescent becomes more determined and focused to move off the streets. What is important is the "will" to try and change his thinking to realistic and achievable goals with education and training. This mindset change brings a whole new identity and completes his paradigm shift from street life to a socially acceptable lifestyle.

CHANGE IN IDENTITY

A paradigm shift for the street adolescents meant a transformation in the way they perceived events, people, their options, environment, and life. The shift has a dramatic effect on their lifestyle and on their vision of the future. The shift is a formation of a new identity, where they give themselves more options within this paradigm as a form of retaining this identity.

Adolescents select and appropriate characteristics from peers, parents, teachers, relatives, religious leaders, and famous people to gain a unique identity. The new person or identity is not their final self, but it forms the basis of what they will become. If adolescents manage to work through the contradictions of this process, they develop positive and healthy feelings towards themselves. Role experimentation allows street adolescents to find their niche in their street culture and the way they pass through this stage has a profound impact on their future. Mindset change in street adolescents leads to personality change and change in identity.

Arif, who completed the Five Phase Program, says, "When my friend told me about the Residential Home where he was staying for a couple of months, I really had no idea what to do." He says when he was on the street he got no respect, he was badly treated by the police, he was not recognized as a human being, he felt he was a non-entity (no identity). Arif became a peer educator after undergoing a paraprofessional training course. He goes for outreach looking for new children on the street. Often the police catch him, thinking he is a street boy. But whenever he shows the NGO's identity card to police personnel, they set him free. Such incidents make him feel good. He says, "I feel happy about the way my street friends look at me now. Thank God, I have chosen this alternative instead of being on the street."

Arif has options to work with other NGOs or in housekeeping. He said. "*I am now an uncle.*" He has built his capacity to stay within the "safety net."

CAPACITY BUILDING

The street adolescent with his new mindset sees vocational training as a guarantee to remain "within" his new identity status. Economic strengthening activities are most effective when they target those young-sters who are at a point in their lives when they are ready to leave the

street or want to find alternative livelihoods. This comes with maturity associated with age or the result of life skills training in self-confidence, self-awareness, and an enhanced sense of the future. After staying at the Residential Home, the adolescents feel they have chosen a better path because they have been performing well not just academically but in terms of gaining a new identity. During our Society's centenary celebrations, the children at the Residential Home remarked, "*We are not street children, we are children of a Home.*"

Ravi, who completed the Five Phase Program, did not have a birth certificate or any other proof of his identity when he went to apply for a driving license. He only possessed the residence proof letter which we had given him from the Residential Home. He was sent back to make a court affidavit of his birth and get a skull test done to determine his age. Ravi, at that time, wanted to enroll in the NIOS. He wanted to build his capacity to work, to education, and so he began planning the possibilities to acquire these. A school certificate would give him the much needed age and identity essential for a passport, a voter's card would give him his rights as a citizen. Hence his motivation was to get the most important certificates that would give him the right to access other services that are the basic rights of every citizen. To do this he had to go through adversities such as being rejected at the driving school due to lack of proper certificates, having to wait for a year to get enrolled into the NIOS school as the requisite documents were not in order and he could be accepted only in the new academic year. He developed his own coping strategies during this waiting period.

RESILIENCE

Resilience has been defined as the positive adaptation of an individual within the context of significant adversity (Luthar et al., 2000). Simply put, resilience is the successful adaptation of an individual despite adversity. It has two requirements (Masten and Coatsworth, 1998): there must be a significant threat, adversity, or trauma, and an individual must be able to overcome these threats or crises through positive adaptation. Several key characteristics are found in the lives of resilient children.

- First, they are socially competent; they are able to establish and sustain caring relationships and to maintain a sense of humor despite the hardships in their lives.
- Second, resilient children are resourceful. They think critically and creatively about the problems in their lives in an attempt to develop possible solutions. They know when to turn to others for help and when they need assistance with a problem.
- Third, resilient children are autonomous. They have the ability to act independently and exert control over their environment. They know that they are masters of their own fate and do not have to accept the adversity in their lives.
- Finally, resilient children have a sense of purpose in their lives and a positive outlook for their future.

All the thirty adolescents I had started with were addicted to chemical substances. They had been on the streets for periods varying from one month to ten years before entering the program. They had to fight to survive the rains and crackdowns by police. Nearly three out of five street children reported that they had been beaten at least once or twice by the police while on the street.[5] Their resilience in the face of these adversities demonstrated their evolving identities. Most of the children I dealt with over the years have demonstrated the following traits of resilience:

- They recognized that they wanted something better for themselves. It is not that they lack the effort or will, but the "medium" (institutional/home care) to obtain it and a systematic method. Their thinking, mindset, and consequent measures are directed to attain that "something better."
- They helped each other in looking for food and money and shared it amongst themselves.
- They demonstrated courage despite being bullied or abused, by staying in the same area as the "tormentor."
- They persevered in adversity and accepted challenges to survive. In sustained crack downs by the police, they had a way of overcoming it and resurfacing in the same areas.

---

[5] "Effectiveness of the Rehabilitation Program," 2003 (internal, unpublished report).

- They had keen powers of observation and would give information on what illegal activities were going on in the area, which civil servant would be waiting to take bribes and where, or the car numbers that came to pick up hashish or other drugs from the local peddler.
- They analysed the phenomenon of educated persons getting into vices—that if you are educated, you can get away with illegal activities, which the poor, uneducated/vulnerable street child is pulled up for.

These are some of the characteristics that typify the street child's resilience. This resilience comes into play when he has a mindset change to pursue a goal. His resilience and ability to cope with adversities in pursing his goals helps him sustain his new lifestyle, which has been a result of his new mindset.

SUSTAINED NEW LIFESTYLE

The cumulative experiences and independence of street youth render them capable of taking on responsibility and surviving from day-to-day, but not of advancing beyond the daily challenges and envisioning or planning for the future. In my study on eight groups of marginalized adolescents (D'Souza, 2005), I found the street children's dependence on institutions to be a major concern. If they were in an institution from an early age, their study and job training period kept them there for over 7/8+ years. Moving out of the institution was a painful experience, often leaving them embittered. In the Five Phase Program, this was taken into consideration while formulating an exit policy with inputs from the adolescents. In Phases III and IV, the experience of practical cooking, living on their own for a few months prior to moving out, all simulated much of their out of institution care situation and made the transition process smoother.

Children are agents of their own development, rather "agents of change in their own lives." Their participation is critical to improve adaptation to societal expectations. Through this entire process of adaptation, the adolescents are led through a mindset change in their thinking, reflecting,

and resilience which brings about an identity change. This resilience is supported by their desire and working to sustain this lifestyle. All the six who completed the program went through the above process successfully.

Shekar said, "I lost three jobs in one year because of my boss going bankrupt, not getting more business, no money to pay me. But I know how to live, I manage."

When the guiding principles of youth empowerment and peer education are used to improve self-esteem and adequately treat substance abuse, it can ultimately yield sustainable results. This sustained lifestyle is the penultimate step to a more permanent and settled form of living independently.

SETTLED INDEPENDENT LIVING

Therapeutic centers are drug-free residential settings with treatment stages that reflect increased levels of personal and social responsibility. Peer influence, mediated through a variety of group processes, is used to help individuals learn and assimilate social norms and develop more effective social skills. Individuals are motivated to change through their interaction with others, including their peers from the streets. The original TC approach was developed to treat serious substance abusers in a residential program by changing their behavior and thinking. The guidance and support of the staff and peers of the adolescent is important for the transition. An atmosphere conducive to reflection and analysis, therefore, has to be created.

Independence from care is a painful process. If not weaned in a gradual process in participation with the adolescent, it makes the individual bitter, leading to negative reactions. Independence and starting a family of his own and becoming well settled is a matter of pride for the youngster. His bonding is to the place and to the persons who cared for him and nurtured his growth process. The aim is not to provide another form of dependence on the institution but encourage them to seek peer support and role models.

REFLECTIONS

These 13 steps symbolize the journey of questioning how my experience could be documented systematically not only to improve my practice but also to contribute significantly to the street adolescents. Although it has been researched within the framework of and adapted to the Five Phase Model Program, it is a pattern that cuts across cultures, generating possibilities that can give the street adolescent a concrete and realistic future.

7
The Enduring Image
CONCLUSION

Street youth are potential assets to their communities and society. We must open doors for them to become full participants and reintegrate into their communities.

Whilst trying to understand the lifestyle and mindset of the street adolescent, one asks again:

What is it that triggers instant decision-making?
Does he apply critical thinking to his decisions?
Is going back to the streets the only option available to him?
Does he choose this option in the absence of knowing about other alternatives?

The street is his comfort zone, his "survival niche."

It is more a pattern of thinking that the street child gets habituated to while reacting to situations. This pattern of thinking does not give him the liberty or time to think of the consequences at that instant of decision-making. Those who manage to overcome this pattern of thinking, go through a process of unlearning it (often with failures), yet this is an exercise in learning. Motivated, the street adolescent takes recourse to the experience of his successful colleagues, institutional supports, and his own attitudinal and mindset change. Yet, his movement off the streets is entrapped in a cycle of attempts and failures which I believe, is misconceptualized as his survival repertoire.

Is addiction to street lifestyle a pull factor? It is the street adolescent's critical thinking and mindset that either keeps him in that cycle or gives him the impetus to change his lifestyle. Once he has got it "sorted out in his mind," he manages to cope with challenges and impulses, and endeavors to sustain his newfound identity.

FINDING EQUILIBRIUM: MINDSETS AND TRANSFORMATION

For many street youth, family and community support disintegrate under the pressures of poverty. Once on the street, the children seek out a network that will enable them to stay on the street, thus rendering it difficult for them to leave the situation. Whether children stay on the street or leave has to do with how they cope and use the opportunities they have on the street and how these opportunities serve as exit mechanisms.

Most children on the streets find adequate coping techniques including a niche in the economic market which gives them sufficient income to eat and clothe themselves, find and take advantage of programs that serve them. They are sufficiently informed about their physical health to stay reasonably healthy, form close friendships with peers, and if possible, maintain some connection with their family of origin. In fact, contrary to popular opinion, the street boys' very resilience is indicated by the coherent, goal-oriented efforts they make to meet their pressing survival needs. Resilience is based on the belief that persons are able to cope with stress, adversity or trauma, depending on the balance of risk and protective factors. Although many street children tend to be drop-outs from school, the skill and creativity they display in surviving and managing their lives on the streets indicate that they do not lack intelligence; thus their dropping out of school is mainly due to environment-related factors.

These children are rarely perceived as social actors capable of making their own decisions based on options available to them. However, these street children are not helpless, pathetic victims. They have built their lives from their own resources and within their own community. They are self-reliant, independent, and have succeeded in surviving within an often hostile and unsafe environment. Their experiences may leave them emotionally drained, yet they harbor a strong will to survive; philosophical issues are not a priority. Their thoughts are directed more towards where the next meal will come from and where they can find a place to sleep. Thus, I think, it is important to help them use their ability to think, reflect, and analyze and overcome their confusion and low self-worth. Such support enhances their chances of escaping the degenerative cycle of poverty.

Street children tend to be viewed more as a problem to be solved rather than as an asset to be worked with. Undoubtedly there are problems: the multitude of push and pull factors, the lack of street-children-centered policies, and the inadequacy of grassroots services. I used the problem tree analysis along with my team to identify the basic problem, specifying its cause and effects. This step-by-step approach enabled me to arrive at a consensus and an understanding of the problem to be addressed, how and under what constraints. The entire organization with the staff went through this exercise, to bring ownership and quality service to the children in 2004 (refer Appendix 3: Problem Tree).

The participation of street children in research and planning via a methodology that empowers them is of crucial importance. Participatory Action Research seeks to generate knowledge through self-inquiry and reflection. Education helps children to develop curiosity, a love of learning, and a problem-solving attitude. This involves mental processes of cognition such as comprehension, inference, decision-making, planning, and learning.

The key to helping street children off the streets is their ability to be reflective through a guided thought process. Reflecting on my experiences and observations over the past 26 years, I am of the opinion that children are sustained in their situation on the streets largely due to their limited opportunities to think critically, reflect on their situation, and their future. *Their cognitive thought processes are mainly geared to survival, immediate situation management and instant gratification of the senses.*

A paradigmatic shift can take place in street inhalant abusers through a guided thought process. Starting with the premise that a street child's actions are guided more by impulse than by rational thought, I created exercises designed to stimulate thinking which, in turn, helped develop openness to new ideas and new learning among the street boys (D'Souza, 2004). Once the boys were ready to learn, there was an almost simultaneous unlearning that took place—the breaking of myths and misconceptions such as their feelings of being worthless, being incapable of a better future, and that their situation could not be changed due to their *karma*. If the boys at this stage were confronted by others with similar experiences, they tended to learn and assimilate from them and move towards critical reflection of their own experiences in the light of their new learning. This process set up the next stage for the development of a future vision and a search for alternatives, leading to a change in mindset. The street adolescents now had a high degree of self-confidence and self-worth, it made them feel capable of acquiring skills that would promote and sustain their new productive lifestyle. The process, which first began in their mind and attitude, found its culmination in a move towards settled/independent living.

The movement towards a self-sustaining lifestyle is typified by the cases of Farooq, Dhawal, and Ashley. Farooq took the oft-trodden road to the city, but with the permission of his parents. He started as a *zari* worker working from 9 am till midnight on a salary of ₹750, but realized that the city of Mumbai offered many opportunities to move up the economic ladder. He worked in a restaurant, where his salary rose to ₹1500. He sent money home, but his parents disapproved of his "hotel work" and asked him to take up a "good job." Farooq returned to the streets, but did not stay long—the "lure" of the streets in the form of drugs, sex, and other "freedoms" did not hold him. He met an old friend, Mushtaq, who was at the Maria Ashiana Therapeutic Centre, Lonavala, India. Mushtaq convinced him to join the Centre. Farooq joined Phase 3 of the program, as he was not addicted and the medical tests proved that he had no toxins in his system. Farooq not only completed the therapeutic program successfully, but also helped the staff with the boys both within the institution and at the outreach. His career graph is one of those unusual movements of managing to complete the program, go beyond, retreat, recover, and restart. He completed his training, took up a job, went back to the streets, was despondent, but with help and inner courage, he transcended his situation to take up not one job, but two—one during the day and another at night.

Farooq's self-improvement report read as follows:

- Was successful in learning English and Hindi
- Did his paraprofessional course
- Passed SSC creditably

- Developed a positive self-image
- Learned about hygiene and its importance

Dhawal and Ashley also typify the struggle to succeed. Dhawal came to us from Kolkata when he was 12–13 years old. He was an excellent artist and had won several competitions. Seeing his talent, I prevailed upon a friend of mine to take him on as an apprentice, creating and designing thermocol cut-outs for weddings. Dhawal managed to finish Standard 12, went into full-time designing, and landed in a job in South Africa.

Ashley, too, has traversed a similar path and now works in a multinational company. When he came into the shelter, he was 10 years old, traumatized by the earthquake that had destroyed most of his village at Latur in the state of Gujarat, India. He had a bitter experience with a policeman who asked him to shine his shoes. When Ashley asked him to pay up, the policeman threw his shoeshine kit into a nearby drain and also took away his earnings. When Ashley met me, he asked me for a loan of ₹100 to buy a new shoeshine kit. Unfortunately, he had a similar negative experience with another policeman. He started scrap-picking, but then gave it up in favor of selling pens onboard trains. Repeated incidents with the police who took away his earnings without reason caused Ashley to observe that it was actually the police who were responsible for turning street boys into thieves—they did not allow them to earn honestly.

Perceiving Ashley's innate smartness and his interest in learning English, I enrolled him for the National Institute of Open Schooling (NIOS) which he passed in his first attempt. Following this, he started working as an office boy at the Residential Home, entrusted with administrative duties. His keen interest in computers saw him getting enrolled for a computer course. However, he ran away briefly from the Residential Home when one of his former friends from the streets beckoned him. During this period, he earned by undertaking catering jobs during the wedding season. He wanted to return to Latur and try to locate his mother. He failed in his first attempt and returned depressed to the Residential Home. I gave him some money and asked him to try again. This time, he managed to locate his mother and stayed with her for a while before returning to the Residential Home, pursuing his degree in computer applications, and finally getting a job in a multinational computer company.

ETHICAL CONSIDERATIONS AND DILEMMAS

There are two basic ethical issues that are pressing:

- Those involving therapeutic interventions.
- Those involving the research process.

Often these two would mix to become a dilemma for me as an interventionist. My daily tasks required me to make decisions on therapy; these decisions were not for purposes of research alone, but as reflections to enable me to make improved decisions.

Ethical frameworks address three primary issues:

- **Access** (consent/permission from the participants).
- **Safeguarding rights** (assurance of confidentiality, right to withdraw from the research at any time).
- **Assuring good faith** (securing permission from those whose stories we report).

As participatory action research is carried out in real world circumstances, and involves close and open communication among the people involved, I paid close attention to certain ethical considerations:

- All participants were allowed to influence the work, and the wishes of those who did not wish to participate were respected.
- The development of the work remained visible and open to suggestions from all participants.
- Issues of informed consent and of ensuring the confidentiality of data with regard to the study of my employees and the adolescents in my care posed ethical questions; therefore, I sought permission at various points of time to make relevant use of the data.
- Informing them about the descriptions of their stories and points of view were negotiated with those concerned prior to writing.
- Confidentiality was maintained.

- The children have been accorded the same respect in print as conveyed in our face-to-face situation.

There have been many ethical dilemmas that surfaced at different points of the study and programs:

- *Complex role play—Changing roles from guardian to researcher*
  In the program, I had been the guardian/father figure to these children. For the scientific rigor of the research, I had to shed this role and slip into the role of a researcher. The change in roles had to be done through tact and reinforcement.
- *How does one ensure staff/team motivation?*
  In my experience, if the staff members do not reorient their goals or are not trained appropriately, there is the possibility of staff burn out and loss of enthusiasm within a couple of years. How should this issue be managed? Constant training, reorientation of goals, redefining roles and a consistent "thinking" on emerging issues maintain staff motivation.
- *Can children make life-course decisions?*
  It was an ethical dilemma to let children aged 7–13 make a "life-course decision." Maintaining a professional distance in these decisions was as much a dilemma as it was a need. I questioned whether I should respect the boy's decision to leave in the middle of his treatment/medication, even when he had habitually run away and returned in a worse condition each time? It stretched my understanding of the child's participation in his decision and my dilemma as a researcher at times wanting to get into a guardian's role.
- *Should a regular runaway be reinstated?*
  An adolescent who repeatedly runs away, keeps taking away a few boys each time from the program. Should we keep taking him back when he returns, when in need? This is a question I have asked colleagues and counselors in other shelters in the country. Each case needed special consideration.
- *How does one help terminal cases on the outreach?*
  In "terminal situations" when they ask us for help on the outreach, how do we manage this issue? I thought it was necessary to

understand the focus and objective of the organization. This, in practical situations on the streets, is easier said than done.

- *How does one deal/interfere/do away with power relationships?*

I have come across several cases of the "protector–utility boy"[1] relationship on the streets, wherein the "protector" does not allow his "utility boy" leave the streets to join a program to get off the streets as he is abusing him and is under his control. How do we deal with this power relationship? As a method to counter this, I developed the camp method for groups of street boys from particular areas of outreach. We targeted these types of relationships and worked on them for three–four days of the camp.

- *When does one wean the child away from the institution?*

If children stay for long periods of time in a shelter, they tend to lose their street survival skills and become dependent on the institution, often making their exit from the institution traumatic. The phase-wise movement in an exit policy adopted by the institution helped to get the children prepared for independent living.

- *How does one limit NGO shopping?*

We have several instances of children "shopping" for NGOs when they do not get what they want from one organization, when they are unable to accept the demands made of them or when repatriation or rehabilitation efforts are sustained against their will. Yet for their long-term good, they "hide/move" into another organization. Should they be pursued and should their ability to shift to organizations be termed as resilience, survival strategy or taking advantage of the system? Networking with other NGOs and sharing information have helped limit these incidents of "shopping."

- *How do we balance religious beliefs/mindsets with growth?*

"This is my karma/my fate," has been a major block to the adolescents' positive movement "off" the streets. They tend to view it more from a cultural/religious angle, which makes their

---

[1] Protector–utility boy: Big boys who use the younger boys for sexual pleasure and to run small errands, whilst protecting them from other bullies on the streets.

mindset all the more difficult to deal with. How do we balance their religious beliefs with challenges for positive growth? Role modeling was one of the motivational factors that worked well.

- *Ex-addicts as "nurse attendees?"*
  I have questioned whether it is right for the organization to keep ex-addicts as "nurse attendees" to take care of those who are admitted into Phase 2 of the Therapeutic Program. Is it taking advantage of their vulnerability, of their helplessness? I viewed it as contributing to their image as positive role models and giving them a sense of self-worth, too.

- *To join or not to join the institution? Whose decision is it?*
  I have questioned the efficacy of the outreach program in encouraging children to get admitted into an organization. Is it the street child's need to join a program or is it the need of the institution? Is it the need to have the numbers to sustain the institution's survival? When should the institution leave it to the child to decide to join its program and leave him to join without "pressure"? In order to enable as many children as possible to get "off" the streets, we found that it was best to offer opportunities for them to participate in the program without coercion.

- *Where does one draw the line?*
  Organizations in their admission policy face a dilemma as to where to draw the line. How many children should they cater to? When should they stop fresh admissions? The compromise is between quality and quantity. I have come to understand that qualitative service has its efficacy in journeying along with the fewer numbers who are helped towards independence rather than with those who are kept for protection from the streets. The focus/objectives of the organization must be kept in mind.

- *What should be the extent of caregiving?*
  How does one define the term "holistic care of street children"? Where does this spiral or chain reaction in caregiving end? This dilemma often results in the organization losing out on individualized caregiving.

- *Should caregiving be extended to street boys detected with HIV/ AIDS?*
  Street boys are at high-risk for HIV/AIDS due to the everpresent dangers of abuse and of establishing relationships with women

on the streets. These boys are sexually active from the age of 13+; many are abused by older boys (at a far younger age). Some boys have sexually transmitted diseases, some test positive for HIV. Since we did not have care facilities for HIV cases, we did referrals and worked in the area of prevention. I always faced a dilemma in testing the youngsters. Some boys were unwilling to be tested, some unwilling to accept that they tested positive. In one instance, a street adolescent residing with us refused to accept the fact that he had tested HIV positive. On one occasion, he was seen deliberately giving his razor to another boy to use. I was faced with the moral dilemma of whether to keep this boy on at the Residential Home or to reveal his health status to the others. In these instances, we at the Residential Home tried to get the affected boys to settle independently. HIV always posed a major dilemma because of the ever-present risk of indulging in sexual activity outside the institution and returning to us for residential care.

- *How does one counsel street adolescents who enter into long-term relationships with older women on the streets?*

Boys from the Residential Home, educated or trained in a skill and well on their way to independent living, were often attracted to older women residing on the pavements outside the Home. The psychological need for affection and attention of the female sex entrapped many boys who converted their long-term relationships (with these 40+ women with four–six children) into marriage, which was a regression in many ways—physically they were vulnerable as these women continued in their way of life, that is, having multiple casual sexual relationships with truck drivers and others; economically, their meager savings were depleted, what they had spent on themselves, now had to be stretched to feed a ready-made family of five or more; psychologically, a strong binding sustaining relationship dwindled into faithlessness. Now the boys were caught in a trap with mounting debt, emotional scars, and a bleak future.

These questions and dilemmas have constantly impinged upon my work and research with the children. I have tried to deal with them and put together some of my insights into the ensuing ethical issues.

LESSONS LEARNED

"How do I improve my practice?"—this question motivated my research, helped me to be reflective; the practice engendered by my undertaking of this Participatory Action Research informed much of my learning. It helped to make my tacit knowledge more explicit. I feel that the cyclic processes of action, observation, reflection, and planning have created a platform for new thinking and for "the embodiment of new pedagogical ideas and professional practice" (Whitehead and McNiff, 2006). The breaking up of my experience into different cycles helped me analyse, reflect, and put into perspective my queries; the change in my reflections helped the emergence of theory in my practice. My autoethonographic account helped me observe more clearly, seek other perspectives, and be more informed in team decisions.

Making street youth think critically is perhaps one of the best ways to get them to make socially acceptable permanent choices that would help their rehabilitation. The children have knowledge of actions harmful to them, yet they give in to their detrimental consequences. Working on their thought processes and mindsets is essential to help informed choice. When the approach is person-centered, it places much of the responsibility for the therapeutic process on the boys themselves. They determined the direction of their movement, while informal questions enhanced the boys' insights and self-understanding. All this led to increased self-esteem and stimulated greater openness to experience as well as an increased capacity to experience and express feelings. It fostered better self-understanding, lowered levels of defensiveness, guilt, and insecurity, and promoted positive relationships with others; all of these helped to increase the congruence between the boys' idealized and actual selves.

Knowledge/information should follow understanding, assimilation, decision, and appropriate action. The mindset of the children requires to be guided from their "instant gratification," "live for the day" and on the spur of the moment decision-making to a well thought out, reflective and cognitive approach. This is essential for their progressive movement off the streets and taking responsibility for their actions.

During the first pilot experimental project I conducted for drug addicted street youth in 1993, I met 22 year old Fernandes. In my eight years (until then) on the streets, he was the first boy from my community, hailing from my native land. He spoke in my mother tongue; this gave me added impetus to try and help him out of his situation. He was consuming heavy doses of "brown sugar" (impure form of heroin), but informed me that he was not interested in changing his situation. I tried to talk to him several times, but to no avail. Every day I met him I offered to help him, but he refused, saying he was happy as he was and did not need any help.
— First Camp Evaluation Report, June 1993, Mumbai

The episode with Fernandes taught me a lesson I remembered for the rest of my life. *A person who needs to change has to have the desire to do so.* In the course of my evaluation of the situation, I realized that I needed to be open to all communities and treat every child as one belonging to my community. Fernandes taught me to make the entire street children's community "My Community." I needed to be equally zealous in my interaction with all children on the streets. He taught me:

- to offer and yet leave the final decision to him;
- to push but not to force, yet wait;
- to help him in his decision, while at the same time, ensuring him his freedom;
- to learn to accept my personal disappointment and yet not get discouraged;
- to learn to be professional as an interventionist; and
- to understand that I am working for the children and not a particular community.

In experiential learning, reflection leads to self-awareness and reflexive thinking.

Invariably, those in institutional care expect the child to understand the dangers of living on the streets and think that the children will "automatically" make the choice of leaving the streets. In the reconnaissance phase, I wondered:

When it was difficult to get food and shelter and be at the mercy of the police, bigger bullies and harsh situations, why could the children not come to live at the Residential Home? Why could they not see that their life revolved around sitting outside the dargah begging in a "terminal situation"? Why not see and learn from your counterparts who have been rehabilitated? It seemed logical for me, but it is through an experience, a shift in their thinking that would get them there. Till then they are a part of the "street child genre."[2]

This led to further questioning—how working with the street adolescents' mindsets as an educative method through preparation and small exercises on the part of the adolescent can help them make decisions that are well informed. This reconfirms that sustained cognitive inputs can bring about long-term behavioral changes provided the adolescents have a strong positive intention and motivation to change with requisite skills within a "friendly/guided environment."

This had a learning for all involved—it was not only the adolescents but also we as staff, who needed to be reflective. We have to reorient our objectives, reflect on practices long in use, and keep the issue and understanding of the street children "alive" through our proactive stance.

Before I was placed in the Residential Home in 1994–95, at every monthly mela since 1987 there was a slogan repeated: "saddak chaap" (street life) and the boys would shout in unison "zindabad!" (long live). I thought it rather demeaning although many felt that it gave the boys an identity. My perception was that this slogan was meant to: (a) remind the boy where he came from; (b) the streets or street life was not one that society accepted or glorified; (c) intrinsically this slogan meant street life had our tacit approval; (d) it meant that we did not put forward our Residential Program as one that could wean them away from street life but discreetly encouraged their status quo on the streets. We had a consultation with the staff and some of the older street and ex-street boys. One of the first measures they suggested was removing the slogan and from late 1995, we stopped using it altogether.

— Residential Home Annual Report, 1995

Thus, research with street children has been a collective team effort. The reconnaissance phase generated questions which were researched, reflected upon, and answers sought in unison with the adolescents and the team.

A street child whether on the street or in an institution has certain insights and reflections which may not always be vocalized, but which have

---

[2] Street child genre: Living, thinking, and experiencing the lifestyle of a street child who does not think of changing his situation.

to be taken into consideration. Farooq had listed a few of his thoughts, some of which I incorporated into my program.

- Small boys tend to run away mainly due to pressure from the bigger boys.
- Inaction on the part of the staff often prompted the boys to run away.
- It was difficult to convince the boys about the program as many had had negative experiences with other NGOs.
- Attempts to elicit information from the boys succeeded only when Farooq shared his story; many boys were reluctant to open up and discuss their stories.
- Poverty was the main reason why the boys ran away.
- Very few were literate.
- Smaller boys evinced more interest in studying.
- The rest were keen on working for which they had to obtain the requisite training such as in cooking, two-wheeler mechanics, driving, and so on.
- There was a lack of trust among the street boys.
- Covering up their true story with a made up one till trust was built.
- Initially, many boys would sit quietly in a corner, but after some days, interaction and bonds grew. However, minor fights were frequent.
- Although there was an initial resistance to routine, adjustment took place and discipline set in.
- A period of apprenticeship should follow training, so that the boys could be assured of work soon after.

This inclusive approach gave meaning to my years of experience and the direction to help research and practice in the mindset of street children.

Street children represent a complex set of factors which require a multitude of resources and efforts to address the issue, primarily through an attitudinal change. This can be brought about through influencing and setting in motion cognitive changes leading eventually to behavioral modification, adoption of an alternative lifestyle and sustaining this over a long term. Although a slow process, this is an innovative method, as it lays the foundation for a generalized approach that cuts across multiple cultures and models/approaches to the street children issue. It has served as a platform to crystallize the observations and experiences of those working in the field of substance-abusing street addicts. Isolated, charity-based approaches will not address the issues of street children or the problems confronting children "at the margins" adequately. Hence, all approaches towards street children—preventive and protective—must rest on a foundation that is rights-based and holistic.

According to Richard Petty (1995: 210), among the attitudes relevant to drug abuse prevention are attitudes toward *oneself* (e.g., low self-esteem may contribute to drug use), *figures of authority* (e.g., parents, government officials, and teachers who eschew drug use or who advocate new treatment approaches), *peers* (e.g., friends and colleagues), the *drugs themselves* (e.g., are they seen as harmful or exciting?), and *new drug treatment* programs (e.g., are they seen as beneficial or ineffective?). Assessments of drug prevention efforts sometimes have focused on the new knowledge acquired rather than on attitude and behavior change per se. Attitude consists of three components: affect (emotional aspect), cognition (beliefs and knowledge), and behavior (responses/actions). Therefore any attempt to obtain long-term behavioral change must necessarily address these three components. However, knowledge change in the absence of individual and/or community attitude change is unlikely to result in behavior change. Attitude to oneself is thus at the top of this "hierarchy," as it changes everything else.

My work on mindsets underscores the importance of changing attitudes; especially with reference to the street inhalants who formed the core of my study. A person's attitude is an important mediating variable between the acquisition of new knowledge and behavioral change and, therefore, changing attitudes carries with it profound implications. First, attitudes often have a direct impact on behavior. Second, if the attitudes of a large number of individuals of a particular community change, then there is openness to the group's attitudinal change, encouraging change in the behavior of other members. Hence, normative pressure can produce behavior change even if an individual's own attitude does not change. Third, unless there is a change in the children's attitudes, they may lack the motivation necessary to acquire new skills or break old habits that allow new behavior to occur. This change, I think, has to be paralleled with a change in institutional attitudes and interventions.

THE CHANGING FACE OF STREET CHILDREN

During the reconnaissance phase, I observed the "typical" street child run away from the village, struggling against all odds for survival, rummaging through the garbage or begging for food, working as a shoe shine boy, or as a ragpicker, or in occupations associated with the destitute and the marginalized. The 1990s witnessed a change in the identity and the image of the street child, wrought by a change in the interventions and strategies of different organizations. Several services for street children began springing up in smaller towns and cities, increasing emphasis was given to rehabilitation, repatriation, and education by these service providers, which shifted the focus to development of the child and the need to move him off the streets.

There was a paradigm shift, with street children acquiring a new identity and wanting to be counted among the middle class with appropriate ambitions, skills acquisition, and values. They now saw that it was possible to change their situation, by making use of the opportunities given to them. In their individual identity lay their collective strength, wherein they got inspiration from those who were rehabilitated. The visibility of the changed lifestyle, attitudes, and thinking patterns led to a manifold increase in the numbers of children leaving street life and being rehabilitated and repatriated.

The street children of today, however, are more middle class savvy as is reflected by their aspirations and attitudes. They no longer want mere education, but strive towards specialized courses. Those in institutions particularly do not like to be labeled as "street kids" and consciously try to distance themselves by dressing better and not mingling with the new entrants from the street. Few agencies have been able to handle the challenges posed by these street children and adolescents, who have learnt by necessity, "to be self-sufficient, quick-witted, suspicious, and at times rebellious" (Sauvé, 2003). These agencies refer to themselves as being youth-centered, but most are still driven by the traditional paradigm of adult control over children and adolescents; they assume the responsibility of telling these adolescents what to do, how to behave, and what is important. Little thought is given to the children's own voices or experiences. Thus institutions dealing with such groups send out a message to them that they cannot contribute anything to the program and that they are only there to receive and learn. Through their behavior, they tell the youth that they cannot help themselves but must depend on adults for help, that youth should respect these adults even though these adults do not respect them. Those institutions that have applied a participatory approach with the children have had fruitful experiences that have gone beyond mere numbers.

REDEFINING PROGRAMMATIC STRATEGIES

Working with street youth involves uncertainties, risks, and unexpected issues. One has to constantly reinvent strategies, objectives, motivations, and be prepared for any eventuality. In addition, they may not produce the measurable outcomes typical of more controlled programs. In India, for instance, the *Juvenile Justice (Care and Protection of Children) Act, 2000* is the key legal framework that ensures the right to protection of children. Based on the Indian Constitution, this Act conforms to the *UN Convention on the Rights of the Child*, the "Beijing Rules," and the *United Rules for the Protection of Juveniles Deprived of their Liberty*, and all other relevant national and international instruments. Formulated in 1986, the *Juvenile Justice Act* was amended in 2000, and again in 2006. Government of India, in a positive step towards the care and protection of children, asked all state governments to make provision for its complete execution by first studying it in their given contexts and promulgating the rules to their specific contexts.

The Act has a child-friendly approach underlining proper care, protection, treatment, and rehabilitation and reintegration of children below 18 years. While outlining the measures to meet the needs of these children, the *Juvenile Justice Act* refers to the role of the police and NGOs.

It states that it is imperative for the "individuals concerned with children" to fill the spaces, in order "to advance the child rights approach."

The Child Welfare Committee (CWC) took on a lead role in ensuring the care and protection of especially vulnerable children. The NGOs, who had registered themselves under the Charity Commissioner and the Registrar of Societies, had now to register themselves under different categories of the *Juvenile Justice Act*. The Residential Homes need to have a license, a fit institution certificate, etc. These requirements, necessary to streamline the quality of care of children, have in some cases been a challenge for many existing child care service providers.

Standard requirements of spaces for those already existing homes, shelters, day care and night shelters are subject to their own space limitations in urban areas. The challenge of "obligation" to accept referrals of court committed children to institutions that do not fit into the specific objectives/focus of the receiving service provider (NGO) is a difficulty that needs to be addressed.

This referral situation changes the character of the organization and their focus of care. Most care givers make long-term goals with each individual child in their care. This often includes repatriation and rehabilitation plans. Incorporating the suggestions of the *Juvenile Justice Act* procedures to these children's plans that were in place earlier has proved to be a challenge to service providers.

The *Juvenile Justice Act* directive that a child grow within his cultural milieu is a distinctive and positive move in the upbringing of the child. This aspect has sometimes been a regression for a child (from a backward state) who has already been placed in an educational institution within a cosmopolitan context offering better facilities for his future.

The *Juvenile Justice Act* has to be commended in its move to standardize the care and protection of the child all over the country. The quality standards measurement has been a move in the right direction. Involving various informal systems and community-based welfare agencies in the protection, care, treatment, development, and rehabilitation of children is the final objective. Its particularities are best treated in formulations of the *Rules Act*, 2007[3] to be laid down by each state.

---

[3] "The State Governments in collaboration with civil society shall develop and make available simplified and child-friendly versions of the Act and the rules in regional languages." [R.16. (4), *The Juvenile Justice {Care and Protection of Children} Act, 2000]*

This calls for radical rethinking in terms of how we in institutions deal with street children and adolescents. If we view street youth as being contributory and having something to offer rather than as empty vessels needing to be filled and helped, we should design programs that reflect this thinking. We should respect street youth as whole beings with complex and interconnected life experiences. Interventions should be founded on what youth bring to the institution: their stories, dreams, and choices. Rather than foster dependency, efforts should be made to allow young people to articulate their own reality and define their goals and objectives. Local culture and prejudices often prevent street youth from accessing basic social and health services and hinder their efforts at breaking away from social stigma.

It is important that there is a secure and non-judgmental environment wherein street youth can openly contemplate the daily risks and decisions they take, reflect upon possible consequences (intended and unintended), and then discuss their choices and safer alternative lifestyle knowing that their personal autonomy will be respected.

> Exploring cultural models of difference and the ways in which these are
> used to create inequalities can at times make space for sensitization about
> prejudice and discrimination as an integral part of the participatory process.
> (Cornwall, 1998: 56)

The models of care for street children should be encouraged to celebrate differences amongst them, to challenge discrimination and to work together cooperatively and democratically in a manner that transforms and challenges much of their existing experiences of exploitative relations (O'Kane, 2003).

RECOMMENDATIONS

1. Working on the thought processes of the street adolescent requires a step-by-step understanding of his situation, reflecting on his lifestyle, analyzing it, and making an informed decision. This is the key to initiating behavior change. This is best done after he goes through a process of unlearning street thought processes while

simultaneously learning those processes of cognitive behavior that encourage positive development. For this positive development, it is essential to work on a paradigm shift in his mindset of the streets. From a mindset that "this is my fate" and "I cannot do anything about changing it" to motivating him to change his attitude, through role models, counseling, goal-setting, exercises in thinking and reflecting, change in identity, and mechanisms to cope and sustain a lifestyle different from that on the streets, is what sustains his mindset change and identity.

2. Conceptualizing street youth as a manifestation of the political and socioeconomic climate, and not simply pathologizing them, indicates that healthy development of street youth should be understood in the context of other societal problems. Such factors as poverty, unemployment, lack of housing, lack of education, and inadequate welfare and infrastructure combine as push and pull factors responsible for youths taking to street life and should also be taken into account in order to understand them as individuals (Tudorić-Ghemo, 2005).

3. Support services for street youth are often guided by a problem-oriented perspective, that is, a tendency to view their life experiences as symptomatic of pathology and risk. It would be more effective to develop an understanding of how street children perceive their life experiences before engaging and supporting them to make positive transitions in their lives. Programs serving adolescents must be tailored for them. It should ideally commence during the critical pre-adolescent period, meet standards of care and be guided by theory. Most programs tend to fail when not guided by sound theory. The use of innovative and flexible methodology can enable a detailed understanding of street children's lives, the finer nuances of their relationships, social networks, and most importantly, help them move off the streets.

4. While working with street boys, it is important to take cognizance of the fact that their everchanging multiple identities (shaped by their very mobility) affords them endless opportunities and resources that enhance their survival strategies on the street. Therefore, institutions should recognize the importance of

mobility in the lives of street boys as an inescapable part of their survival and work their programs accordingly.

5. The transition from low to high self-worth is slow and requires an attitudinal change on the part of the street adolescent. The staff team may make the efforts to enhance the self-worth of the boys through motivational talks and sessions, engage them in recreational activities and various other creative means, but what is critical is professional counseling. These counselors serve as confidants; their availability to be there for the youngsters when they need them, giving them sound advice/direction, to move forward is important.

6. Recognition and acceptance by service providers/institutions that street survival (through gambling, sexual promiscuity, power relationships ("protector–utility boy," abuse of glues, solvents, and other inhalants) is important to the street boys, and their lives revolve around these. It is important to develop a holistic picture of substance abuse by identifying individual, family, and social problems leading up to it. For dealing with the problem of substance abuse among street adolescents, there needs to be a set of theoretical and operational guidelines for multilevel interventions, whether community-based, center-based, or street-based.

7. The street boy's thinking that the "freedom of the streets" is lost if he joins a program, is often the reason for resisting change and is symptomatic of psychological trauma. Service providers need to identify such misconceptions and work on the thinking process that shapes such views. Addressing these street cultural issues is an important element of any street therapy program. It effects a change in the street adolescent's mindset, a dissociation between "freedom" as he had perceived it when he started life on the street, which came from an unstructured way of life, to "freedom from want" which would be the outcome of a structured therapeutic program. Phase-wise movements in programs must encompass inhalant abuse, the need for psychological healing of the adolescent, skills acquisition as well as a clear cut exit policy that fosters independence, rehabilitation, and repatriation.

8. Children derive a great deal of positive satisfaction from contributing to the household income through employment;

it gives them a sense of utility, self-respect and self-confidence. Currently, there is a move towards vigorous livelihood support to vulnerable youth not just as a complement to the provision of outreach services and primary health interventions, but as a necessary component of integrated programs that can empower young people to act on their knowledge and skills.

9. Employment training is insufficient to keep boys off the streets altogether; hand-in-hand, there should be a sound understanding of how the boys end up on the streets and what keeps them there. The complexities of their lives mean that the boys come onto the streets for different reasons and they will also move off the streets upon "answering/addressing" those issues. Skill and vocational training programs do not totally equip the boys with the personal and social resources necessary to move into the economic mainstream. Most of the programs that run small scale hobby centers producing items such as paper bags, candles, cards, and other curio items, often leave the youth moving out of the institution stranded, as these skills are not apt for his survival or for the job market. Vocational training must be highly professional and attuned to the labor market. Street adolescents face enormous difficulties in obtaining and maintaining employment and constructing their lives around their jobs. Practical preparation for this phase of their lives and a follow-up program are important aids.

10. Facilities and programs should be geared towards keeping the boys engaged constructively. A weekly progress chart developed along with the adolescent is an important factor to motivate and help him position himself and view how others perceive his progress. Planning and implementation of service-provision should be done with the participation of the boys for whom it is meant. This helps ownership and sharing of responsibilities for the adolescents' progress.

11. Participation and encouragement of "critical enquiry"/reflection by street adolescents helps them to understand power relations, to challenge negative perceptions held against them, and to assert their rights as children and as human beings. Thus, it is important to create platforms for street youth to express themselves, advocate

their cause, and draw attention towards investing more in street children programs. Sufficient attention must be paid to their street–shelter–street cycle lifestyle. A collective review and a reflective assessment of program interventions, a collaborative networking with other NGOs in tackling this issue is the need of the hour.

12. An enabling and supportive environment should be created that goes beyond mere provision of services, and lays emphasis on initiating and sustaining boys' participation. The emphasis should change from "assistance for the boys to assistance by and from the boys." Only then can their dependency on the institution be reduced and they can become self-determining and independent individuals.

13. To ensure staff retention, programs should provide adequate and ongoing training, offer adequate salaries to reduce turnover, and develop support systems for staff members, such as team meetings, counseling, case discussions, and professional consultations.

14. Effective programs start small and grow in small steps to ensure multilevel involvement and promote local ownership of the program.

15. The government's responsibilities lie towards the realization of rights for children, and provision of at least minimum legal and regulatory frameworks. Governments should check quality, coordinate, and ensure that services are properly developed, executed, monitored, and implemented with a minimum standard requirement.

16. Practice should be reflective and dynamic, responding to changing environment and changing needs. They should be rights-based, where the child's protection is accorded primacy.

17. Emphasis needs to be placed on returning the child to his home, wherever possible, after having carried out the requisite checks. This must be accompanied by regular follow-up. Ultimately the decision of whether or not to return to the family needs to be taken by the child himself. For this, he must be provided all the support he needs to take an informed decision. When an organization is unable to take on repatriation as an intervention,

it should not be hesitant in stepping back. Such stepping back should not be considered a failure on the part of the organization; any attempt to repatriate the child without adequate orientation to his individual reality is potentially dangerous. Collaborating with other organizations involved in repatriation is the alternative.

18. Religious belief systems greatly influence the way street youth perceive themselves ("this is my fate, I cannot change it"). This, in turn, often influences their survival behavior. Working on the positive aspect of their beliefs, helps their positive movement off the streets.

19. Organizations and agencies need to assess typical personality characteristics of street youth in order to understand individual differences in autonomy, resilience, and capacity to resist stresses.

20. Street education should play a pivotal role in reaching out to a greater number of street children who cannot otherwise be reached. Training of ex-street children on methods of peer-to-peer counseling have proved to be an effective tool subject to judicious use. However, selection and training of such ex-street children or peer educators needs to be well organized.

"How do I improve what I am doing?" This question could be adapted, put forward to the street child to help him reflect and analyse his own life. The "transformation" or socialization and reintegration of street children, some of whom are addicted to street life, is challenging. Their problems need to be addressed with a commitment to empower them towards self-reliance, according them respect for their dignity and potential. The focus must shift from reasons for children coming on to the streets to a clear understanding of their departure from the street and how they are sustained thereafter.

REFLECTIONS

This narrative account of my systematic enquiry, the process of understanding that emerged and the growth of knowledge through a creative struggle to understand the lived reality with the male street inhalant abusing adolescents, offer a method of dealing with this phenomenon. The participatory action research has allowed situated reflection on both performance and learning at the workplace, leading to new insights and new working practices between the staff and the boys and, thereby, empowering all involved.

Annexures

APPENDIX 1
ADMISSION POLICY OF THE DRUG
DE-ADDICTION CENTRE

Note: The staff decided to come up with an admission policy to stream line those cases that were going beyond the focus of the organization. It was becoming difficult for the staff to care for the physically and mentally challenged as they were not specialized to do so. The policy was made for referrals coming from the street contact center as well as from referring agencies.

The Drug De-addiction Centre has certain criteria that define its admission policy for children from the street as well as for those referred from other centers. This policy helps to ensure fair treatment, transparency, and equality of opportunity for all vulnerable children who seek help. The contents of the policy are as follows:

A. INTAKE POLICY:

1. The recommended age for the children should be between 6–14 years.
2. No physically or mentally challenged children will be admitted.
3. Drug-addicted children will not be admitted unless they have gone through the detoxification and therapeutic phases.
4. Children suffering from chronic/life threatening illnesses will not be admitted to the Residential Home.
5. No admission for Childline referrals.

6. No admission for community referrals.
7. Only admission for orphans or street children from the community.
8. While re-admitting ex-boys (i.e., drop-outs and repatriated), the boys have to attend the Child Court of the Residential Home.
9. Preference will be given to boys who know regional languages.
10. Complete physical examination (blood group, health status, height, weight, identification marks, X-ray, STD, HIV/AIDS) will be done within 24 or 48 hours of contact before admission of any child.
11. New boys need to be prepared by the Drop-in Centre for further programs at the Residential Home.
12. Drop-outs are readmitted after follow up at the Drop-in Centre for a period of two months during which they have to go through an orientation camp.

B. Admission Policy for Referring NGOs:

1. The process of detoxification should be completed by the referring organization (NGO). Staff has to be constantly present while the process of detoxification is on. Moral support is required to be rendered in completing the detoxification process.
2. If NGO referral boys run away from the Therapeutic Centre, the Residential Home is not responsible for that.
3. After completion of three months, the boys should be taken back by the referring (NGO) organization for further training (Phase V—to be carried out by the collaborating organization).
4. The staff of the Residential Home will train collaborating NGO staff for street preparation, i.e., methods and strategies to be followed while doing outreach.

APPENDIX 2
BOYS' FOLLOW-UP FEEDBACK FORM [BFF]

Note: The Boys Follow up Feedback form evaluates the progress of each boy enrolled in relation to their education, health and hygiene, behavior, and future career. The evaluation can be done on a weekly and monthly basis to understand the areas that require improvement.

1. Name
2. Age
3. Residential Address
4. Religion
5. Education
6. Medium of Education
7. Occupation
8. Family History: A) Total Members in Family
                          B) Family Atmosphere
                          C) Socioeconomic Status
9. Reasons to run away from home
10. Street Life—A Summary
11. Admission in Shelter
12. Physical/Mental Health Status
13. Hobbies
14. Skills Known/Learnt
15. Future Career Goals
16. Follow-up Co-ordinator's [FC] Remark

Data as applicable:

	Date: In/Out	Reason	Place	Referred: To/By	Reason	Remarks
Drop-out						
Repeater						
Transfer						

FC's Name:
Signature:
Date:

Progress Chart [PC]

Name   Month

A) Shelter Education

	Week 1	Week 2	Week 3	Week 4	Week 5	Monthly Remarks
Excellent						
Good						
Above Average						

	Week 1	Week 2	Week 3	Week 4	Week 5	Monthly Remarks
Average						
Below Average						
Poor						
Weekly Remarks						

B) Health/Hygiene

	Week 1	Week 2	Week 3	Week 4	Week 5	Monthly Remarks
Excellent						
Good						
Above Average						
Average						
Below Average						
Poor						
Weekly Remarks						

C) Global Behavior

	Week 1	Week 2	Week 3	Week 4	Week 5	Monthly Remarks
Excellent						
Good						
Above Average						
Average						
Below Average						
Poor						
Weekly Remarks						

D) Future Career Plans

	Week 1	Week 2	Week 3	Week 4	Week 5	Monthly Remarks
Excellent						
Good						
Above Average						
Average						
Below Average						
Poor						
Weekly Remarks						

FC's Signature:
Date:

APPENDIX 3A: PROBLEM TREE

Note: The entire organization engaged in a problem tree analysis in 2004, to bring ownership and quality service to the children. This analysis with the team helped to identify the basic problem, specifying its cause and effects. This step-by-step approach enabled me to arrive at a consensus and an understanding of the problem to be addressed, how and under what constraints.

APPENDIX 3B: OBJECTIVE TREE

Note: The objective tree represented desirable conditions that were opposite to those in the problem tree, i.e., a state where there was no drug consumption among the street boys and where the long-term end of moving into settled independent living was satisfactorily achieved.

Appendix 3A: Problem Tree

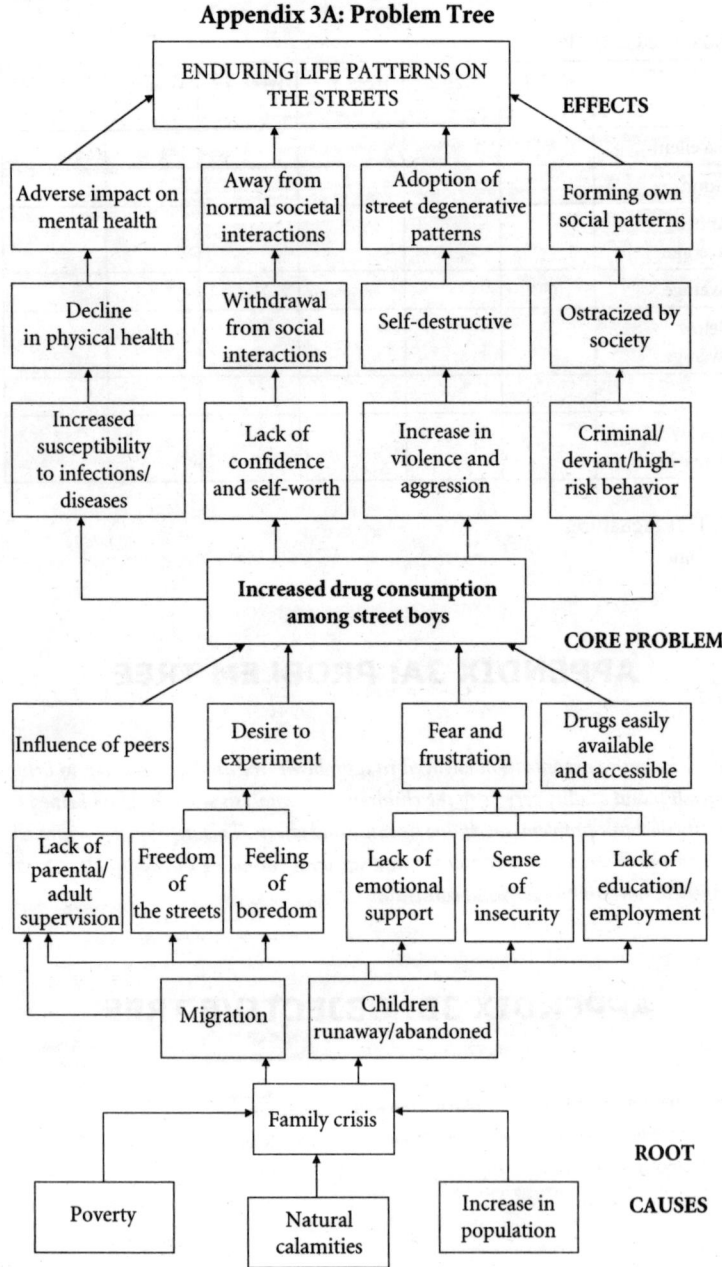

Appendix 3B: Objective Tree

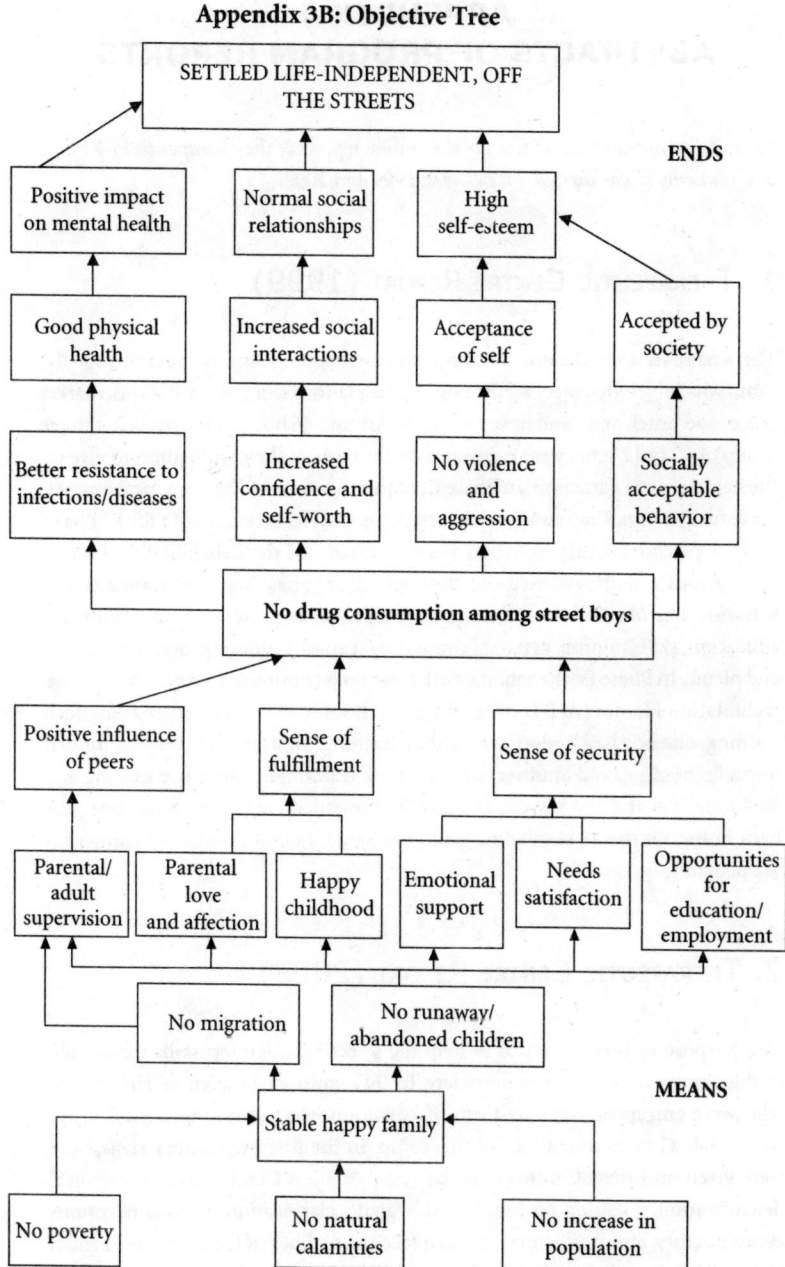

SETTLED LIFE-INDEPENDENT, OFF THE STREETS

ENDS

Positive impact on mental health

Normal social relationships

High self-esteem

Good physical health

Increased social interactions

Acceptance of self

Accepted by society

Better resistance to infections/diseases

Increased confidence and self-worth

No violence and aggression

Socially acceptable behavior

No drug consumption among street boys

Positive influence of peers

Sense of fulfillment

Sense of security

Parental/ adult supervision

Parental love and affection

Happy childhood

Emotional support

Needs satisfaction

Opportunities for education/ employment

No migration

No runaway/ abandoned children

MEANS

Stable happy family

No poverty

No natural calamities

No increase in population

APPENDIX 4
ABSTRACTS OF PROGRAM REPORTS

Note: Below are abstracts of some of the annual reports of the Therapeutic Five Phase program which was carried out between 1999 and 2007.

1. THERAPEUTIC CENTRE REPORT (1999)

The Khandala second camp started with street contact and preparation for the camp which included meeting the boys on the platforms of railway stations, market places and beach areas and in some NGOs. Around 46 boys on the street in the age group of 12 to 17 years were counseled on the basis of their willingness to give up the habit of drug addiction. In Phase II, of the 36 boys admitted in a local hospital for detoxification, 8 ran away and the rest completed it successfully. In the III Phase, various psycho-spiritual activities were conducted at the Rehabilitation Centre. The various activities carried out throughout the phase were yoga, meditation, behavior control, mind control, not going back to street, group discussion, informal education, skill training, personal counseling, games, outdoor programs, prayers, and picnic. In Phase IV (Rehabilitation), three boys continued to stay in Alternative Habilitation Homes (AHH) or rented group homes, two boys were sent for Tech training, one boy had undergone welding training, another three boys continued formal schooling, and another two boys took training in paper bag making and *bandhini* (Tie and Dye) work. In Phase V (Resettlement), three boys were sent back home. Of the 28 boys admitted to the Rehabilitation Centre, 13 completed the program successfully.

2. THERAPEUTIC CENTRE REPORT (2002)

The purpose of this camp was to help the street kids develop skills that would enable them find an identity in society. In this camp, ex-Residential Home boys who were entrapped in some form of addiction, were given preference. There were in all 41 boys who attended this camp. In the first preparatory stage, boys were given an orientation towards the Rehabilitation Centre, need for medical detoxification, a session on health and hygiene, clarification of misconceptions about doctors, and finally how they can face the realities of life in the Residential Home. The second stage (medical detoxification) saw the admission of the kids in local hospitals where they stayed for about one week to ten days for blood tests, X-rays, and other screening tests. After this, these kids were taken to the Rehabilitation Centre. At the Rehabilitation Centre (third stage), various activities such as spiritual classes, sessions on adjusting to a new environment, new friends, different way of life, behaviors, recreation activity, work therapy, interaction with visitors, and picnics were conducted during a span of four months. About 22 boys successfully completed the program, whereas the rest left the program midway.

3. THERAPEUTIC CENTRE REPORT (2004)

The main objective of the Rehabilitation Program was to concentrate on the younger street children who indulged in drug addiction, because of their ever-increasing numbers in Mumbai. The target group therefore was the school going street boys in the age group of 8–14 years. In the 1st Preparatory Phase, the outreach staff approached the street children on different stations of Mumbai city to trace addicted boys. A group of 24 boys were taken for a Pre-detoxification camp to a youth village during which orientation about the youth village, sessions on street life, and effects of drugs on the body and the importance of medical detoxification were provided to the children. In the second stage, the boys were sent to different hospitals according to their levels of addiction. Eighteen boys were sent to different hospitals and six boys were sent for education to the Residential Home. The various activities held at the hospital included counseling by the social worker, games, drawings, puzzles, occupation therapy, pre-preparation for the third phase, and providing medicines. The boys were oriented about the therapeutic community's rules and regulations in the third phase. Regular activities and sessions on sexual behavior, adjustments in new environment, anger management, self-discipline, care, personality development, individual meetings with children, case studies, and so on, were conducted in the third phase to help the children follow a disciplined life. In the fourth phase, 17 boys were transferred to the Residential Home followed by home settlement in the fifth phase.

4. THERAPEUTIC CENTRE REPORT (2007)

The purpose of the therapeutic camp January–November (2007) was to help children from the street to develop their skills for a better "drug free" life in their future. With that purpose Outreach was done in Mumbai city in different main railway stations, e.g., CST (Chatrapathi Shivaji Terminus), Dadar, and Bombay Central, etc., daily to engage with the boys, identify them and to prepare them if they wished to join the program (Phase I). A group of 91 addicted boys were taken for detoxification by the Therapeutic Centre (Phase II). All the 91 boys had undergone detoxification treatment for four days at the Sion hospital in Mumbai. OPDs were done at the Sadhu Vaswani hospital, Lonavala. Initially they were given a general examination, counseling and treated for minor illnesses with the focus on detoxification. In the third phase several programs were undertaken for the holistic and all round development of the boys. The boys at the Centre had undergone a rigorous schedule in order to help them get away from their drug-taking habit. Their timetable consisted of yoga, meditation, non-formal educational classes, physical exercise, sports, and creative activities. In this phase, there was more focus on English and computer education to help the boys adjust in society. According to the special capabilities and interest of the boys, they were sent to different training programs/institutes for training such as housekeeping, electrician, tailoring, two-wheeler mechanic, four-wheeler mechanic, driving, etc. (Phase IV). Out of the 91 boys here, 25 boys were sent to Karjat youth village for pre training, 13 boys were sent for schooling, another 18 boys to different training institutes, 2 boys for higher college education and 16 boys to the Residential Home. The success of the whole program can be measured by the fact that 17 boys benefited from home placement in 2007 (Phase V).

APPENDIX 5
STUDY FOR THE REHABILITATION
OF DRUG ADDICTS

Note: Prior to the establishment of the 5 phase program in 1999, I decided to conduct a study on the rehabilitation programs that were available for them and what were the key areas I would have to delve into in our program.

In the 1990s, there was no specific program for street drug addicts' rehabilitation. Just one organization in the city had commenced a program that was more an outreach program that a Therapeutic Centre-based program. The study hence focused on the indigenous and governmental medical resources that the street addict had at his disposal to overcome his addiction.

It was found that 65 percent of the street addicts graduated from sniffing drugs to more hard core drugs like heroin. The general view was that there is no way out of the addiction cycle and that they cannot get help from anyone. The government hospitals only exacerbated their stress. The age group at which the boys were generally introduced into sniffing was between 11 to 13 years. The older street addicts found it difficult to pick up a trade if they were employed by some skilled roadside workshops and soon gave it up. Their skills, capacities, and attitudes were already formed and hence they found it difficult to learn new trades and skills. Their preferred occupations were working at wedding sites or picking scrap for recycling. Those addicts who took the decision to go home were referred to as being rehabilitated, though there was no evidence to prove the same. In the absence of a structured program, a measured and focused rehabilitation was seen to be lacking for the street addicts.

APPENDIX 6
EFFECTIVENESS OF THE
REHABILITATION PROGRAM (2003)

Note: The need was felt to open a larger facility as the numbers for admission were swelling. I was asked to do the above mentioned study to find out the impact and effectiveness of the program from 1999 to 2003. This study helped shaped the new facility and its amenities.

The Rehabilitation Program had been in existence for 4 years. There were a large number of children seeking admission, but the facility could support just 20 percent of those coming for the orientation camps. Before going in to build a larger facility, a need was felt to study the impact of the program on the children who had gone through it in the past four years and accordingly make amenity and facility changes apt for the program. The study was made based on the different phases and their impact on the children during that phase.

The street contact phase was seen as more of an exploratory period when the children wanted to "feel" what it would be like; they had heard about it from their peers. It was an experimentation—40 percent went for the orientation camp thinking it was a picnic. In some cases it was to escape police crackdowns, the rains or just to join their friends. In the second phase, 20–28 percent dropped out as they could not face the loneliness in the hospital or its medical procedures, the fear of what was to come. Those that stayed on did so largely due to the presence and example of some of the ex-addicts who had gone through the program. In the third phase, towards the end of that mending period, they were asked to make their choices for their future. Many of them would make decisions that kept them with their friends, even if they barely knew what it meant to pursue further studies or be a mechanic. In the fourth and fifth phases, stability was common, as they identified themselves with normal society and no longer as street children.

Those who dropped out of the first three phases of the program ascribed reasons such as poor quality and quantity of food (48 percent), bullying by the other boys (34 percent), neglect by the staff when they needed attention for their medical or other needs (28 percent). This study helped focus on the areas that needed attention in the program.

APPENDIX 7
INITIAL PROFILE FORM

Note: Initial Profile of the Child form (IPC) is the one where details and background information of a street child is collected during different phases of interaction with him. Such information includes personal details regarding education, health, family, duration on street, intake of drug, progress in the Residential Home, training undertaken, and so on.

PERSONAL REFERENCE CARD

Name: -   Age: -
Gender: -Male
Alias Name: -   Date of Birth:-
Mother Tongue: -   Languages Known:-   Photograph
Contacted By: -   Date of First Contact:-
Referred to: -   First Contact Point:-
Categories: - Slum/Street/Slum based Street/Abused Child/Child
              Labour/Affected by Natural Calamities/Missing

Current Place of Stay: -   *In Mumbai*
Duration on the Street: -
Education:-
Current Occupation/s: -
Previous Occupation/s:-
Health:-
Identification mark on the body:-
Religion:-
Native Place Address:-
Reason for leaving home:-
Reason for Referral to Open House
a. Food   b. Bath   c. Medical

Reason for Referral to Residential Home
a. Special Case   b. Medical   c. Repatriation
d. Referral to other NGO

Name of the Staff_____Signature_____Date_____

FAMILY STATUS:-

No.	Name (Biological/Step)	Age	Relation	Living/ Dead	Education	Occupation	Income
1							
2							
3							
4							
5							
6							
7							
8							

Complete narration of child's life before coming to Shelter:-

HISTORY OF STREET LIFE
(Areas frequented, contact and experience with various groups on the street)
Mobility of child:-
Runaway with whom:-

PROBLEMS FACED ON THE STREET *(Physical/Psychological/Economic):-*
Peer Influence:-
Source of Earning:-
Earnings per Day:-
Money spent on:-
Savings:-
Help from Other N.G.Os/Agencies:-

INFORMATION ON SUBSTANCE ABUSE
WHICH SUBSTANCES HAVE YOU ABUSED:-

i) Beedi   ii) Cigarette   iii) Tobacco   iv) Solution   v) Charas   vi) Ganja
vii) Syringe   viii) 10 No. Goli   ix) Alcohol   x) Any other (specify)

Since when have you been abusing the said substance and in what quantities

(To get an idea of the progression as also the amount of substance that could have affected him physically and psychologically) :-

What are the reasons for drug abuse?

i) Makes me feel good   ii) Helps forget my problems   iii) Releases tension
iv) Nothing to live for/suicidal   v) Peer pressure   vi) Any other (specify)

GUIDANCE AND COUNSELING REPORT
     Areas of Intervention: (Education, Vocation, and interpersonal relations)

Follow-up

Area of Interest: -
Psychological problems: -
Physical problems: -
Future Interventions: -
Counselor's Note: -

APPENDIX 8
SUMMARIES OF PUBLICATIONS

Handbook for Children in Difficult Situations, Volume 1 (2003)
Activity Manual for Marginalized Adolescents
By
Barnabe D'Souza and Dr Reeta Sonawat

This is the first in the series of four and is targeted towards adolescents between 11 and 16 years of age. Meant primarily for use by staff working with vulnerable adolescents, this manual provides a comprehensive list of participatory learning activities, which will be very useful for individual and group assessment. It offers a range of interesting activities, verbal and non-verbal, which may be used ad per requirements. Learning takes place through use of diverse mediums such as focus group discussions, drawings, role-plays, story narration, outdoor games songs etc.—all of which will help sustain interest of not merely the target group but also the staff.

Handbook for Children in Difficult Situations, Volume 2 (2003)
A Manual for Non-formal Education
By
Barnabe D'Souza and Ms Rupal Vador

Education plays a vital role in improving the quality of life of the people. Despite the efforts of governmental and non-governmental organizations to bring all children into the fold of formal education, many children still continue to be out of school. Low socioeconomic status of parents constrains them to send their children to earn at an early age, rather than to school. Therein lies the need to cover these children under the non-formal education scheme.

This manual on non-formal education (mainly for children between the ages 3 and 13) aims to bring about overall development of these children while at the same time gives them a chance to learn skills which are practically applicable in their daily life, so that they may enter mainstream society. It comprises short games and activities that a social/field worker can use while imparting non-formal education. It indicates different ways of explaining a single concept to the children, all cost efficient and at the same time ideal for the setting in which the class is conducted.

Handbook for Children in Difficult Situations, Volume 3 (2004)
A Manual for Adolescents
Undergoing Therapeutic Processes
By
Barnabe D'Souza

A Manual for development of children undergoing Therapeutic Processes is a resource manual designed to answer the urgent need for a holistic therapeutic program catering to the marginalized children. It is created for the facilitators or social workers, who like to deal with the target group in innovative and effective ways.

The manual is divided into three sections. The first section includes sessions for coping with the past life of the participants. The sessions help them to accept themselves and their past. The second section deals with reconstructing the present by polishing the participant's personality, communication skills and general understanding of self and society. The third section comprises planning for the future, implementation and follow-up.

Handbook for Children in Difficult Situations, Volume 4 (2005)
A Manual For Outreach Strategies
By
Barnabe D'Souza, Dr Sunita Shanbhag and Ms Rupal Vador

An outreach program is one of the most powerful tools used as a support system for marginalized children and adolescents (between 3 and 18 years of age). The aim is to strengthen the child and build up his capacities in his natural setting, rather than to bring him to an institution where, in the course of his stay, he frequently loses his edge, his resilience, and instead becomes dependent. This volume is targeted towards enhancing the street enablers diversity of intervention at different levels of interaction with children and adolescents—it comprises counseling strategies for individual and group contact, as well as planned sessions on issues like drugs, HIV/AIDS, education, health, hygiene, group life, sex education, entertainment, planning for their future and so on. This manual will be a handy reference guide to all outreach workers and the organizations working with marginalized children.

Understanding Adolescents at Risk (2004)
Edited by
Barnabe D'Souza, Dr Reeta Sonawat and Dakshayani Madangopal

As society becomes increasingly complex, the social context of adolescence has undergone tremendous change and many are getting uprooted and marginalized in their attempt to fulfill their survival needs. This necessitates the recognition of adolescents, particularly marginalized adolescents as a special category for systematic study. This book is a collection of research studies and review papers on different aspects of marginalized adolescent development. It is hoped that this book will provide the necessary impetus, inspiration and commitment to promote the human capital in our youth by accommodating and addressing adolescent issues and concerns as a part of national human development.

Adolescent Issues and Perspectives (2005)
Edited by
Barnabe D'Souza, Dr Reeta Sonawat and Dakshayani Madangopal

The phenomenon of adolescence has always evoked considerable interest among researchers and all those involved with their care. This book is a collection of

12 selected research and review articles contributed by experts in the field. Youngsters pose a constant challenge due mainly to their erratic temperament and shifting moods.

The book presents an academic overview from acclaimed practitioners and covers topics as diverse as health, high-risk behavior, pro-social behavior, substance abuse, runaways and so on. This book is meant to enable all those working with youth to chart out a plan of action in building social capital and bringing about meaningful change in the lives of young people.

Healthy Food—A Challenge (2004)
By
Barnabe D'Souza and Ms Purvi Gilani

Food deprivation through poverty is the root cause of malnutrition, and in vulnerable children, both malnutrition and infection are widespread. Interaction with diverse groups of marginalized children and adolescents reveal that despite the vast amount of literature available on nutrition, the staff of various organizations often finds it difficult to plan out a suitable diet for children. This booklet aims to provide valuable information regarding basic foods and the nutritive values of each, interspersed with catchy illustrations to sustain the reader's interest.

Pivoting Peripheries (2005)
By
Barnabe D'Souza and team

A participatory study pertaining to the development of marginalized adolescents was carried out by the International Federation of Catholic Universities, Paris, in association with Shelter Don Bosco, Mumbai. This book comprising six chapters, focuses on this vulnerable yet neglected section of society, those adolescents who survive on the fringes, who have forsaken the joys of childhood in order to take on all the burdens of adulthood. The book is meant to serve as a stimulus to action for all those responsible for the welfare of children and youth at risk, to enable them to fulfill their promises for the future.

A Guide for Social Workers as Counselors of Vulnerable Children (2006)
By
Barnabe D'Souza and Ms Rupal Vador

This manual tries to integrate knowledge of children into a framework that facilitates action. Divided into three major sections comprising basic skills in counseling, the process of counseling and issues involved, it lays emphasis on working together with vulnerable children to understand their subjective life experiences and the dynamic interplay of various inter-relationships. Each topic is substantiated by real-life examples or learning exercises, and encourages the readers to place themselves in the role of the social worker, internalize learning and practice specific counseling skills.

Walking with Vulnerable Children (2006)
Edited by
Barnabe D'Souza

This is a compilation of the rich and varied experiences of those who work in the social and developmental sector. It is a first-hand account of social workers who have been closely associated with the lives of the marginalized and destitute. The book reflects the complexity of interactions, the associated problems and the simple strength of the social workers' convictions.

The book can be an effective aid to youngsters and others involved in the field of social work. Drawing inspiration from the enriching experiences highlighted in this book will serve to enhance their commitment to making a difference in the lives of the under-privileged.

Children in Adult Garb—The Street Children's Reality
A Research Study in Mumbai (2008)
By
Dr Barnabe D'Souza

This book presents a holistic profile of street children in Mumbai, based on research carried out over a period of five years. It contains micro-studies of different aspects of their everyday lives including their food habits, health problems, high-risk behaviors and the NGO services they access. It offers reflective analysis and comparisons with slum children and other potential at-risk groups. The findings pertaining to multifarious aspects of street children's lives are synthesized in this book.

Eliciting People's Participation in Community Development—A Manual (2009)
By Rev. Dr Barnabe D'Souza
Edited by Kennedy Saldanha

This manual explores the process of community participation in terms of the numerous elements and sub-processes that it involves. It has elements of conceptual discourse as well as lessons from actual practice. It is meant to serve as a guide for those with an interest in community development who wish to enhance their understanding of some of the fundamentals of community participation—the concept, the process and resources—and who want to initiate or further develop community participation processes. The process is what has been stressed in this manual.

Marginal Zones: Development-induced Displacement in Mumbai (2010)
By
Barnabe D'Souza and Dakshayani Madangopal

This book on development-induced displacement in Mumbai, India, captures the subtle nuances of people's experiences and traces processes that reflect movement in time, from the destitution caused by displacement through deconstruction, construction and finally to reconstruction and recovery in resettlement. This insightful social–scientific analysis attempts to answer certain ethical questions by highlighting the impact/consequences of displacement, the causal connections between displacement and development, the multidimensional nature of the displacement experience and the importance of choice and informed consent among those displaced. It presents a positive view of displacement and sees it as setting the stage for profound social and cultural changes, which opens new vistas of opportunity to the displacees, the chance to acquire new skills and resources that can help them towards effective resettlement. The new resettlement paradigm proposed by the book gives an indication of some of the mitigation and monitoring mechanisms that can counter the negative impact of development-induced displacement.

Responding to Development-induced Displacement: A Training of Trainers Manual (2011)
By
Barnabe D'Souza and Dakshayani Madangopal

Over the past few decades, the problem of development-induced displacement has become larger, more complex, and geographically more widespread. Often, situations of internal displacement require communities, local, and national and international authorities to develop innovative responses quickly and under stress. Strategies for reinforcing the protection of vulnerable populations should help promote the stability required for their long-term recovery. This compilation provides practitioners a variety of examples from the field of development-induced displacement, based upon the experiences of those who have wrestled with this phenomenon and its diverse manifestations in different political, cultural, and developmental contexts.

Glossary

Adda (Hindi): Location of comfort, where the street boy knows his specific area for food, shelter, recreation, earning and friends.

Addiction to the streets: Captivated by the environment/lifestyle of the streets and the "freedom" it offers.

Agent: An employer, a charitable individual who takes on the role of guardian or a family that sires the child for his progressive movement off the streets or a mafia goon picking up children on the station to sell to small restaurants or workshops for a price.

Aur ek chance (Hindi): Last chance, one more chance.

BBH: Bosco Boys Home, a training center for the boys.

Best time for outreach: Night time is considered the most suitable time to meet the street child. While the city sleeps, he is a conspicuous by his presence on almost deserted streets. He does not have work and is often in a group by night.

Betul: Training center for the boys.

Bollywood: The Hindi film industry.

Brown sugar: Drugs—a derivative of heroin.

CCVC: Coordinating Committee for Vulnerable Children, an umbrella organization of 44 NGOs in Mumbai.

Chai (Hindi): Tea.

Coolie (Hindi): Porter, at the train stations.

Dada (Hindi): The local goon/bully/gang leader of the area.

Dargh (Hindi): Islamic religious place of worship, outside which free food is distributed.

Didi (Hindi): Elder sister.

Diwali Mela (Hindi): A fair organized for 5,000 street and marginalized children during the Hindu festival of lights.

Don Boys' Group: Formed in the Residential Home for those who were being prepared for schooling, training or for jobs. It entails imbibing a certain routine, discipline, responsibilities, values, and work ethics.

Drop-in Centre coordinator: Department Head at the Drop-in and Outreach Centre.

Experience by proxy: Wish to experience what the other is doing, so take joy, relive or listen/go to meet the other person who has been undergoing that experience.

GO: Governmental organization.

Instant gratification: Desire for immediate results; inability to postpone satisfaction.

Izzat (Hindi): Respect.

Kaka Hotel (Hindi): A place where the boys get free food distributed by religious donors.

Kamchor (Hindi): One who avoids work.

Kuch to banna hai (Hindi): I want to be someone in life.

Limbo state: Period of transition/indecisive state of mind.

Line mukkadam (Hindi): A supervisor who picks up street boys to give them work at marriage parties. Considered the highest position a street boy can reach while on the streets and working at marriage parties (*wadikaam*).

Maal chunna (Hindi): Sorting scrap/recycling materials.

Maidan (Hindi): A large recreation ground often used to sleep or take drugs.

Marriage seasons: According to the Hindu religion, certain periods in the Hindu calendar are considered auspicious to marry.

Mela (Hindi): Fair, where 500–700 children come to my organization every 19th–20th of the month since 1987. It is an event to celebrate the lost childhood of the children, to get information about services in the city, to meet other peers in the same situation, have an identity, recreate, have food, get health and hygiene services, stay in the Residential Home or use such services.

Mukkadam (Hindi): The supervisor/employer who picks up street boys to work at wedding parties (*Wadi*).

My society: The Salesian Society of Don Bosco, an international religious men's congregation whose charism is to work mainly for youth.

Naka bandi (Hindi): Patrolling by the police, especially at road intersections, checking for miscreants and deviant persons, mainly a preventive action.

Need fulfilling trait: Guided by satisfaction of immediate impulses compulsively.

NGO: Non-governmental Organization.

NIOS: National Indian Open School—An adaptive curriculum and formal education system set up by the Delhi Board of Education, to help children who cannot go to formal school due to various reasons. To complete their high school.

Other class people: Generally regarded as those people who do not mix with the street children. It could be the middle and upper class people.

Outreach staff: Team working at the Drop-in Centre and reaching out to the children at their locations of stay on the streets, railway platforms and such places, where the children live/congregate.

Outreach boys' camp: A group of 20–30 plus boys are taken from the streets for 3 days for an orientation program about the Five Phase program go to a place outside the city. They return to the streets if they choose not to join the program.

Own language: Own slang words of the streets.

Peer educator: Someone who has undergone similar experiences and serves as a positive role model for others, influencing them directly or indirectly. He plays a leadership role or a role given with responsibilities to assist the process of rehabilitation of street children.

Pivoting Peripheries: A three-year qualitative research study of several groups of marginalized adolescents (D'Souza and team). Two of the eight groups included were street drug addicts and street children. The team came up with a model of working with institutionalized children.

"Protector–Utility boy": Big boys who use the younger boys for sexual pleasure and to run small errands, whilst protecting them from other bullies on the streets.

Quasi-street children: Those children having families living in the slums or pavements of the city. The children spend more time/live/earn on the streets away from their families.

Quotah: A certain number of cases registered is the target set to monitor the duties of particular police stations.

Rakhi (Hindi): A band tied on the wrist of a boy by a girl on Rakshabandan day (Hindu festival), signifying that she is his sister and he as her brother will protect her for life.

Rehabilitation Program Coordinator: Department Head at the Rehabilitation Program Phase Three.

Research and Documentation Coordinator: Department Head at the Research and Documentation Centre.

Residential Home Coordinator: Department Head at the Residential Home.

Residential Home Samachar (Hindi): Quarterly newsletter of the Organization, publishing information and news regarding the happenings at the Home and its various projects.

Retrospectively: Writing (during reflecting/writing of my thesis) my 21 years experience in hindsight, using case stories, special events, questions, peculiar learning experiences, similarities and reflections that intrigued me.

Saddak Chaap (Hindi): Term commonly used to refer to those with a street mentality and behavior.

Saddak Chaap Zindabad (Hindi): Long live street life! (a slogan).

Shelter Samachar (Hindi): Quarterly newsletter highlighting current happenings in all the departments of the rehabilitation program.

Serial manner: Keeps on oscillating constantly between the institution and streets.

Solution: Typewriting correction fluid. It has an acetone base and its components are toxic. It is commonly inhaled on a piece of cloth by young street addicts. It is highly addictive and is a common drug of choice among street children.

Staff team: Entire team working in the five phase therapeutic program.

Street child genre: Living, thinking and experiencing the lifestyle of a street child who does not think of changing his situation or moving off the streets.

Street enabler: A staff team member who goes on outreach contact on the field to enable the street child with services for their well-being.

Sulabh toilets (Hindi): Public toilets and shower facilities (pay and use), availed off by slum dwellers and street children.

Survival mode: Making use of the system and resources available on the streets to their advantage. It is not to get off the streets, but to use the benefits given by NGOs for immediate relief from a particular situation minus the long-term goal of the agencies.

Survival strategy kit: The different coping mechanisms and behaviors used by street boys to deal with his situation on the streets, often detrimental to his future, body, or value system.

Thanda days (Hindi): Days when there is no work, days on which no earnings are received.

The terminal situation: A situation wherein a street child has lived out his childhood on the streets and is now a grown up adult. He is heavily addicted to substances, unable to work and earn, lives on charity, outside charitable institutions (on the streets). He does not have a fruitful future, no agency to support him. In this situation he is staring at a difficult death situation on the streets.

Three "pillars" of social reintegration: Housing, education/vocational training, and employment.

Uncle: On the streets it refers to a male outreach social worker of an NGO.

Utility boys: Big boys who use the younger boys for sexual pleasure and to run small errands, whilst protecting them from other bullies on the streets.

Value Education Camps: Held for a group of boys of the various projects at a location outside the city for three days, wherein intense sessions on personality development, abuse, sex education, budgeting, and relationships are conducted. It has one main theme on which the entire group and trainers focus. At the end of the camp, certain decisions are taken by the group for their betterment.

Vardi (Hindi): Free food donated as alms outside religious places by the devotees.

Vasuli (Hindi): A form of protection money, to be permitted to work or stay in that area by the local goon/toughie.

Wadikaam (Hindi): Catering and related services done at big marriage parties. Most street children above 14 yrs enjoy this work as there is lots of food, fun, and drugs. The payment is good, but it is only seasonal. A street boy may get work for 40–50 days in the whole year.

Zari work (Hindi): Fine embroidery work using gold thread, often children between 5–6 and 14–15 years are employed for 15 plus hours. Often they are sold by their parents from their villages of north–central India, to come to work in *zari* workshops in the city.

References

Agrawal, R. 1999. *Street Children: A Socio-Psychological Study*. New Delhi: Shipra Publications.

American Psychiatric Association. 1994. *Diagnostic and Statistical Manual of Mental Disorders*, 4th edition. Washington, DC: American Psychiatric Association.

Anandalakshmy, S. and M. Bajaj 1981. "Childhood in the Weavers' Community of Varanasi," in D. Sinha (ed.), *Socialisation of the Indian Child*. New Delhi: Concept Publishing.

Bandura, A. 1986. Social Foundations of Thought and Action: A Social Cognitive Theory. Englewood Cliffs, NJ: Prentice-Hall.

Beazley, H. 2003. "The Sexual Lives of Street Children in Yogyakarta," *RIMA: Review for Indonesian and Malaysian Affairs*, 37(1): 17–44.

Bennett, Susan. 2004. *Autoethnography: Writing—about the Self Analytically*. Retrieved from www.hymboldt.edu/~cpf/autoethnography.html on 3 March 2008.

Bernstein, B. 1975/1977. *Towards a Theory of Educational Transmissions*, Volume 3 of "Class, Codes and Control." London: Routledge.

Bowlby, J. 1969. *Attachment and Loss: Attachment*, Volume 1. New York: Basic.

Byrnes, J.P. 1996. *Cognitive Development and Learning in Instructional Contexts*. Boston: Allyn and Bacon.

D' Souza, B. 2003. "Effectiveness of the Drug Addiction Program," unpublished in-house study, Shelter Don Bosco, Mumbai.

D'Souza, B. 2004. *A Manual for Adolescents Undergoing Therapeutic Processes*. Mumbai: Tej-Prasarini Publications.

D'Souza, B. 2005. *Pivoting Peripheries*. Mumbai: Shelter Don Bosco Research, Documentation and Training Centre.

D'Souza, B. 2008a. "Frail Bodies...Adult Realities," in *Children in Adult Garb—The Street Children's Reality*, pp. 111–34. Mumbai: Tej-Prasarini Publications.

D'Souza, B. 2008b. "Some Say I want More...Others Say I want Something," in *Children in Adult Garb—The Street Children's Reality*, pp. 77–110. Mumbai: Tej-Prasarini Publications.

D'Souza, B. 2008c. "Travelling the Road to Experience," in *Children in Adult Garb—The Street Children's Reality*, pp. 135–70. Mumbai: Tej-Prasarini Publications.

Dewey, J. 1933. *How We Think: A Restatement of the Relation of Reflective Thinking to the Educative Process*. Boston: D.C. Heath.

Dimenstein, G. 1991. *Brazilian War on Children, 1991*. London: Latin America Bureau.

Dweck, Carol S. 2006. *Mindset: The New Psychology of Success*. New York: Random House.

Ennew, J. 1994a. "Parentless Friends: A Cross-cultural Examination of Networks among Street Children and Street Youth," in F. Nestmann and K. Hurrelmann (eds), *Social Networks and Social Support in Adolescence*, pp. 409–426. Berlin: Walter de Gruyter.

Ennew, J. 1994b. *Street and Working Children—A Guide to Planning*. London: Save the Children.

Environmental Health Perspectives. 2005. "Inhalant Abuse: Supporting Broad-based Research Approaches." Retrieved from http://findarticles.com/p/articles/mi_m0CYP/is_8_113/ai_n15343377/?tag=mantle_skin;content

Eysenck, H.J. and M.W. Eysenck. 1985. *Personality and Individual Differences: A Natural Science Approach*. New York: Plenum.

Fernandes, G., P. D'Souza, and V. Samuel. 2002. *Resilience: A Joyful Growth, Report of the Action Research in Promoting Resilience in Children*. Mumbai: Research Unit, College of Social Work, Nirmala Niketan.

Freire, Paulo. 1970. *Pedagogy of the Oppressed*. New York: Continuum.

Gigengack, R. 2006. Young, Damned and Banda: The World of Young Street People in Mexico City, 1990–1997. Doctoral Thesis: University of Amsterdam.

Gilligan, R. 2003. "Promoting Children's Resilience—Some Reflections," Paper presented at the launch event for The Glasgow Centre for the Child and Society, University of Strathclyde, Glasgow, Scotland, 18 March 2003.

Glanz, K., B.K. Rimer, and F.M. Lewis. 2002. *Health Behavior and Health Education. Theory, Research and Practice*. San Fransisco: Wiley & Sons.

Gollwitzer, P.M. 1990. "Action Phases and Mind-sets," in E.T. Higgins and R.M. Sorrentino (eds), *The Handbook of Motivation and Cognition: Foundations of Social Behavior*, Volume 2, pp. 53–92. New York: Guilford Press.

Gollwitzer, P.M. 2003. "Why We Thought the Action Mindsets Affect Illusions of Control," *Psychological Inquiry*, 14: 259–67.

Hatton, N. and D. Smith. 1995. *Reflection in Teacher Education: Towards Definition and Implementation*. The University of Sydney: School of Teaching and Curriculum Studies.

Hecht, T. 1998. *At Home in the Street: Street Children in Northeast Brazil*. Cambridge: Cambridge University Press.

Hutchby, I. and J. Moran-Ellis (eds). 1998. *Children and Social Competence: Arenas of Action*. London: Falmer.

Johnson, V., E. Ivan-Smith, G. Gordon, P. Pridmore, and P. Scott. 1998. *Stepping Forward: Children and Young People's Participation in the Development Process*. London: Intermediate Technology Publications.

Johnson, V., J. Hill, and E. Ivan-Smith. 1995. *Listening to Smaller Voices: Children in an Environment of Change*. London: Action Aid.

Joubert, J. 1899. "Ch. XVIII: Of Education," *Joubert: A Selection from His Thoughts*, trans., Katharine Lyttelton. New York: Dodd, Mead & Co. Retrieved from http://www.bartleby.com/354/18.html

Kumar, K. 1993. "Study of Childhood and Family," in T.S. Saraswati and B. Kaur (eds), *Human Development and Family Studies*. New Delhi: Sage.

Lucchini, Ricardo. 1997. "Between Running Away and Eviction: The Child Leaving for the

Street," English version of the Working Paper "Entre fugue et expulsion: le départ de l'enfant dans la rue,' translated by Daniel Stöcklin. University of Fribourg, Switzerland. Retrieved from http://www.unifr.ch/socsem/Fichiers%20PDF/Between%20running%20away.pdf (accessed on 5 August 2011).

Luthar, S.S., D. Cicchetti, and B. Becker. 2000. "The Construct of Resilience: A Critical Evaluation and Guidelines for Future Work," *Child Development,* 71(3): 543–62.

Masten, A. and J. Coatsworth. 1998. "The Development of Competence in Favorable and Unfavorable Environments: Lessons from Research on Successful Children," *American Psychologist,* 53: 205–20.

Matza, D. and G. Sykes. 1961. "Juvenile Delinquency and Subterranean Values," *American Sociological Review,* 26(5): 712–19.

Mayer, J.D. and P. Salovey. 1997. "What is Emotional Intelligence?" in P. Salovey and D. Sluyter (eds), *Emotional Development and Emotional Intelligence: Implications for Educators,* pp. 3–31. New York: Basic Books.

Murphy, L.B. 1953. "Roots of Tolerance and Tensions in Indian Child Development," in G. Murphy (ed.), *In the Minds of Men.* New York: Basic Books.

NIDA and WHO. 2000. "Street Children and Drug Abuse: Social and Health Consequences," Marina Del Rey, California: International Program Office of Science Policy and Communications, National Institute on Drug Abuse (NIDA) and Department of Child and Adolescent Health and Development, World Health Organization (WHO). Retrieved from http://bajik.wikispaces.com/file/view/StreetChildrenfromSean%5B1%5D.pdf

NIDA. 2001. "Facts about Inhalant Abuse," National Institute on Drug Abuse (NIDA) Archives, 15 (6). Retrieved from http://archives.drugabuse.gov/NIDA_Notes/NNVol 15N6/tearoff.html

O'Kane, C. 2003. "Street and Working Children's Participation in Programming for Their Rights," *Children, Youth and Environments,* 13(1): 4. Retrieved from http://colorado.edu/journals/cye

Panicker, R. 1993. "Study on the Situation of Street Children in Six Cities of India: Major findings," *Street and Working Children,* 8: 1–2.

Petty, R.E. 1995. "Creating Strong Attitudes: Two Routes to Persuasion," in T.E. Backer, S.L. David, and G. Saucy (eds), *Reviewing the Behavioral Science Knowledge Base on Technology Transfer,* pp. 209–24. NIDA Research Mongraphs No. 155, National Institutes of Health, USA.

Piaget, J. 1995. "Explanation in Sociology," in L. Smith (ed.), *Sociological Studies,* pp. 32–96, New York: Routledge.

Ryan, R.M. 1995. "Psychological Needs and the Facilitation of Integrative Processes," *Journal of Personality,* 63: 397–427.

Sauvé, Stephanie. 2003. "Changing Paradigms for Working with Street Youth: The Experience of Street Kids International," *Children, Youth and Environments,* 13(1), Spring. Retrieved from http://colorado.edu/journals/cye and www.streetkids.org/assets/pdf/2003/SKI_paradigms.pdf (accessed on 7 May 2004).

Scheper-Hughes, N. and Daniel Hoffman. 1995. "Kids Out of Place," in Fred Rosen and Deirdre McFadyen (eds), *Free Trade and Economic Restructuring in Latin America: A NACLA Reader,* pp. 226–37. New York: Monthly Review Press.

Seligman, M.E.P. 1975. *Helplessness.* San Francisco: Freeman.

Strickling, B.L. 1998. "A Moral Basis for the Helping Professions," Paper presented at the 20th World Congress of Philosophy, Boston, USA.

Tudorić-Ghemo, A. 2005. Life on the Street and the Mental Health of Street Children—A Developmental Perspective. Dissertation, University of Johannesburg.

UNICEF. 2007. "Child Protection from Violence, Exploitation and Abuse." Retrieved from http://www.unicef.org/protection/index_orphans.html

UNODC. 2004. "Solvent Abuse among Street Children in Pakistan," Islamabad: United Nations Office on Drugs and Crime (UNODC), United Nations System in Pakistan. Retrieved from http://un.org.pk/undcp/glue%20sniffing.pdf

Veale, A., C. Hegarty, and S. Finucane. 1997. "An Examination of Self-Concept and Self-Esteem among Ethiopian Street Children and Children of the Traveling Community in Ireland," Paper presented at Fifth European Congress of Psychology, Cross-Cultural Section, 6–11 July 1997, Dublin, Ireland.

Visano, L. 1990. "The Socialization of Street Children: The Development and Transformation of Identities," *Sociological Studies of Child Development*, 3: 139–61.

Whitehead, J. and J. McNiff. 2006. *Action Research: Living Theory*. London, Sage.

WHO. 1993. *Street Children Project, NIDA and WHO 2000*. Report from CYP Africa Centre, Lusaka.

Wolin, S.J. and S. Wolin. 1993. *The Resilient Self: How Survivors of Troubled Families Rise Above the Adversity*. New York: Villard Books.

Index

About the Author

Barnabe D'Souza, PhD, was the Executive Director of Shelter Don Bosco (SDB), Mumbai, as well as the founder and driving force behind "Maria Ashiana," a Don Bosco therapeutic center in Mumbai. He is currently Director, "Balprafulta," a child rights organization. He holds a masters degree in Social Work from Mumbai University and was teacher and vice-principal of Don Bosco High School (1982–85, 1993–94). Dr D'Souza was awarded PhD degree from University of Coventry, College of Worcester, UK.

He has more than two decades of experience in working with marginalized children and has authored several publications till date.